S0-ARN-706

Vivien Leigh

ALSO BY MICHELANGELO CAPUA

Montgomery Clift: A Biography
(McFarland, 2002)

Vivien Leigh

A Biography

by MICHELANGELO CAPUA

McFarland & Company, Inc., Publishers
Jefferson, North Carolina, and London

Vivien Leigh was named Vivian Mary Hartley by her parents, but for professional resons she later changed the spelling of her first name from Vivian to Vivien. The spelling change is explained on page 22, after which this book uses the spelling "Vivien" throughout.

LIBRARY OF CONGRESS CATALOGUING-IN-PUBLICATION DATA

Capua, Michelangelo, 1966–
    Vivien Leigh : a biography / by Michelangelo Capua.
      p.   cm.
    Includes bibliographical references and index.

    ISBN 0-7864-1497-9 (softcover : 50# alkaline paper) ∞

    1. Leigh, Vivien, 1913–1967.   2. Actors—Great Britain—
Biography. I. Title.

PN2598.L46C37   2003
792'.028'092—dc21   2003001319

British Library cataloguing data are available

©2003 Michelangelo Capua. All rights reserved

*No part of this book may be reproduced or transmitted in any form
or by any means, electronic or mechanical, including photocopying
or recording, or by any information storage and retrieval system,
without permission in writing from the publisher.*

Cover photograph: Vivien Leigh in the 1940s *(courtesy Ken Galente collection)*

Manufactured in the United States of America

McFarland & Company, Inc., Publishers
  Box 611, Jefferson, North Carolina 28640
   www.mcfarlandpub.com

To my mother

Acknowledgments

I have benefited from the help of many informants and institutions, and for assistance and support I am indebted to friends without whom the completion of this project would have been impossible. I would like to thank Michela Cinotti; the late Ken Galente and his wife, Irma; Walter Federico Salazar; Don McCulty and the Vivien Leigh Society in West Virginia; the staff of Bobst Library, New York University; the staff of the New York Public Library for the Performing Arts at Lincoln Center; the Museum of Television and Radio of New York; the staff of the British Library's Humanity Reading Room, St. Pancras, London; the staff of the British Library newspaper collections, Colindale; the staff of Vancouver Public Library, Vancouver, British Columbia; and the Museum of Modern Art of New York, Still Archive section. Finally, I give special thanks to Yvette Tenberge for her invaluable help with my English translation.

Table of Contents

Introduction

"Scarlett O'Hara was not beautiful, but men seldom realized it when caught by her charm...."

Although Margaret Mitchell, the author of *Gone with the Wind*, opened her novel with this description of her heroine, the words do not apply to Vivien Leigh, the British actress who gave an unforgettable performance as the southern belle. Vivien Leigh possessed a beauty that men seldom failed to notice, but her tendency toward neurotic and obsessive behavior, as well as her anxiety about achieving perfection in her art, would overshadow this beauty.

Vivien became a legend who was idolized for an appeal and a charismatic magnetism that radiated both on screen and in person. Yet her obsessive love for Laurence Olivier and her habit of reaching for more in life than she could possibly attain, combined with a terrible disease that would carry her from madness to death, tragically marked her existence. Analyzing her career today, it is easy to note how often her acting appeared false when she was not captured by the same excitement she felt when she played Scarlett in *Gone with the Wind* or Blanche in *A Streetcar Named Desire*. Nevertheless, it is undeniable that Vivien Leigh was at the center of one of the most important events in film history, and that she was at the center of one of the most romantic and tragic marriages in Hollywood. It was her part in both of these widely read scripts that sealed her lasting fame.

Chapter One

Scent of India

I won't sing, I'll recite.
—Vivian Hartley at age three and a half

On Saturday, July 8, 1967, between 10 P.M. and 11 P.M., London's West End theaters dimmed their front house lights in memory of one of Britain's greatest actresses, Vivien Leigh, who had died the previous day. Inside the playhouses the performances continued uninterrupted in order to honor a remarkable statement Vivien once made: "Being a film star—just a film star—is such a false life, living for false values. Actresses go on for a long time and there are always marvelous parts to play. I don't ever want to retire—I want to act until I am ninety."[1]

Vivien Leigh's sudden death at age 53 put an end to a career made up of forty-three stage appearances, twenty films and two Academy Awards. To many, however, she has always remained Scarlett O'Hara from *Gone with the Wind*, one of the most popular characters in the history of cinema. She played O'Hara brilliantly, and achieved a sense of immortality, which made her a kind of myth.

Vivian Mary Hartley (who later changed the spelling of her name to "Vivien") was born to Ernest Richard Hartley and Gertrude Jackjee on November 5, 1913, in Darjeeling, India. The couple had married in London a year before, moving to Calcutta shortly after the wedding.

The origins of Vivian's parents have often been fictionalized by Hollywood producers in order to make them more interesting to moviegoers. David Selznick, the producer of *Gone with the Wind*, often maintained that Vivian's parents were Irish and French as were Scarlett O'Hara's parents, but this statement was far from reality. In fact, Ernest Hartley was born on the island of Islay in the county of Yorkshire on February 19, 1882.[2] He was the last of seven children, and his father was an administrator in the Civil Service. As a child, Ernest was greatly influenced by the books of Rudyard Kipling, a writer of English descent who had lived in and written about India. Inspired, Ernest left England for India to seek his fortune.

Once Ernest arrived in Calcutta, he was hired as a stock exchange broker by the firm Piggot, Chapman & Co. In the beginning, the radical change of lifestyle was quite shocking for him, but he quickly learned how to live and act the role of a British gentleman in India.

From cricket games to polo tournaments, from racehorses to amateur theatricals, Ernest participated and enjoyed all of Calcutta's high-society social events. He was an extroverted and friendly man who loved to earn money and live well, and he had a particular passion for horses.

Contrary to what previous biographies have erroneously stated, Vivian's mother, Gertrude Jackjee, was born not in Yorkshire but in Darjeeling, India, on December 5, 1888, as her passport reveals. Gertrude's background was Indian and British, and she was raised Catholic. She was extremely beautiful, with perfect features, a peachy skin tone and sparkling blue eyes.

One night, Ernest, who was riding in his friend Geoffrey Martin's car, whispered, "Who is the girl sitting in the front?" "It's the chauffeur's sister," was his friend's answer. That was Ernest and Gertrude's first meeting.

A couple of months later, he proposed to her. The news caused a big sensation in Calcutta due to the social difference between the two lovers. But without worrying about people's comments, the couple sailed on the *City of Sperta* to London, where they were married on April 9, 1912.[2]

Shortly after this, the newlyweds returned to India. To avoid Calcutta's terrible summer heat, they left again by train for Darjeerling, at the foot of the Himalayas. In November of that same year, Vivian Mary was born. She was a beautiful baby, exactly as one might have expected in view of an old Indian superstition: any mother who looks at the peak of Mount Kanchenjunga just before her baby's birth will have a child with a perfect face. Although Mary was the name Gertrude preferred for her daughter, Vivian was eventually chosen out of respect for a tradition in Ernest's family. (Gertrude later tried to have another baby, but she prematurely delivered twins who lived no longer than a week.)

Ten days after Vivian's birth, the Hartleys, accompanied by two servants, returned by train to Calcutta and moved into a rented two-story villa in the elegant residential neighborhood of Alipore.

Vivian spent most of her first weeks of life in a luxurious garden, which her mother was personally taking care of. Flowers were baby Vivian's first contact with nature, and they would become an important constant in her daily life. A bouquet of fresh flowers in a vase would always be present either in her dressing room, hotel suite or home, together with her collection of French impressionist art. These works, specializing in floral subjects, were part of her traveling luggage.

Another childhood characteristic of Vivian's was her liveliness—a restless energy which only allowed her a few hours of sleep a night. This worried

Vivian, age three and half, reciting "Little Bo Peep," 1917.

Gertrude, but a doctor assured her that there was nothing wrong, saying that she was just "not a sleepy baby."[3]

By this time, Ernest Hartley was ready to go back to England, but he was persuaded by some friends to join the Indian Cavalry and put his horsemanship to the service of His Majesty the King of England. Gertrude and Vivian followed him to Mussoorie, a small village close to Darjeeling, where Ernest started his cavalry practice. Two years later, he was transferred to the military station of Bangalore, where the Hartleys lodged in the suburbs of Ootacamund.

Every day Gertrude insisted that the family move back to England, because she was particularly worried about Vivian's religious education. At that time, the little child was cared for by a Catholic nanny, Miss Holden, who replaced an unsophisticated Indian amah. Vivian would spend her days carefree, listening to their mother read Hans Christian Andersen and Lewis Carroll's classic tales. But she preferred, as did her father when he was a child, the adventures written by Kipling and the stories of ancient Greek mythology, which she learned by heart.

While her father was still in the Indian Cavalry, Vivian Hartley debuted on stage at age of three and a half performing the children's rhyme "Little Bo Peep." As the little shepherdess, she wore a white pastoral-style dress with a floral hat and held a shepherdess's crook trimmed with a large silk bow.

The Hartleys' marriage was going through difficult times, due to Ernest's frequent escapades. One night, tired of pretending to be naïve about her husband's infidelity, Gertrude had a dinner party to which she invited all the women suspected to be romantically or sexually involved with Ernest. The story caused a considerable stir in Indian high society amongst those who knew of Mr. Hartley's affairs. Later, Vivien Leigh would tell her friend Radie Harries that her mother knew exactly when Ernest was having an affair because he would give her expensive bracelets in order to ease his guilt.

Luckily, little Vivian was not present when her parents' marriage was on the rocks. Gertrude and Ernest had agreed to send their daughter to Roehampton, a small village not far from London, to the Convent of the Sacred Heart, where she would receive a better education than she would in India. Hence, Vivian, at the age of six and a half, left her native country. She would not return until 1964.

Chapter Two

Inside a Convent

When I leave school, I'm going to be a great actress!
—Vivian Hartley to her schoolmate Maureen O'Sullivan

In early January, 1920, the Hartleys along with Vivian and Miss Holden, boarded the ship *City of Baronda*, bound for England. They arrived in London on April 5, where they lodged for a few days at the Hotel Carlton. Shortly after this, they continued the trip to Waterville in the county of Kerry, where Vivian met her grandparents for the first time. Before they returned to India on the S.S. *Dongola*, Gertrude and Ernest left Vivian at the Convent of the Sacred Heart at Roehampton, where she was educated for almost eight years. She did not see her mother again for sixteen months, her father for much longer.

In the convent she was appointed student number 90. At six and a half years of age, she was the youngest student ever accepted there. Vivian was never afraid of the rigid discipline imposed by the nuns under the strict direction of the Reverend Mother Ashton Case, and she would remember those eight years at the convent as the happiest time of her life.

Vivian's wardrobe at the convent consisted of sixteen dresses: six embroidered, four colored, three lace, and three morning dresses, along with eight pairs of socks and eight pairs of warm stockings. Because of her young age, she was allowed to keep a white kitten, which she had adopted from her grandmother. The kitten served to alleviate some of her initial loneliness, and was an exception to the severe rules of the convent, where pets were strictly forbidden.

Vivian soon made friends with a schoolmate two years her senior,

Maureen O'Sullivan (later popular as a Hollywood actress and especially known for her portrayal of Jane in the *Tarzan* films opposite Johnny Weissmuller). Vivian's friendship with Maureen helped to dispel her intense sense of solitude.

The strict education in the convent discouraged friendship between girls: letters were read and censored, and rooms were often searched in case there was any offensive literary or personal material. The day would start at 6:30 A.M. with an early mass at 7:15. Breakfast was followed by long hours of study, and then by sport and musical activities. The day would conclude at 9 P.M. sharp, when all the lights would be turned off.

The austere dormitory where the girls slept was dominated by a big picture of the Virgin Mary. There were roughly 20 beds in each room, separated by long white curtains. Illumination was by gaslight, and there was no heating. Before going to bed, Vivian, like all the girls, had to fold the clothes she had worn during the day and leave them on a stool placed in front of the bed. A nun would collect the clothes and take them to the laundry, replacing them with clean ones for the next day. Folding her underwear and clothes onto specially made embroidered silk squares would became a daily ritual for Vivian, almost a fetish, which would last throughout her life. She would continuously buy new squares, made exclusively of silk or pure cotton with lace edges.[1]

During her stay at the Sacred Heart convent Vivian took violin and cello lessons. Literature and history became her favorite subjects and math her least favorite. In one of the many letters Vivian wrote to her mother during that time (all written on lilac-colored notepaper, one of Vivian's favorite colors), she stated her particular interests in Egyptian history: "The more I hear about Egypt, the more I wish that we could dig all the sand away and that all those marvelous sphinxes and temples and buildings could be seen again.... Do take me out to the places like Egypt etc. when I am grown up."[2]

Despite being the youngest girl in the convent, Vivian soon showed herself to possess extraordinary poise. Her communicative personality made her one of the most popular students at Roehampton. Lady Patsy Quinn Lambert, who had also studied at Sacred Heart, remembered: "What people noticed most in her as a young girl was her perfect manner.... She had many friends at school and we never felt jealous of her in spite of her beauty and personality, and she seemed quite without jealousy on her side."[3]

Her self-confidence naturally came out through acting, an activity strangely not repressed by the stern education of the convent. In fact, the girls often staged plays and Vivian acted with great enthusiasm the parts of the Fairy Mustardseed in Shakespeare's *A Midsummer Night's Dream* and Miranda in *The Tempest*. During holiday breaks, the girls, escorted by lay sisters, would go to London to visit museums and art galleries or to see a ballet or a concert. It was after attending the classical ballet *Where the Rainbow Ends* that Vivian decided to take ballet classes. But among all the shows she attended, *Round in Fifty* was the one that impressed her the most. It was a comedy starring George Robey at the London Hippodrome. Vivian saw the show sixteen times, collecting ten autographs from the star of the play, who soon became her favorite actor.

Gertrude visited England every summer, but Ernest did not see his daughter again until 1926. He would try to quench his sense of guilt with presents sent from India. In the beginning, they were beautiful toys, which gradually gave way to expensive objects like strings of pearls, Indian ornaments, silk stockings, or baskets of exotic fruits, which Vivian would share with her schoolmates.

During the summer of 1926, Gertrude and Ernest took their daughter on vacation with them to Ireland. Finally, Vivian had the chance to spend all her free time with her father, fishing for trout with him or just taking long walks. She disclosed to her parents her passion for the theater, and she shared her dream with her father, who had the same interest when he was young. She hoped that one day, if she ever returned to India, they could perform together at the Royal Theatre. Ernest answered vaguely, telling her that it would be very difficult because of his lack of spare time.

Vivian stayed at Roehampton until the summer of 1928, and then she traveled with her parents to the South of France, where at Dinard, a small summer resort village, she was enrolled into the local school convent.

Ernest was still working for Piggot, Chapman & Co., but the Wall Street crash of 1929 forced him to return to Europe. In the meantime, Vivian was transferred the next semester to the Sacred Heart Convent in San Remo, on the Italian Riviera. Even though the sunny weather and the happy atmosphere of the little Italian town was better than the gloomy and cold English climate, it did not help to lower the intense sense of pressure present inside the convent.

Vivian quickly noticed the difference from her previous convent, where she spent the best years of her childhood. She began to detest the new school, not only because of the frequent hints of lesbianism between girls and nuns, but mainly for the religious hypocrisy involved.[4] Her behavior became more rebellious and insubordinate, resulting in frequent punishments.

Her adolescent exuberance, in contrast with her refined and gentle manners, appeared to be a sign of Vivian's personality, which manifested itself in sudden mood changes that would turn into real manic-depressive symptoms. As a friend recalled: "Vivian would get along fine for a few hours, other times a day or more. But when it happened, we'd see a completely different girl—moody, silent, petulant, rude, often hysterical. None of us understood it, not even the school mistresses."[5]

Although the short educational experience in San Remo allowed Vivian to improve her Italian (she did not learn it as well as French), it did nothing to satisfy passion for acting. Vivian celebrated her fifteenth birthday in Italy, the same year that her parents finally moved back to Europe. In fact, the Hartleys arrived in Marseille in the spring of 1929, and they finally removed Vivian from the school in San Remo.

She spent that summer lightheartedly in Aasleagh, Ireland, where former schoolmate Patsy Quinn visited her. Gertrude moved to the little town of Biarritz on the French Atlantic coast, where she started a beauty products business in order to contribute to the family's shaky financial situation after the losses of the 1929 economic crisis.

Now at sixteen, Vivian needed "the final touch" to complete her education, and her mother decided that Paris was the best choice. She enrolled her in a little private school in Auteil, not far from Paris, where independence among students was strongly encouraged, something much different from the other schools Vivian had previously attended. She could finally wear the clothes she liked and spend her free time as she wished. Her grades improved considerably, and the study of languages and French literature, along with acting classes, became her favorite subjects.

The school headmistress, Madame Manileve, had hired the acting coach Mlle. Antoine, an actress from the Comédie Française. The teacher's method was not simply based on acting, but also on lessons in elocution and deportment. Vivien Leigh later said "[Mlle. Antoine] was a most inspiring teacher and I owe a great deal to her care in correcting my diction and to her encouragement ... 'I believe you have a future in the theatre, *mon enfant*,' she told me, 'but you must go back to England and work ... work ... work.'"[6]

Vivian's Christmas holidays were spent in Biarritz with her family, followed by a long trip to Switzerland. While there, she was enrolled in her next stage of education, a non-convent school in Bad Reichenhall near the borderline of Austria and France, not far from Salzburg. Gertrude's main purpose in arranging this was to have Vivian learn German. While there she started to appreciate opera, in particular Wagner, and often traveled to Vienna's Opera House.

Living in a little village in the Alps, she often spent time outdoors, skiing and riding her bicycle, but because of an inner-ear problem she found balance tricky and never excelled in any sport.

During one of her frequent visits to her daughter, Gertrude noticed extraordinary changes in her behavior. Vivian confided her intention to marry immediately because, in her opinion, if she delayed she would never get married. She also told her astonished mother that she was already engaged to two German boys. Gertrude did not pay too much attention to her daughter's statements, thinking of them as adoles-

Vivien Leigh, early portrait.

cent fantasies. However, a couple of days later, while they were having dinner together at an hotel in Munich, Vivian kept staring at the young waiter who was attending their table. All of a sudden, she said to him in German, "You deserve to be kissed." Gertrude instinctively slapped her.

Vivian's official education ended in the summer of 1931, after four semesters at Bad Reichenhall. On her education she later would comment, "I learned to speak French and German fluently and Italian [her facility with foreign languages let her personally dub her own films in French and German, something very unusual for an actress at the time].... Formal education ... very little. I never passed an examination until I was in Germany and I only won a prize for Scripture. My school reports used to say 'Must concentrate more' and I can't really add six and four."[7]

"I had an opportunity of studying diction and the theatre in many countries, I met people of all types and nationalities. They gave me that flexibility of mind which is so necessary to an artist, and taught me, I hope, understanding."[8]

Although her last year in school was Vivian's happiest, her excitement of finally going to London did not diminish.

Chapter Three

Wedding Interlude

---

*"Leigh Holman looks the perfect Englishman.
I'm going to marry him."*

"He's almost engaged to my sister Dulcie."

"That doesn't matter. He hasn't seen me yet."

—Vivian Hartley and Claire Martin

At eighteen years old, Vivian was the perfect debutante, and she was eager to enjoy all the worldly and cultural opportunities that London had to offer. But because Gertrude was often in Biarritz, busy with her business, Vivian was always alone at home with her father and spent her time reading, playing music or dreaming about her future.

There are two stories that detail how Vivian decided to seriously start her career as an actress by attending the Royal Academy of Dramatic Art in London. In the first version, Ernest suggests it to her one night at dinner: "You know, Vivling [his affectionate term to address to her; a contraction between the words Vivian and darling], you might make an actress yourself." Those words gave her a definitive push toward a desire already inside of her.

But it is more plausible that she was constantly thinking about a possible career as an actress (she later stated to the press: "I always wanted to be an actress.... When I was seven I said to Maureen O'Sullivan.... Not a just an actress but a great actress"[1]), and she was encouraged by watching her former schoolmate Maureen O'Sullivan, who was only two years older and already in the big Hollywood production *A Connecticut*

12

Yankee. This caused her to announce to her parents that she would make acting her full time profession.

Ernest was pleasantly surprised and immediately enrolled her into the Royal Academy of Dramatic Art. Since it was only the beginning of February, Vivian had to wait until May 1 when the classes began. The Hartleys' financial situation, however, was still very shaky. The investments and the stock market speculations that Ernest made did not gain the expected profits, even though he was confident that there would be a fast recovery of the British economy, which was still in full recession. Suddenly, however, Gertrude's successful beauty business brought a sizeable income to the household budget, making it possible for the family to afford Vivian's onerous tuition at the Royal Academy of Dramatic Art.

After months of living in hotels, the Hartleys rented a house in Falmouth in West County. It was quite easy for Vivian, with her outgoing personality, to meet new friends, like the four Martin sisters who were living in Teighmounth, not far from her new residence.

One day, while Vivian was strolling with Hillary and Claire Martin down the street of a little village in the same county called Halcombe, one of the sisters was cordially greeted by a man on horseback.

"That's Leigh Holman," Claire Martin said. "What do you think of him, Vivian? Isn't he handsome?"

"I think he looks the perfect Englishman. I'm going to marry him," was Vivian's quick answer.

"He's almost engaged to my sister Dulcie," Hillary said.

And Vivian replied: "That doesn't matter. He hasn't seen me yet."[2]

A couple of days later at the South Devon Hunt Ball, Vivian Hartley was officially introduced to Herbert Leigh Holman. Leigh was thirty-one years old, a handsome man with blond hair and clear eyes, whose reserved manner made him attractive and interesting. He bore a resemblance to Leslie Howard, one of Vivian's favorite actors. He was educated at Harrow and Jesus College, Cambridge, and like his father, he was a barrister-at-law two years later in the Middle Temple in London.

Vivian's "joie de vivre" and her radiant beauty immediately appealed to Leigh, who paid her a compliment on her magnificent sea-green ball gown that matched her eyes.

Leigh's great maturity and refined manners greatly impressed Vivian, who tried every possible way to meet with him again. For days after the ball she stayed in a trance-like state, telling all her friends that she was madly in love. Although Leigh was thirteen years older than she, Vivian said he was the man of her dreams. She spent her afternoons watching long, boring squash matches that Leigh would play with his old Cambridge friend Hamish Hamilton. After a couple of days, Leigh completely forgot about Dulcie Martin, who had refused his marriage proposal because she was not ready for such an important step.

A few weeks later Leigh had to go back to London to resume his legal work. Vivian asked her parents for permission to go back to the city earlier than the scheduled date of the beginning of classes, in order to be closer to him. But Gertrude was worried about the compromising situation and, instead, decided to send her daughter to the Hartley grandparents in Bridling, using the fact that the old couple was not healthy as an excuse. She told Vivian that the presence of their granddaughter would help them to feel less lonely.

Six long weeks of daily correspondence began between Vivian and Leigh. All of a sudden, the days seemed too long to pass in that "deadly hole."

Vivian would read Colette, knit and shop, but above all she was thinking exclusively of Leigh and making plans for the future. Finally, on March 1, she returned to London to participate in the Pegasus Ball and was accompanied by Leigh. Ernest forbade her to stay in Leigh's bachelor apartment and obliged her to be hosted by some family friends.

During this time Vivian passed her admissions test to the Royal Academy of Dramatic Art (RADA); the examination consisted of auditioning as Lydia in a love scene from the play *The Rivals*. RADA's director, Sir Kenneth Barnes, along with the teacher Ethel Carrington, were so deeply impressed with Vivian's physical presence on stage that they immediately announced her admission to classes, which commenced on May 1, 1932. Her first two roles were from Shakespeare's *As You Like It* and *A Midsummer Night's Dream*.

Through Leigh Holman, Vivian met Oswald Frewen, a retired Royal Navy commander and landowner, and the cousin of Winston Churchill. The old man was Leigh's very good friend and confidant.

"I might marry Viv," Leigh told Frewen one day.

"They'll make another nice couple," wrote the friend in his diaries.[3]

The following month Leigh bought an engagement ring with a green stone for thirty-five pounds at Mappin and Webb's and officially proposed to Vivian, filling her with excitement and happiness. She instantly accepted, and ran to her mother to share the news and to show her the ring. Gertrude tactfully explained to her daughter that the ring had to be returned to Leigh because the green stone would bring bad luck in the marriage. Vivian followed her mother's advice and Leigh returned the ring to the jewelry store, exchanging it for a classic diamond engagement band.

The marriage was not approved by Leigh's mother, a woman with a fierce character who completely disapproved of her son's choice to marry a "little girl" with an uncertain family background, something that was unacceptable to the Holmans' standards. Gertrude also had reservations and tried to tell Vivian that she and Leigh were not a perfect match. She reminded her that, in the Catholic religion, a marriage is a commitment for life, and she suggested that she consult a priest. Vivian did not listen to her.

As a matter of fact, Vivian and Leigh did not share the same interests. While she loved the theatre and would go accompanied by friends, he was completely devoted to his profession, which left him very little free time. But the way in which they met and their courtship had all the romanticism Vivian needed, and it was enough for her to believe that she was in love and sure of her choice.

They were married on December 20, 1932, in the Roman Catholic Church of St. James, Spanish Place. Patsy Quinn and another friend, Jane Glass, were her bridesmaids. Vivian looked very pale and skinny, as is noticeable from the photographs of the ceremony. She wore a simple white satin gown with a white crocheted Juliet cap, looking even younger than her nineteen years. As soon as the ceremony was over, Vivian removed her wedding band to show it to friends and relatives. The gesture made Gertrude extremely upset; she was very superstitious, and begged her daughter not to do it again because it was terribly unlucky and could endanger the length of her marriage.[4]

Immediately after the reception, the couple left on their honeymoon to ski in the Alps on the border between Germany and Austria. They returned to Leigh's apartment in St. John Place only two weeks later.

Vivian had left RADA with the intention of dedicating herself solely to her marriage and housekeeping. This decision was principally made due to her husband's insistences.

But Vivian's energetic and restless character was not suited to a boring, domestic life. To be more independent, she took driving lessons using an older car, which she drove to go shopping with her girlfriends. But after only a few weeks Vivian was longing to go back to her studies. So she attended some weekly French classes given by Madame Alice Gachet at RADA and then added other classes.

The slow progresses Vivian made at RADA gave her an awareness of some physical blemishes on her own body. Her big hands and thick wrists became a real obsession. From that moment on, she would use gloves and purses not only as mere fashion accessories but also as devices to balance the optical effect. She also started to wear many different big

Vivien Leigh

rings, which distracted people's attention from her hands, which Vivian used to call "my paws."

Later, as photographer Angus McBean remembered, the actress would also complain about her neck, believing that it was too long and that her legs were too big, fat and short. "So I told her that she had one very small fault. At the right hand side of her mouth she had a tiny raised muscle.... It was caused by a small dental misalignment, which made her use her teeth on that side more than the other."[5]

In June 1934, when Vivian was presented at court to George V and Queen Mary (her presentation was sponsored by Leigh's sister, Awyn Holman), she attended the ceremony wearing long white gloves to cover her hands, and a string of pearls adorned her long neck.

"What a lovely girl," Queen Mary would comment.

In February 1933, Leigh's mother died. Vivian was just in time to tell her that she was pregnant. Not even her pregnancy stopped her from attending RADA, where she acted as the protagonist in George Bernard Shaw's *St. Joan*, her last appearance on the stage of the Academy.

The summer of 1933 was very frantic. In anticipation of the happy event Vivian and Leigh moved into a bigger apartment at No. 6 Little Stanhope Street in the neighborhood of Mayfair. Vivian was now involved in decorating her new place with antique pieces. Her knowledge of, and skill at, antiquarian markets was rather instinctive, as she would often buy very valuable pieces for little money in London flea markets. Her showy taste always prevailed over Leigh's more discreet taste.

On October 12, 1933, a month before her twentieth birthday, Vivian wrote in her diary: "I had a baby—a girl" after a very complicated and painful delivery at the Rahere Nursing Home on Bulstrode Street.

During her hospital stay, a small tubercular patch was discovered on her lungs. At that time it was nothing serious, but it was the first sign of something that would dangerously reappear later in life, something with which she would pay with her own life.

Vivian named her baby Suzanne. She returned home from the hospital a couple of weeks later, and the baby was immediately given to a professional nanny who was hired by Leigh, along with a cook and a maid to take care of the house and allow Vivian to rest. The baby's birth did not cause any radical change in Vivian's life; motherhood did not suit her, therefore she resumed all her activities as if nothing had happened, upsetting Gertrude and Leigh a great deal.

She later maintained in an interview,

> I loved my baby as every mother does, but with the clear-cut sincerity of youth I realized that I could not abandon all thought of a career on the stage.... I took the problem to my husband and asked his advice. He was many years older than I was, a deeply kind and wise man, with the rare quality of imagination that implies tolerance and unselfishness. We decided that I should continue my studies at the Royal Academy of Dramatic Art ... and got a good nanny for the baby.[6]

As Fabia Drake, Vivian's close friend and a successful actress remembered, "She was bored with her marriage to a barrister. She told me she'd married Leigh Holman because she thought he was intelligent and that she found him a bore."[7]

To all the friends who were invited to the Holmans' on Little Stanhope Street, the marriage appeared to be picture perfect: the young and beautiful wife, the devoted lawyer husband, and the lovely baby in the care of a nanny. But in reality Vivian needed more excitement and joy, and she hated all the typical conventions of a bourgeois marriage.

Chapter Four

A Star Is Born

"I changed my name again today: I'm Vivien Leigh"
—Vivian Hartley Holman to Leigh Holman

An opportunity to break her daily monotony came unexpectedly when a friend, who was working for an advertising company, told her that they were looking for a girl to use in an advertising campaign for cigarettes. Vivian went to the casting for fun and was instantly chosen as the ideal model.

In August 1933, the Holmans took a long holiday on the Baltic Sea. The vacation had been planned for long time; however, in Copenhagen, about halfway to the destination, Vivian received an important cable from London. There was a possibility that she could have a little part in the film *Things Are Looking Up*, starring popular British actress Cicely Courtneidge. Vivian did not want to miss such a unique opportunity and decided to return home immediately. Refusing to listen to Leigh's arguments, she boarded the first ship to Southampton and left him to continue the journey by himself.

Once she arrived in England she had to wait many days before starting work, because the film production had been delayed. Finally, filming began, and each day Vivian drove to the studios in Lime Grove in her two-seater car, leaving detailed instructions for her servants at home as to what to do in her absence.

She was unpleasantly surprised when she got the script and noticed that her part as a high school student had only one line in the entire movie (which was later cut in the editing room): "If you are not the headmistress, I shan't come back next term!"

That one line, though, guaranteed her a salary of thirty shillings per day. On the set Vivian met Anne Wilding, another extra who was playing a student. The two actresses drove together every morning for two months to Cobham Hall in Kent, where the movie was being shot. During the long breaks between takes, Vivian would do the crossword puzzles from the *Times* with Anne. From that moment on, crosswords and reading would be her favorite hobbies.

It was during *Things Are Looking Up* that Vivian learned how to raise one eyebrow, a mannerism that would became a characteristic of both Scarlett O'Hara in *Gone with the Wind* and of Blanche DuBois in *A Streetcar Named Desire.*

The film opened in England in April 1935 and received decent reviews, but Vivian's name was never mentioned. She was excited by the experience, however, and she started to look for new parts to play in films. She would go out to London nightclubs with other actresses, like Gillian Maud and Beryl Samson, with the hope of being noticed by a producer or director and getting another job.

At that time in England the film industry was less difficult than Hollywood, and actresses like Vivian could freely work either in the theater or in films without a contract tying them solely to one acting world.

During the summer of 1934, Beryl Samson recommended Vivian to a young agent called John Gliddon, who had recently opened an agency and who was scouting for new talents to represent. Gliddon had been an actor himself, but had little success. As a journalist, he had also written some articles about the entertainment world, but he eventually decided to become an agent. In fact, he became the first agent of many actors who later became stars, like Deborah Kerr.

"Here was a very beautiful girl who possessed that rare gift—star quality."[1] With these words Gliddon described his first meeting with Vivian at his little office at 106 Regent Street. She truthfully confessed to him that she had only one previous professional experience, the little part in *Things Are Looking Up,* but the agent promised that he would help her to obtain major roles.

But his first priority was to change the name Vivian Hartley. Vivian immediately suggested "Susan," "Suzanne Hartley," then her maiden name "Mary Hartley," but none of these, including "April Morn" and "April Maugham," that she later proposed, seemed right. There are two different versions as to who was the first to propose Vivian Leigh. One story has Oswald Frewen quoting the Edgar Allan Poe poem "Annabel Lee," and another story centers around a conversation that Gliddon had with actor Victor Novello in which he mentioned Vivian's husband's name.

A couple of nights later, Gliddon had dinner at the Holmans to discuss Vivian's professional future with Leigh, and to reassure him of the potential qualities his wife had as an actress. He also talked about the possibility of signing an exclusive, long-term contract with his agency.

In the following weeks Gliddon took Vivian to all the social events in which the moguls of the English film industry participated. Every night she would wear a different dress to impress everybody with her sensational beauty, and she eventually got little roles in films and in plays. But the beginning of her career was not very promising. In fact, she got a little part in a play called *Murder in Mayfair* starring the popular actor Ivor Novello, but she had only one line to deliver and was fired along with other extras before the play opened.

Leigh was not jealous that his wife was going out with Gliddon every night to restaurants and nightclubs like the Ritz, the Savoy Grill or the Colony Club. He accepted the fact that it was just public relations that had the potential to help his wife's career. On one of those evenings Vivian and her agent met Leslie Howard. Gliddon asked him if he knew of any future projects in which Vivian could have a part. The actor referred him to his director and business partner Adrian Brunel, who in turn introduced Gliddon to John Payne, who was running a casting agency for low budget films.

After meeting with Payne, Vivian was offered two leading female roles, one in *The Village Squire* and another in *Gentleman's Agreement*. The first movie was a low-budget production in which Vivian played the daughter of a rich landowner, played by David Horne, who fell in love with a young actor who was acting in a local production of *Macbeth*. Vivian received a salary of twenty-five guineas for five days of work, and for the first time her name appeared in the film's reviews.

In *Gentleman's Agreement*, which she made a month later, she was a young typist, again opposite David Horne. The actor immediately became very fond of her and recommended her to director and producer Matthew Forsyth, who was looking for a girl to cast in the romantic play *The Green Sash*, which was set in Florence. The part was not easy, but Vivian obtained it and had a salary of five pounds a week.

It is interesting to read Vivian's biographical profile in the original playbill of the show, because it is erroneously stated that *The Green Sash* was her debut on the London stage after playing for two years in the "Comédie Française." The misunderstanding began during the audition when the owner of the theatre, Leon M. Lion, asked Vivian about her previous experiences. Vivian said: "The Comédie Française…" and she was immediately interrupted with a request to deliver some lines. She was about to add: "would send to my school in Paris a teacher to improve our acting technique." The director and the producers were all impressed with her beauty and her presence on stage and they signed her on, but the mix-up remained and it was included as Vivian's sole stage professional experience.

The night after *The Green Sash* opened, Charles Morgan, a critic for the *Times* used adjectives like "precision and lightness" to praise Vivian's performance in the play.[2] The article was the reason Gliddon had a meeting with film and stage director Basil Dean, who, after reading the review, was interested in meeting Vivian.

Dean was a former schoolmate of John Gliddon's and he had opened the Associated Talking Pictures Studios at Ealing just a few years before. He was interested in Vivian mostly because of her striking beauty and offered a contract to play in his next film, *Look Up and Laugh*, a musical comedy based on a screenplay by J.B. Priestley, starring Gracie Fields in the leading role opposite Vivian, who would now receive a total salary of three hundred pounds—considerably higher than the five pounds a week she was earning for the play.

The filming of *Look Up and Laugh* started in the spring of 1935. Every morning Vivian would wake up at 6:30 A.M. to be on time at the set, even though her presence was usually not required until 4 P.M.

Basil Dean was considered more of a despot than a director. He would often remind Vivian, in front of the entire crew, of her total lack of experience, insulting her nearly to the point of tears. "She was so uncontrollably nervous that for quite a while she seemed unable to take directions," remembered Dean.[3]

The film did not do justice to Vivian's real beauty; cameraman Bob Martin would often complain to Dean about Vivian's long neck: "It's a swan!"[4] On the set between takes, Vivian would study Russian, fulfilling her desire to learn other foreign languages. At the end of the filming, Dean was dissatisfied and did not give any sign to either Gliddon or Vivian that he was interested in working with her again. He still considered her little more than a beautiful woman without talent as an actress.

On her side, Vivian was even more impatient to move on with her career. It was very difficult for her to stay home and dedicate herself to Leigh or Suzanne, who got used to rarely seeing her. Little of her time was invested in nourishing familial affections; instead, she was completely devoted to cultivating her ambitions as an actress.

One night, Vivian, in the company of Beryl Samson, went to see *Queen of Scots* at the Theatre Royal. Laurence Olivier was the star of the play, and the previous year Vivian had seen the show *Biography*, by Richard

Kurt, in which he also starred. She was completely hypnotized by Olivier's charisma and his magnetism, confessing to her friend, "That's the man I'm going to marry." Samson disconcertedly replied, "I just remind you that you are married and so is he." "It doesn't matter. I'll still marry him one day!" she declared. After that night, she returned to the Theater Royal many other times, and at the end of one of the performances she was finally able to see Olivier backstage.

Theater producer Sydney Carroll, who had been an actor and a critic for the *Daily Telegraph* and *Sunday Times*, was looking for an extremely beautiful actress to be the lead in *The Mask of Virtue*, a play in costume written by Carl Sternheim. The rehearsals, directed by Maxwell Wray, were scheduled to start immediately at the Ambassadors Theatre. The director had previously tried to cast Peggy Ashcroft, Diana Churchill and Anna Neagle, but none of them, nor any other famous actress who he thought would be right for that part, was available. He was in a panic, so he called his old friend Aubrey Blackburn and asked if he had any actresses to suggest to him. As soon as Wray specified "this girl has to be spectacularly beautiful," "Vivian Leigh," was Blackburn's immediate reply.[5]

So Vivian arrived at the office of Sydney Carroll on Charing Cross Road accompanied by Gliddon. She was wearing a wide-brimmed black hat and a simple black dress, which emphasized her pale skin and her long straight black hair. The agent left Vivian in the waiting room with dozens of girls. Gliddon wanted to talk to producer Carroll and director Wray alone, specifying immediately that his client had only one professional experience on stage; however, if beauty was the main requirement, then she was the right girl. Wray opened the door of his office and went into the waiting room for a moment, when he came back he said, "If Vivian Leigh is the girl dressed in black sitting at the end of the table in the outer room, then as far I am concerned, the part is cast."[6] He was fascinated with her appearance. Carroll was also impressed with Vivian's appeal, remembering that he had noticed her a few days earlier in a restaurant. He confirmed the director's choice.

Before Vivian signed the contract, Carroll, who was keen on fortune telling, asked her to have her hand read by a palmist. The producer was impressed with Vivian's extraordinarily long line of success; therefore, he instantly offered her a contract with a salary of ten pounds a week.

Carroll had only one demand: that her name be changed from the ambiguous "Vivian" (a name used for either men or women) to "Vivien." In order to obtain the part, Vivien accepted the terms at once, and that evening when she came back home she exclaimed to her husband, "I changed my name again today: I'm Vivien Leigh."[7]

The rehearsals of *The Mask of Virtue* were extremely tiring for Vivien. Although she was very determined and beautiful, she still looked too young and inexperienced in the eyes of the company. She had to literally be coached line-by-line by another actress,[8] who also helped Vivien with some respiratory and vocal exercises. In addition, director Wray used all the possible devices, from make up to the right lighting, to make Vivien look dazzling in her period costumes.

On May 15, 1935, the opening night at the Ambassadors Theatre, Vivien Leigh became an overnight success on stage and an instant star. The audience was hypnotized by her presence and her striking beauty. It seemed impossible not to look at her when on stage, even though her voice, especially in two scenes where she had to cry, was not totally convincing. Once the curtain fell, thought, she received twenty minutes of applause.

Many of Vivien's future friends were in the audience that night: Noël Coward, John Gielgud, Terence Rattigan and Hungarian producer and director Alexander Korda. Korda was obsessed with motion pictures, and he did not have any interest in any other art forms unless they could be a source of inspiration for a possible film. Therefore, he would rarely go to the theatre, and the opening night of *The Mask of Virtue* was an exception. As Paul Tabori wrote in his biography of Korda,

> That night Korda, Joseph M. Schenck, Murray Silverstone and Monty Marks were dining at the Savoy Grill.... About nine o'clock Korda suddenly remembered that he had two tickets to the opening of a show in his pocket, one that a film critic had asked him to attend in order to see a new leading lady. The two Americans decided to go along, even though it was getting rather late. They reached the theatre in the middle of the last act. A strikingly beautiful young girl was on stage, and all four of the late-comers were instantly struck by her looks and her talent.... After the play ended, with many curtain-calls, the two Americans and Korda held a hasty conference. The Americans agreed that Korda should have 'first go.' If he could sign her up, they would retire from the competition. If he couldn't—well, then let the best man win.[9]

Vivien had visited Korda's office a couple of months earlier, but Korda, who at the time was the most famous and powerful film producer in England after the international success of *The Private Life of Henry VIII* and *The Scarlet Pimpernel*, was not impressed by her. In his opinion, she looked beautiful and charming, but she lacked those charismatic qualities necessary to make her a star. Moreover, Vivien reminded him of Merle Oberon, his last discovery, and an actress with whom he had an affair.

Therefore, he was not interested in someone so similar to her. But that night, a few lines delivered on stage by Vivien were enough to change his mind. Without knocking, he entered her dressing room, apologizing immediately for the mistake he had made judging her too hurriedly: "Even an Hungarian can make a mistake."[10] After congratulating her, he scheduled an appointment at his office for the following day.

Vivien was radiant with joy, and after she removed her make-up and changed, she went with her parents and Leigh to a party thrown for the cast at the Savoy and then to dance at Florida, which at the time was the trendiest club in London. She stayed awake and waited until 4 A.M. for the reviews to come in the morning papers.

The critics were all enthusiastic: "A Star Is Born," "A New Actress," "A Triumph" were some of the headlines that appeared in London's major newspapers. The public's enthusiasm and that of the critics kept growing in the following days. Every day, on the doorstep of her home, Vivien would find a journalist who wanted to learn more about her private life. All the articles from that period describe her as a young, talented actress with a very promising future. They all mention her great ability to balance her profession with the difficult task of being a good mother. Unfortunately, motherhood seemed to be the least of Vivien's priorities. She would have reporters take photographs of her holding little Suzanne in her arms, stating that she hoped that one day her daughter would be an actress, too. But then, right after that, she would leave the child in the care of a nanny, who often complained about how obstinate and bossy Suzanne was. Vivien's dry comment in a letter to Leigh was, "Silly old bitch, her own fault for spoiling her."[11]

Vivien did not understand that giving special attention to her daughter was the only way to make up for her lack of maternal presence, which would only appear in the form of long notes with instructions to the nanny. Suzanne was destined to be raised as a child with few memories of her mother. She spent more time with her grandmother Gertrude and her father, who would try to spend every moment of his spare time with her.

In the meantime, the contract between Vivien and Korda took almost six months to be signed due to exhausting negotiations between the producer and Gliddon. Finally, along with the approval of Leigh Holman, the producer and agent agreed to an exclusive five-year contract in which Vivien committed herself to make two films a year and receive a total salary of 50 thousand pounds. In addition, the contract allowed for the possibility of acting in a play during a six month period each year. The contract details were immediately disclosed to the press, who announced the news with great clamor, giving the impression that Vivien had already received the agreed amount. She would actually be paid in five yearly installments. As a token of appreciation for her new contract, Vivien gave Gliddon a silver cigarette case inscribed with the words "With love, Vivien Leigh."

Due to the great success of *The Mask of Virtue*, the play was transferred from the Ambassadors Theatre to the larger St. James Theatre. But there the low tone of Vivien's voice was lost in the void; the theater was simply too big. The play could not go back to the original location, so the company started a tour and carefully selected the theaters so that the problem would not arise again.

The first to notice Vivien's vocal problem was theater critic James Agate, who wrote in reviewing the play: "[Vivien Leigh] gives to this part all it asks except in the matter of speech. If this young lady wants to become an actress, as distinct from a film star, she should at once seek means to improve her over tone, which is displeasing to the fastidious ear."[12] Vivien immediately followed the advice and started phonetic lessons.

Once the running of the play terminated, she did not work for a while. Every day she became more impatient to go back to work. Finally she received simultaneous offers to play Ophelia opposite Leslie Howard in a Broadway production of *Hamlet* and a call from Korda, who had decided to start a film version of *Cyrano de Bergerac* starring Charles Laughton with her as Rosanne.

As suggested by Gliddon, Vivien sent a telegram to Howard asking him to wait for a couple of weeks until Korda confirmed the project. Howard accepted the request to wait, and in the meantime Vivien took a screen test for the film. The studio requested that she dye her hair blonde, but she was reluctant and obtained permission to wear a wig. The only time that Vivien would change her hair color was to play Blanche DuBois in *A Streetcar Named Desire* on stage because she was convinced to do so by Laurence Olivier, who was the director.

While she was waiting for an answer from Korda, Vivien was living an intense, worldly life. One night she met John Buckmaster, the son of her friend Gladys Cooper and Herbert Buckmaster, the founder of "Buck," an exclusive St. James club for men. John was two years younger than Vivien. He was extremely handsome, a male version of his mother, an expert tennis player and a sophisticated man, who later became an actor and nightclub entertainer in New York. The friendship between Vivien and John was intense, and he instantly became her companion on many evenings instead of Leigh, who detested any sort of fatuous social event. Eventually, Buckmaster would turn out to be the first man Vivien would have an affair with during her marriage.[13]

Vivien's sexual needs were probably not satisfied by marriage, and the idea of cheating on Leigh apparently did not cause her any sense of guilt, despite the fact that she knew that committing adultery in England was still consider a crime. Buckmaster was not the only person who was Vivien's lover. Some, such as actress Eve Philips, stated that for a short but intense time Vivien had an affair with Alex Korda, before later starting her stable, adulterous relationship with Laurence Olivier, who was also married.[14]

As a matter of fact, Korda and Vivien had many things in common: they were both born outside of England, but they adopted it as their country and considered it their real home. Vivien had been educated in Europe and Korda had started his work in Paris and Berlin. In addition, they both loved living comfortably and having an intense social life.

The project of *Cyrano de Bergerac* came to nothing when Charles Laughton said that he would not be interested in the part. On Vivien's insistence, Gliddon immediately cabled Leslie Howard to confirm her availability for *Hamlet*, but the communication arrived too late, and Howard had already cast another actress.

In the meantime Vivien kept busy by working as a model for several women's magazines. Among the jobs was the promotion of "Matita," a beauty skin cream, and a portrait by Cecil Beaton for Vogue in which Vivien was wearing a dress by the famous designer Victor Stiebel, who later became Vivien's close friend, often sending her new designs created exclusively for her. Each time Vivien wore a dress by a famous designer she would order some custom changes, like different buttons or the addition of cuffs or hems, personalizing her wardrobe according to the occasion in order to make it unique.

Some days before the play closed, Laurence Olivier and his wife Jill Esmond attended one of Vivien's performances of *The Mask of Virtue*. The actor described in his autobiography the impression he had of Vivien that night: "Apart from her looks which were magical, she possessed beautiful poise; her neck looked almost too fragile to support her head. She also had something else: an attraction of the most perturbing nature I had ever encountered. It may have been the strangely touching spark of dignity in her that enslaved the ardent legion of her admirers."[15]

Two months later Shakespeare's *Romeo and Juliet*, starring Olivier and John Gielgud, happened to be the event of the theatrical season of 1935. The two actors alternated the roles of Romeo and Mercutio. For the first time, the main character was performed with an extreme sensuality rather than the typical romantic sensibility. This new way of playing Romeo aroused lively interest among critics.

Vivien attended the opening of the show and saw it several times. She was completely mesmerized by Olivier. At the end of one of the performances, she showed up in his dressing room, and in front of other people exclaimed: "I'm Vivien Leigh and I just had to tell you how marvelous you were."[16] Then, a few minutes later when she remained alone with him, as Olivier remembered, she gave him a soft little kiss on the shoulder before leaving.[17]

The next encounter happened some nights later at the Savoy Grill. Vivien was in the company of John Buckmaster at a table not far from Olivier and his wife. The actor had shaved his beard and mustache to look younger for his role as Romeo. "What an odd little thing Larry looks without mustache," commented a laughing Buckmaster, who knew Olivier. Vivien found his comment strangely irritating.

"I was very indignant and I said rather pompously that he did not look funny at all!" Vivien recalled. "Then Larry came over as we were leaving and he invited me to join a party that the weekend. I said that he presumably meant the two of us—my husband as well—and so we went and we played football, and I remember Larry roaring around one minute and then accountably falling fast asleep under the piano next."[18]

That was not a particularly romantic beginning for a romance, and that weekend was not an occasion to get to know each other better, even though the reciprocal attraction between the two was obvious.

Vivien was offered a leading role opposite Ivor Novello in *The Happy Hypocrite*, a musical comedy written by Clemence Dane and Richard Addinsell, based on the novel with the same title by Max Beerbohm. Because the show was opening in April, Vivien also had the opportunity to be part of the cast of Shakespeare's *Richard II* at Oxford University. The department of dramatic art would often ask for the presence of professional actors and actresses in their productions. John Gielgud called Vivien to audition for the part of the queen. Although she was very nervous, Vivien got away with it perfectly and was cast by director Glen Byam Shaw, who was firmly convinced that Vivien would bewitch the exclusively all-male audience of Oxford.

Although her role was not very long, Vivien was very convincing, especially wearing the magnificent period costumes. During the running of the play, she would take her meals at the University cafeteria, and during her breaks she would write long letters to Leigh, expressing her solitude and her feelings of homesickness.

On February 17, 1936, *Richard II* opened. The *Times* wrote a despicable article on Vivien, who did not pay too much attention to it, being too busy rehearsing her next role in *The Happy Hypocrite*, in which she had to sing. She accepted the difficult part because she was enormously fascinated with the challenge of participating in something new.

Before debuting in London, *The Happy Hypocrite* was first presented for a short run in Manchester and Southport. Vivien would spend her resting time playing cards with her colleagues, mostly during the long trips by train. Cards, along with crosswords, were her favorite pastime; sleeping was the least of her interests, and after playing canasta or bridge, she would spend the rest of the night reading and chain-smoking. She would sleep no more than five hours a night.

One night, the cast of *The Happy Hypocrite* went to see Lillian Gish in *The Old Maid*. Everybody laughed at the dramatic performance of the actress, while Vivien and Novello were intensely moved to tears.

The Happy Hypocrite was warmly received, and on the night of the opening in Manchester, Gertrude and Ernest were applauding in the audience.

As usual, Vivien would write to Leigh every day until the show opened at His Majesty's Theatre in London's West End on April 8, 1936.

Although the reviews were mixed, Vivien received good mentions. "Vivien Leigh's performance was of exquisite sensibility—a foreshadowing of how much to come in later years."

On the opening night Olivier and his six-month-pregnant wife Jill went backstage to congratulate Vivien. Olivier had recently told his wife that if the child were a boy, he would name him Tarquin. After the initial compliments, Vivien kept looking at Esmond's pregnant belly and couldn't stop saying: "And how's little Tarquin?" Olivier's embarrassment was evident. It was, in fact, like a public announcement that Vivien was his mistress.[19]

That same night Leigh went alone to ski at Davos in Switzerland, leaving Vivien in the hands of her companions.

During the rehearsals of *The Happy Hypocrite*, Novello introduced Vivien to the photographer Angus McBean. "I've found a girl with a dream of a face, which will give you no trouble." Those were the words spoken by Novello over the phone to McBean, who was chosen to take some production photographs of the play's cast.[20]

"By the end of her first night in the play, I think I had fallen in love with her ... for weeks afterwards Vivien and her beauty were very much on my mind."[21] And from that moment on, Vivien, along with Audrey Hepburn in the 1950s, became McBean's favorite model, and he her official photographer.

The audience did not understand the obscure symbolism of the play and *The Happy Hypocrite* was forced to close two weeks in advance.

Although 18 months had passed since Vivien had signed her contract with Korda, she had yet to make a film. In a letter addressed to Gliddon, Korda's attorney expressed his regret that no appropriate roles had been found for Vivien. For a while, she started to doubt her look and decided to make an exotic change. She started wearing more colorful dresses and heavy make-up.

As he did every year, Sydney Carroll organized an open-air production in Regent Park.

Vivien, early portrait

Through her agent, Vivien got the part of Anne Boleyn in Shakespeare's *Henry VIII*. This seemed to her to be a good opportunity to improve her experience in the classical theatre. She would later state in an interview, "I like playing Shakespeare better than anything else, because I think he wrote the greatest plays.... And I think one learns more through acting in classical plays than one does through anything else.... Classics require much more imagination and more training."[22]

Due to a rainy summer, the acting troupe ended up working on the play beneath a canvas tent. Vivien's voice lost strength because of several colds she caught while acting outdoors. To improve her vocal ability, Vivien would take daily lessons from Olivier's former teacher Elsie Fogerty. Fogerty's method began by having Vivien remove her high heel shoes and stand in her stockings while exercising her voice. This would allow Vivien to feel her voice vibrate through her entire body.

In the last six months of 1936 Korda cast Vivien in three films; one of these was *Fire Over England* opposite Olivier, who she was regularly seeing in secret.

Chapter Five

Larry, Larry, Larry

"I'd rather live a short life with Larry than
face a long one without him."
—Vivien Leigh to a friend

Laurence Olivier was born in Dorking, Surrey, on March 22, 1907. He was the son of a minister in the Anglican church, from whom he received a strict religious education. His mother, who he referred to in his autobiography as "my entire world,"[1] died when he was only twelve. After he studied at the School of Speech and Drama, Olivier had his first professional experiences on the stages of Birmingham and the West End theaters of London.

While in London he met his first wife, Jill Esmond Moore, who was acting with him in John Drinkwater's comedy *Bird in Hand*. Together they were scouted by playwright Noël Coward (Vivien's future close friend), who offered them a role in his last play *Private Lives*, which brought them to New York during its tour. Because of a repressive upbringing, Jill Esmond was Olivier's first sentimental and sexual experience with a female. Unfortunately, the marriage did not work from its first days. The theater was the only place where Larry could escape and vent his frustrations, and it was working on stage that slowly gave him confidence and poise. In a short time he became one of the most promising actors of the English theater along with John Gielgud and his close friend Ralph Richardson.

In 1935, although he was having great success in *Romeo and Juliet*, Olivier went through a difficult period dominated by personal unhappiness, which pushed him to have a brief homosexual experience. This affair ended after he met Vivien and started working with her.[2]

The filming of *Fire Over England* began in July 1936 at the Denham studios. Korda gave Vivien a great opportunity not only to work opposite Olivier, but also to be supported by a first-rate cast, which included Flora Robson and Raymond Massey. An uncredited young James Mason had a secondary role and was also under the supervision of German producer Erich Pommer.

Vivien was cast as Cynthia, a lady-in-waiting for the Queen, who is jealous of the romance between her servant and a handsome naval officer, played by Olivier. The first professional meeting on the set between Vivien and Olivier happened in the corridor of the self-help canteen. When she kindly remarked that she was excited to be working with him, Olivier laughingly replied, "People always get sick of each other when making a film—we shall probably end up by fighting."[3] Nevertheless, during the fourteen weeks of shooting, the two lovers did not have any arguments. When Vivien did not have to shoot a scene she would observe Olivier acting. She would often worry because he did not want any doubles, not even for the most dangerous action scenes.

The love scenes were extended compared to the first draft of the script, and they reflected on screen exactly what was happening in real life. The affair was not a secret to anyone on the set, and with the excuse of rehearsing a scene, Vivien and Olivier would often lock themselves in one of the dressing rooms. Olivier would leave after a long time looking exhausted and worn-out. He confessed to a friend, who noticed that he was always fatigued, "It's not the stunts. It's Vivien. It's every day two, three times. She's bloody wearing me out."[4]

In the following years, Vivien's high sexual drive would be a matter of complaint for Olivier, especially during her manic-depressive crises, when her sexual energy would increase alarmingly. Although her body was delicate and she almost looked as she was made of porcelain, Vivien had an incredible erotic power over all of her men, a strength that she physically had to exercise on a daily basis through sex.

The affair was happening while Leigh Holman was sailing on vacation in Sweden, and while Jill Esmond was at home going through her last days of pregnancy. On the set Korda took on the role of adviser to everyone with a problem. One day Vivien and Olivier went to his office and told him, "Alex, we must tell you our great secret—we are in love and we're going to get married." He smiled and said, "Don't be silly—everybody knows that. I've known it for weeks and weeks."[5] Korda advised the two lovers to be very discreet because if the affair reached the press and the public, they could jeopardize their careers and give bad publicity to the film.

When the shooting of *Fire Over England* was almost completed, Vivien met Winston Churchill, Oswald Frewen's cousin, who Korda had invited to the set. Churchill would become a friend and a big fan of Vivien's films. Vivien loved making movies; however, she felt depressed when she heard that she only had a one-day break between films before she would have to immediately start shooting *Dark Journey* at the same studio.

In addition, on August 21 she received the news of the birth of Simon Tarquin Olivier, whose father had to be next to his wife to celebrate the happy event. Although the separation was for a very brief time, Vivien could not resist the temptation to go to the baby's christening bash. At the party it was noticed that she vanished with Olivier for some time. When they came back separately, Olivier had some lipstick showing on his cheek, and Vivien left right afterward.

Vivien gave the announcement of Tarquin Olivier's birth to Leigh Holman in a letter dated August 26, 1936: "Jill had her baby & I saw it last night. It is really very attractive & very big but not fat. Larry says it is like Edward G. Robinson, which is a little cruel. He has already started reciting Shakespeare to it. We drank its health at the studio yesterday."[6] In the same letter she suggested that her husband not return from his holiday, because she would be busy for the next five weeks filming *Dark Journey* in Dehman.

While Leigh was away, Oswald Frewen went to visit Vivien at home because she was ill in bed with the flu. Frewen found Olivier lovingly looking after her, and sensed that something was happening between the two of them.

The script of *Dark Journey* was a very complicated spy story which Vivien herself admitted in a letter to Leigh that she did not completely understand.

The film was directed by Victor Saville, and took place in Stockholm in 1918. Vivien was Madeleine Godard, the French owner of a fashion atelier and boutique who sewed codes and maps inside the linen of dresses as a spy for the British allies.

Filming with Saville was a pleasant experience for Vivien, because the director was almost always satisfied with the first take, especially when it came to Vivien's close-ups. Vivien learned many technical devices on the set, such as the importance of the placement of chalk marks, how to lean her body too much or too little, and positioning her face to her advantage. *Dark Journey* was made in five weeks, and it was fairly successful and earned positive reviews.

Vivien was supposed to start *Storm in a Teacup*, her third film for

Korda, immediately after *Dark Journey* was completed, but she decided to take a ten-day vacation because she was too exhausted to immediately resume her work. Since Leigh was also busy with his profession, Vivien asked Oswald Frewen to accompany her on her trip to Italy. Frewen, being the perfect gentleman, first asked Leigh's permission, and he agreed without problems.

On October 25 Vivien and Frewen left for Taormina, Sicily. Once they arrived at the resort, they stayed at the Hotel San Domenico, from which they took many excursions, like one to the city of Catania and another hiking to the top of Mount Etna.

The two friends shared the same room, because Vivien did not like to sleep alone, and, as Frewen wrote in his diaries, the sexual tension was very high. In fact he had a crush on Vivien, but he never had the courage to reveal it to her, because he was respectful of Holman and because he knew about the affair with Olivier.

Frewen, like many other friends of Vivien's, noticed around this time that Vivien began assuming many of Olivier's characteristic attitudes and mannerisms. Among those was the continuous use of the word "fucking" which was constantly present in Olivier's sentences. Despite her gentle manners, Vivien never had a problem using profanity while talking. It was a habit that often made other women feel uncomfortable when in her presence, and it would increase during her violent manic-depressive attacks.

After visiting the Greco-Roman amphitheatre in Taormina and shopping along its narrow streets, Vivien decided to go to Naples because she was apparently very interested in visiting the city and the excavations of Pompeii, but her real planned destination was the island of Capri. In fact, Olivier and his wife were on holiday in Capri, and were staying at the Hotel Quisisana.

Although she was afraid of flying (a fear that would be present throughout her life), Vivien was determined to reach Naples in as little time as possible. She purchased a ticket on a seaplane, which arrived at its destination after an entire day of flight due to a strong wind that frightened all the passengers on board.

The arrival in Capri and the embarrassing meeting of the lovers in the lobby of the hotel was described in detail by Frewen in his diary:

> Larry, the other side of the hall cried in a loud voice, "Vivien!" and Viv, my side of the hall, cried loudly "Darling!" and Jill uttered further love-cries as all the three met in the middle of what I could only describe as a joint passionate embrace, the while I smiled with benignity! It was a scene as false in its greetings as in its contrived unexpectedness. The three broke away and both Larry and Viv at the

same moment made an advance on me and introduced Jill.... I was given a room the side of the Oliviers and Viv the other, so we were three in line and all on communal basis—nobody ever knocked to enter and we all used all three rooms at will and Viv confided to me she thought it was 'all right' and that we were not unwelcome.[7]

Tarquin Olivier had a completely different version. "Jill needed a rest from child birth, from London, from the near presence of the woman who threatened all that they had hoped for as a man and wife.... They checked into the Hotel Quisisana in Capri wondering whether the magic of the place would work. Within only a few days they were landed upon by Vivien who was determined to pry them apart.... They were all photographed together, with Jill's unmade-up mauve-veined face swollen with sunshine, and perhaps with crying."[8]

Despite the bad weather Vivien would take long walks across the island, where she visited her friend, the writer Axel Munthe, who had been living in Capri for years and had always invited Vivien to visit him. Olivier, meanwhile, would study literary criticism on *Hamlet* and engage in long conversations about the incestuous feelings of the character toward his mother with the famous psychologist Ernest Jones, who was also vacationing on the island.

Frewen and Vivien left Capri after four days and went to Rome while the Oliviers stopped in Naples. Olivier began missing Vivien intensely, and he called her to tell her how he realized that he wanted to be near her and that he was willing to leave his wife. Frewen was informed of the telephone conversation and begged Vivien not to rush into any decision for their own good, and for the good of their spouses. Later, Vivien explained to her friend that Olivier's feelings for her became clear on the island, when he finally had both her and Jill in front of his eyes for a long period of time.

Upon her return to London, Jill Esmond tried in every possible way to win back her husband, and even tried to get to know Vivien better by having lunch with her and seeing her regularly. But the situation turned out to give Vivien the advantage, since she learned from Jill all that she did not know about Olivier. She discovered his likes and dislikes, which gave her the opportunity to improve herself as his lover.

Despite the fact that Vivien was stealing her husband, Jill basically liked her. The two women eventually became friends, and Jill would often advise Vivien on books to read, which the two would later discuss together. According to Tarquin Olivier, although Vivien spoke French and German fluently, she did not have a great education. However it was very easy for her to learn new things, and she was always eager to improve and cultivate herself as much as possible.

In a moment of intimacy, Vivien asked Jill about her breast-feeding, and Esmond admitted that she had tried from the beginning, but that she had to give up because she was not producing enough milk. This made her feel like a failure as a mother. "Not as much a failure as me," Vivien replied, explaining that she had breast-fed Suzanne and hated it, since it pulled down her breasts and they never recovered their original shape.[9] She had sworn then not to have any children again.

Vivien celebrated her twenty-third birthday during the filming of *Storm in a Teacup*, the first of two movies in which she played opposite Rex Harrison. The story was based on a comedy written by Bruno Frank and had a subject that was completely new at the time: the fight against a dictatorship in Europe, inspired by a dog tax levy in Germany. *Storm in a Teacup* gave Vivien the chance to showcase her perfect French and her ability to play golf.

Although the film was a light comedy, Saville, who was directing Vivien again, was not persuasive enough to convince her to shoot a scene where she was supposed to fall on her buttocks. "I am a British actress" Vivien said simply, which meant "I'm a serious professional and I do not degrade myself to certain levels."[10]

The film received excellent reviews and the couple, Vivien Leigh and Rex Harrison, was compared by the British press to the Americans Myrna Loy and William Powell, who became popular for the *Thin Man* movies. Harrison had a platonic crush on Vivien, who was always talking to him about Larry. This made him shy, and Harrison was never brave enough to be bolder with his advances. "She was very much like a cat," Harrison remembers in his autobiography. "She would purr and she would scratch and she looked divinely pretty doing either…," adding, "I remember that Vivien hoped to go to Elsinore to play Ophelia in *Hamlet*, opposite Olivier, and when she feared she couldn't, she broke down in the dressing room in wild hysteria, anger and anguish."[11]

At that moment, the only thing Vivien could do was patiently wait for a casting call from the project in Denmark and watch Olivier playing in *Hamlet* in London. After her daily takes, she would go directly from the studios to the theater to watch him during his rehearsals, often without stopping at home to change or to say hello to Suzanne.

During the 1936 Christmas holidays, Vivien and Leigh went to ski at Kitzbuhl and Sils in Austria, where she broke her ankle in a ski accident. The situation worsened when she strained some muscles and injured a knee at the beginning of the new year. Forced to rest, Vivien spent most of her time reading. There was one book among the pile that particularly impressed her, a novel written by Margaret Mitchell, an American writer who was having incredible success in the States with her first book, published in May 1936: *Gone with the Wind*.

After her convalescence, Vivien was cast in a small part in the comedy *Because We Must*. The rehearsals began at Wyndham Theatre, where the show debuted on February 5. Her enthusiasm for *Gone with the Wind* grew every day as she voraciously read through the 1000 pages. She gave some copies of the book as gifts to the other actors in the company on the occasion of the London premiere of *Because We Must*.

Two weeks later *Fire Over England* opened in British movie theaters, and a gala premiere was organized at the Leicester Square Theatre, which was attended by the Duke and the Duchess of Norfolk and some military authorities. A crowd of fans gathered to watch the arrival of the celebrities under a heavy rain.

The film received mixed reviews, but Vivien was finally judged as "an actress and not merely a decoration"; "a combination of intelligence, beauty and emotional sympathy." Apparently Adolf Hitler was a great fan of *Fire Over England*, and he saw the film several times and screened it for friends and dignitaries. Winston Churchill would do this same thing with the movie *Lady Hamilton*.

On March 11, 1937, about a month after *Because We Must* closed, Vivien was chosen to interpret a little role in Sydney Carroll's production *Bats in the Belfry*, a funny comedy that allowed the actors to improvise parts of the text when teasing each other. *Dark Journey* opened in those days too, grossing more than 500,000 pounds in just one week. The film gave Vivien enormous popularity; until then her success had been confined to the theater audience.

One night Alexander Korda invited Vivien, Olivier and their spouses to dinner at The Moulin d'Or to explain his next project: a film called *The First and the Last* in which the two lovers would be the leading stars. Filming was scheduled to start in early May, which gave Vivien freedom from work for a while.

The friendship between the two couples became more intense, and the Holmans and the Oliviers visited Oswald Frewen at his estate, The Sheephouse, for a picnic. They also stayed in the same inn in Rye. "Vivien's husband struck me as being a dull man, dry, cerebral, without sparkle; I was quite wrong about this.... He was highly intelligent, clever, but not exciting or outwardly romantic." Later, after many unpleasant situations, Olivier's idea of Vivien's husband totally changed: "I grew to like Leigh Holman very much."[12]

In May 1937, at the studio in Dehman, director Basil Dean started shooting *The First and the Last*. The screenplay was based on a short story with the same title by John Galsworthy; Graham Greene adapted it to the screen. Greene was one of the most important British film critics at the time, and he was not satisfied with the final result of the movie. However his solid friendship with Korda would bring him to collaborate again on two other films: *The Fallen Idol* and *The Third Man.*

Basil Dean found working with Olivier and Vivien very difficult. They would flirt, laugh and tease each other all the time and did not take the plot of the film seriously. At the same time Olivier was coaching Vivien's acting to prepare her for her role as Ophelia. She had, in fact, been chosen by the Old Vic company to be part of Shakespeare's production of *Hamlet* in Elsinore, Denmark.[13] Olivier knew how skeptical director Tyrone Guthrie was about Vivien (he would have preferred Jill Esmond) and he only picked her because Olivier insisted.

So, with great zeal, Olivier tried to coach Vivien so as not to disappoint the director. On a daily basis he helped deliver her lines in the car during the commute to the studios and during every spare moment he had available. To allow the two stars to go to Denmark and visit the real places where the tragedy of *Hamlet* was set, filming was stopped for few days, resulting in an enormous increase in the production budget. Once Vivien was confirmed as Ophelia, Korda did not refuse her permission to leave the set of *The First and the Last* because he was convinced that the Danish experience would be beneficial, not only to her career but also to his films.

Before leaving for Denmark, Jill Esmond, always eager to save her marriage, tried to confront Vivien and openly talk about Olivier. However, once she arrived at the Little Stanhope apartment, she lost her courage and did not tell her what she had in mind. She realized that she had lost her husband forever.

The Old Vic was the first company to bring the castle of Kronborg an all-British cast to play *Hamlet.*

The idea was born from a suggestion made by the Danish Tourist Board in London during the time that Olivier was playing *Hamlet* in the West End. The negotiations were very long because of the doubts Olivier and Guthrie, the director, had. They finally enthusiastically accepted the offer after they visited Denmark and inspected the Kronborg castle, which was built in the sixteen century and located near Copenhagen. They both agreed that the event would be very prestigious for the British nation.

As soon as she arrived at the Danish capital, Vivien sent a telegram to Leigh telling him that she was in good health and that the journey was fine; she was ready to start the rehearsals at the castle.

Anthony Quayle as Laertes and Alec Guinness as Osric were also part of the cast. That summer happened to be the rainiest Denmark had known in 23 years. The rehearsals took place in the large courtyard of the castle with the actors wearing long, rubber overshoes, raincoats and umbrellas to protect themselves from the heavy rain. Due to the bad weather, the atmosphere was very tense. According to Olivier's biographer Thomas Kiernan, Vivien had a strong attack of depression during her stay at Elsinore, switching moods from long moments of silence to hysterical cries, causing many to wonder whether she would be able to work.[14]

Jill Esmond, who was accompanying Olivier, often watched the rehearsals under a waterproof tent, carefully observing her husband and Vivien as they acted in the love scenes. On this occasion the two lovers showed very little consideration for their partners, and they were often caught in public effusions of love. Alec Guinness often took long walks around the lake with Jill, so Vivien and Olivier would not be disturbed. Then Leigh Holman arrived in Denmark by surprise, checking into a single room at the Marienlist Hotel where the Old Vic's company was staying.

The flood that hit the night of the Copenhagen debut forced the cast to present *Hamlet* in the huge hotel ballroom in front of his majesty the Prince of Denmark. The tall crown prince, who occupied a front row seat near the stage area, caused the actors to worry about tripping over his long legs. Although it had only 800 seats, the ballroom was crowded with over 2000 people.

Performing in the hotel ballroom instead of the castle was a huge disappointment to everybody but Vivien, because she knew that a smaller ambiance was more favorable for her tone of voice. Her interpretation was acclaimed with a fifteen minute standing ovation. Vivien was ecstatic; she was playing Shakespeare, her favorite playwright, opposite the man she madly loved. It was a dream come true.

Once they went back to the set of *The First and the Last*, they found Korda directing the film himself. He added new scenes to the script and changed the title to *Twenty-One Days*. The movie opened in January 1940, two years later, when the producer finally sold it to Columbia Pictures, a sale that was helped by the fact that the affair between Vivien and Olivier was now common knowledge. The title was then changed again for the American market into *Twenty-One Days Together*.

Twenty-One Days was a fiasco even though the reviews were surprisingly indulgent. Vivien and Olivier hated it, and when they watched it in the U.S. they walked out before the film was finished.

During one of the last days of filming, while shooting a scene on a boat on the Thames, some members of the cast talked about the highly publicized quest of Metro Goldwyn Mayer for actors to cast in the upcoming screen production of *Gone with the Wind*. Someone started listing all the possible candidates for the leading role: Robert Taylor, Gary Cooper, Errol Flynn and Cary Grant; somebody else suggested Olivier as a perfect Rhett Butler, making him smile. But Vivien quickly stood announcing loudly: "Larry won't play Rhett Butler, but I shall play Scarlett O'Hara. Wait and see."

Vivien's statement was later repeated to a reporter from the *Evening News*, who interviewed her at the studios in Dehman. "I've never been so gripped by anything in my life. It's the finest book I've read, what a grand film it would make! I've cast myself for Scarlett O'Hara."[15]

This announcement was a great mistake, because Vivien should have asked Korda's permission first. Her statement made the director upset, especially since the interview did not help the promotion of *Twenty-One Days*.

Vivien's obsession with *Gone with the Wind* kept growing. As soon as she heard that producer David Selznick had bought the film-rights from Margaret Mitchell and was casting the parts, she asked John Gliddon to suggest her name as the ideal actress to play Scarlett. Gliddon sent a cable to Selznick and the producer answered a couple of days later stating that, at the moment, he was not interested in Vivien. He also added that he had not yet seen her photographs, but promised to watch her in *Fire Over England* once the movie opened in America.

Ten days later, after their return from Denmark and at the end of the filming of *Twenty-One Days*, Vivien told Leigh her intention of separating and living with Olivier. After carefully analyzing the situation, Holman accepted the idea of a separation with the belief that with Vivien's inconstancy, the idea of living with Olivier was only a temporary whim and she would eventually return to him.

Oswald Frewen, Holman's confidant, was in Marseille and therefore could not advise the couple. He was very worried about the delicate situation and wrote in his diaries that knowing Olivier's difficult character, he would not last with Vivien more than five years.[16]

The lovers found and rented a place to live in Durham Cottage on 4 Christchurch Street, in the neighborhood of Chelsea, but they did not move in until a year later after a long renovation.

A month after her separation from Leigh, Vivien wrote him a letter in which she confirmed her decision as final. Leigh told his mother in law Gertrude the details, specifying that he never implored Vivien to come back. He had accepted the decision reluctantly, trying to save at least their friendship, mostly for the sake of their daughter Suzanne.

Vivien and Leigh Holman would always be good friends, and years later when Olivier would leave her, her first husband would once again be close. Holman was not indulgent in the beginning, however, when he initially categorically refused to grant her the divorce.

On Vivien's insistence and through Gliddon, the two lovers met with a lawyer. The attorney's advice was the same for both: to be patient and to wait for their partners to grant the divorce, because without their consent, it would be an endless battle with the possibility of charges of adultery and desertion. Unsatisfied with the consultation, Vivien commented impatiently: "What a ridiculous little man!"

Her dedication to Olivier was total and exclusive, and living together with him left no time for Suzanne. In fact, Vivien had decided that it was best for her daughter to stay with her father. Her role as a mother passed from little to nonexistent. Gertrude was and continued to be the real mother to Suzanne, now six years old, even though Vivien pretended to be a mother by choosing her new nannies, women who were substitutes for her.

Jill Esmond asked the advice of Noël Coward, who wanted to meet alone with Olivier to get a better picture of the situation. After the meeting, the only advice the playwright had for Jill was for her to leave England for a while. Coward was very fond of Esmond, but when he saw the usually self-controlled Olivier so taken by passion for Vivien, he realized that there was nothing to do about saving the marriage .

Jill followed her friend's advice and went to Antibes on the French Riviera. She was convinced that after filming *Twenty-One Days*, Olivier would realize what a big mistake he had made and would go back to being the good husband and father she always thought he was. But Esmond's dream was shattered when she returned to England and heard that Vivien and Olivier were living together.[17]

Durham Cottage was a charming, but small, seventeenth-century house with a nice garden, but it was in need of a radical renovation. Conscious of Vivien's state of anxiety, Olivier organized a brief holiday in Venice. They checked into a little hotel on the Grand Canal and they spent the days strolling between the channels and visiting churches and museums. Olivier soon noticed how good the vacation was for Vivien, who forgot all her anxieties.

When they returned to London, Olivier started filming *The Divorce of Lady X*, while Vivien was busy directing the work and restoration of the house. Vivien decorated it in Regency style with striped and pastel colored curtains and tapestries. She also hung all of her favorite paintings.

As Tarquin Olivier remembers: "She had the gift of making him proud of her, in a way that Jill had never been able to do, with her femininity, little flower arrangements or presents for a friend or some kindness. She always looked frail and beautiful: even if she had worn undercarpet and chains, her long pliant neck and the poise of her movement would have made her yet more regal."[18]

Suddenly, Paramount made Vivien an offer to play a leading role in Cecil B. De Mille's next production, *Union Pacific*. The proposal was very favorable for Vivien because she would earn 3,500 pounds for seven weeks of work, with the option for it to become 14,000 if she agreed to play in another film by the end of that year. She would also receive free, first class transportation and an extra 40 pounds for living expenses. Vivien had Gliddon answer it with a counterproposal that included some extra requests and a higher salary, but no answer came back and the role was given to Barbara Stanwyck.

The major moves in Vivien's career were always made by Korda, who thought that she needed more visibility. For that reason he loaned her to Metro Goldwyn Mayer for the first all-British cast production of *A Yank at Oxford*.

In the beginning Mayer was reluctant to use Vivien, but British MGM's head of production Michael Balcon made him change his mind, explaining that Vivien was living in London and, therefore, no extra travel expenses would be involved. In addition, her salary would be more convenient since she was an actress on loan from Korda. This was much cheaper than paying to have someone imported from Hollywood. Finally, Mayer agreed to cast her in the small but intense part of Elsa, the bold young wife of an Oxford bookseller. Robert Taylor, Lionel Barrymore and former schoolmate Maureen O'Sullivan completed the cast of the film.

Although Michael Balcon was the one who convinced Mayer to hire her, Vivien did not get along with him. She would badly criticize him for being so impatient with the cast and for lacking taste and class; she considered him a "bourgeois."[19]

Vivien was annoyed that her role was smaller than Maureen O'Sullivan's and that it was not suitable to her personality. It was Gliddon who convinced her that the supportive role was more interesting than the leading one, and that it could be an important step in her career.

To better play the part of the bad girl, she wore showy clothes like a leopard fur trimmed suit and "femme fatale" heavy make-up with long eyelashes and fully curled hair. It ended up being a very amusing experience, and more gratifying than she had imagined. The character of Elsa Craddock had undertones of the women Vivien would later play: Scar-

Maureen O'Sullivan, Robert Taylor and Vivien (left to right) in *A Yank at Oxford*, **1938.**

lett O'Hara's stubbornness mixed with Blanche DuBois' high sexual drive. A woman who looked like a beautiful and seductive lady, but behaved in a way that was anything but ladylike.

Francis Scott Fitzgerald was hired by Mayer to review the original script. He rewrote part of the dialogue after the first screenwriter was fired, but did not receive any mention in the film credits.

During the filming of *A Yank at Oxford*, Vivien was always impatient to finish her takes as early as possible in order to run to Olivier. She invented excuses such as a pain in a toe so that she could leave the set early and see a specialist. To be more convincing, she later bought a pair of special shoes as her chiropodist had suggested. But one day Balcon became tired of her daily escapes and said to her: "We can cut a hole in your shoe and that way you can stand up without it hurting you."[20]

Vivien was upset but she did not make any fuss and she followed the suggestion; however, she demanded that MGM reimburse her for her ruined pair of shoes. The money was refunded, but only after long, exhausting correspondence with the film production company.

A few days later Gliddon was invited by MGM to the studios in Dehman. The agent was completely stunned when he heard from an executive of MGM that "Miss Leigh's behavior is incomprehensible and inexcusable. It is making things very difficult for us. Please tell her she must behave herself in the future. If not, we shall have to consider taking up her option when it next falls due."[21] When Gliddon later told Vivien the complaint, she had an attack of fury. "She flew at me," he remembered. "She wasn't shouting now. But it was far more frightening than if she had bawled me out. Her voice turned suddenly hard … rasping … contemptuous. But the worst thing was her eyes—the look in them. They had completely changed from the smiling eyes I was accustomed to seeing. They were the eyes of a stranger."[22]

She then threatened to kick Gliddon out of the house if he would not speak the name of the person who had made such a statement. And she really did it.

A few days later Vivien called him to apologize, embarrassed by what had happened. She admitted that she often had those outbursts of uncontrollable rage that frightened her because she felt she had no power over them. Gliddon forgave her and obtained a couple of days off for her.

When *A Yank at Oxford* opened in New York on February 25, 1938, *Daily Mail*'s critic praised her performance, writing, "Vivien Leigh is the sort of thing that makes anyone want to go to Oxford."[23]

As soon as Vivien finished filming *A Yank at Oxford*, Olivier started playing in Shakespeare's *Henry V*. In fact, Ralph Richardson had encouraged Olivier to concentrate on Shakespeare's plays, not just for professional but also for practical reasons. According to him, if the scandal of living together with Vivien was disclosed to the public, people would be more indulgent of a Shakespearian actor. After the success of *Hamlet* in Denmark, Olivier became a permanent member of the Old Vic Company, which he would leave in 1949.

Vivien had hoped to continue to play opposite him in the next production, as Lady Macbeth, but the part went to Judith Anderson.

Princess Elizabeth paid a visit to one of *Macbeth*'s performances, giving Olivier encouragement. He commented, "It seemed to indicate that the gossip concerning my private life had not reached far or high yet."[24] Ralph Richardson had sensed how important it was for Olivier to have Vivien in the company, and after insisting on her inclusion to the other members he succeeded in getting her in.

Director Tyrone Guthrie offered her the part of Titania in *A Mid-summer Night's Dream*, scheduled to open on December 27 of that year. It was an incredibly beautiful production, not only because of the masterful direction, but also for the memorable interpretations of Robert Helpmann and Ralph Richardson. Music, choreography and stage design were arranged without neglecting any detail.

Vivien was a wonderful Titania, and at the end of one of the performances, princess Elizabeth and Margareth went back-stage to personally congratulate the cast. Vivien and Helpmann bowed simultaneously, and their elaborate headdresses intertwined. They had to leave the room to have them released, making everybody else laugh while they stood embarrassed in front of the royals.

Robert (Bobbie) Helpmann became a close friend of Bibs (as he used to address to her). Although there was a great intimate friendship, it never had any amorous overtones, since Helpmann was openly homosexual.

Charles Morgan's review in *The Times* described Vivien's performance in *A Midsummer Night's Dream* as "nervous." Vivien commented on the criticism in a letter to Leigh: "It is dreadful to consider for a moment that he may be right."[25]

During the rehearsals of the play and on the precise day of her twenty-fifth birthday, Durham Cottage was officially inaugurated with a party. Among the guests were Ralph Richardson and his wife. The actor was having fun shooting some fireworks in the garden of the house, but one of them went straight into the living-room, ruining some of the new curtains. Vivien was outraged, while Olivier was laughing, not only because of the tragic yet comic situation but also because he did not like Vivien's furnishing style.

In March 1938 Vivien wrote to Leigh again asking him for the divorce, but her husband firmly kept his position, as Jill Esmond was doing with Olivier. Vivien had always been honest in admitting that she was not missing Suzanne. Only years later would she regret her inexcusable behavior toward her daughter, calling herself " a bitch" for behaving as a heartless mother. On the other hand, Olivier confessed his sense of guilt in neglecting his son Tarquin, which helped him to be an extraordinary Coriolanus and a sublime Iago in a production of *Othello* directed by Lewis Casson, two roles that marked Olivier's entrance into the history of British theater in the spring of 1938.

Othello had many evident homosexual overtones, something totally different from the classical production staged in the past by Richardson, and it created a stir among the critics. Every night Vivien would watch the show, trying to learn new techniques from her inseparable Larry.

By his own admission, Olivier never considered himself an intellectual, but he enormously appreciated the stimulation Vivien would give to him, suggesting books to read and trying to pass along her passion for opera, classical music and art in general.

During the spring of 1938 Korda loaned Vivien to Mayflower Productions, Eric Pommer's company, to play in *St. Martin's Lane* (later renamed for the American market *Sidewalks of New York*) with Rex Harrison and Charles Laughton. Vivien was not very happy about it; she detested Laughton because she thought he had been responsible for the failure of the project of Korda's *Cyrano de Bergerac*. In fact, Laughton had been opposed to the decision to cast Vivien as Rossana, and he had only accepted it on Korda's insistence, under the condition that she dye her hair blond. Vivien categorically refused, and he never forgave her for such an affront, but later the entire project fell through.

Vivien had the habit of shamelessly cursing and uttering profanities in public. Often, she would swear at personified objects or at herself. Laughton could not bear this language spoken, especially by a woman, due to his strict Victorian upbringing, and the situation became a cause for tension between the two.[26] Vivien, unaware of his homosexuality (Laughton was married to actress Elsa Lancaster), was also afraid of possible "advances" that Laughton might make on her. She tried to avoid him off the set whenever she could.

She detested his massive presence, which the other star of the film, Rex Harrison, recalled: "The most extraordinary thing about Laughton was his size. He was a very large and extrovert actor.… He was also very difficult to act with because of the sheer size of him. If you were doing a two-shot with Charles it was almost impossible to get into the shot. The frame was quite simply full of him.… It was very irritating."[27]

Although the script gave Vivien the opportunity to sing and dance, she disliked her role because, in her opinion, she would not be convincing enough as a street performer and a pickpocket who is noticed by a rich manager, played by Harrison, who falls in love with her and produces her shows.

Sometimes Olivier, when he was not busy at the Old Vic, would visit her on the set, watching many of the love scenes she had with Harrison, many of which were later cut in the editing room. Often Vivien and Olivier would lock themselves in her dressing room for hours and afterwards it would become very difficult for Vivien to go back to work, which provoked discontent among the troupe.

The austere depiction of London's street life in *St. Martin's Lane*, along with Vivien's hardly credible performance, were not received enthusiastically by the audience, and the movie turned out to be a big flop.

Charles Laughton and Vivien in *St. Martin's Lane*.

When filming was over, Vivien fell sick, and a very worried Leigh Holman visited her several times. On doctor's orders she had to postpone all her commitments and take a long period of rest.

Curiously under the suggestion of Laughton, Vivien with Olivier spent her convalescence in France on the "route gastronomique," an itinerary of French locations that combined famous monuments and remarkable landscapes with "haute cuisine" restaurants. They started in Boulogne, went through Paris and crossed the entire country down to the French Riviera. They drove for the whole trip in their old, two seater Ford V-8, leaving their Rolls Royce and chauffeur in London with Holman.

Vivien's convalescence benefited from that holiday. It was the first time the couple traveled completely alone. During their stay in France, they spent a night having dinner with Hugh (Binkie) Beaumont, who had just moved from the famous theatrical agency Howard & Wyndham to H.M. Tennant. Under his management it became the most important production company in London. Over dinner, while Vivien was stroking a Siamese cat she found in the street, Binkie gave her advice that changed her career forever. From that moment on he was one of the few people who would have the power to influence her decisions. "You want to play

Scarlett O'Hara, Vivien," he said, "then you need an American agent. I'm surprised you haven't got one already."[28]

As soon as she returned to London, Vivien complained to Gliddon about the fact he did not have an American agent. Olivier was represented in Hollywood by Myron Selznick, the brother of David, whose office in London was managed by Cecil Tennant.

Gliddon proposed a 50% split commission to Tennant, who immediately accepted in order to represent all of Gliddon's artists, along with his own, on the American market. But Tennant's enthusiasm was connected exclusively to the fact that he wanted to represent Vivien, not because he wanted a relationship with Gliddon. A couple of weeks later, a telegram from Selznick's office arrived, in which the producer asked if Olivier and Vivien were interested in a screen version of *Wuthering Heights* opposite Merle Oberon. But Vivien was not interested in a secondary role, and she knew that Oberon would play the leading part with Olivier.

When they received the *Wuthering Heights* screenplay, however, they found it surprisingly interesting. William Wyler would direct the film. At the time he was completing *Jezebel* with Bette Davis, which would become Warner Brothers answer to *Gone with the Wind* even before that film was in production. Vivien thought that it was not a bad idea to meet with Wyler, who was in London, so she invited him for dinner at Durham Cottage.

The director was still not convinced, after watching *St. Martin's Lane*, that she was right for the role of Cathy. Instead, he tried to convince her to accept the part of Isabella. "Vivien, you are not yet known in the States. You may become a big star, but for your first role in an American film you'll never do better than Isabella in *Wuthering Heights.*"[29]

But he was quite mistaken.

At the same time, Olivier was fascinated by the character of Heathcliff and by the generous salary of $50,000. He decided to accept, even though his biggest worry was what Vivien would do while he was in Hollywood. Vivien did not want to think about a separation from Olivier, so she concentrated on an offer she had received just before she had fell ill: to play in *Serena Blandish.*

Chapter Six

Gone with the Wind

"Hey, genius, meet your Scarlett O'Hara."
—Myron Selznick to his brother David Selznick

On the day of her twenty-fifth birthday, Vivien drove with Olivier to Southampton, where he boarded the SS *Normandie* to New York. As a departure gift, Vivien gave him a small silhouette portrait of the writer Emily Brontë, which she had found in an antique shop in Wiltshire. They said good-bye to each other after a tearful champagne toast, and then Vivien quickly headed back to the Gate Theatre, where she was acting in *Serena Blandish*.

Stewart Granger was her co-star in the play, which was based on a novel by Enid Bagnold. The few memories that Granger has of Vivien during that time are of a beautiful, ambitious and restless woman with two passions: her love for Larry and her determination to play Scarlett O'Hara in *Gone with the Wind*.[1]

During the transatlantic passage, Olivier called Vivien three times, quite an extravagance at the time, but he wanted to be sure that she was fine, and he wanted to express his love and nostalgia for her. *Serena Blandish* was a fiasco, and the show closed about a week after its opening. Once Olivier arrived in Hollywood, he wrote to Vivien almost every day and admitted that he had probably made a huge mistake in accepting *Wuthering Heights*.

He in fact was not getting along with Merle Oberon and was, therefore, unable to reach the kind of rapport the character of Heathcliff needed to share with Cathy. The love scenes were a real "war zone." Oberon would complain that Olivier spat while delivering his lines. He would get angry and would insult her, which would result in her leaving the set. Furthermore, Olivier was not happy with his make-up. He had requested heavy make-up because he was used to the stage, but after producer Goldwyn visited the set one day and saw some takes, he started screaming at William Wyler in his heavy Polish accent: "This is the ugliest actor in pictures. He's dirty. His acting is stagey. He's hammy and he's awful. If he goes on playing the way he is, I'll have to close the picture—or he'll ruin me."[2]

In addition, Olivier was missing Vivien intensely, and he had also developed athlete's foot due to the constant use of a pair of old boots. Those made him limp and forced him to use crutches, which would systematically drop in front of the camera.

At the same time, Vivien was feeling lonely and discouraged. She would smoke like a chimney and sleep only a few hours a night. She also felt the pressure her parents were giving her to go back with Leigh, even after she had asked him again to grant her the divorce.

One day, she impulsively booked a passage on the *Queen Mary*. She thought that even if she was with Larry in Hollywood for five days, the effort of a long trip was worth it. The hope of possibility replacing Merle Oberon was also on her mind, so she told Leigh that she would go to the States for ten days. On November 27, 1938, she boarded the transatlantic to New York.

On the ship she met publisher Hamish Hamilton, an old friend of her husband's, who asked the reason for her journey. Vivien's answer was: "Partially because Larry's there and partially because I intend to get the part of Scarlett O'Hara."[3] Hamilton bet her ten pounds that she would not succeed because the part was only to be given to an American actress. The bet was left unpaid. During the crossing Vivien was reading *Green Mansions*, a book that Olivier had given her as a gift, but she was also reading *Gone with the Wind*, again. Her copy was very worn and filled with notes, and all of the pages relating to Scarlett were earmarked and the parts underlined.

Before leaving, she explained to Gliddon that her trip to Hollywood could be her big opportunity to get a screen test as Scarlett O'Hara. Gliddon was not convinced that such a long trip was worthwhile, knowing Vivien's fear of flying. The trip took five or six days by boat and then more than fifteen hours of flight to reach Los Angeles from New York, with several stop-overs.

The agent wondered if this impulse of Vivien's was another one of her bursts of temperament that she would often have. His greatest worry was that she would not be back in time for *Midsummer Night's Dream* rehearsals, which were scheduled to begin on December 10 at the Old Vic, where she was to play a leading role.

Vivien would return to England a year later.

The American press had been alerted as to her arrival in New York, and once she disembarked at the port a reporter asked her, "Why, Miss Leigh, are you coming to America?" Vivien's quick answer was, "To see Laurence Olivier!" Although only two newspapers printed the news, one of the men from Samuel Goldwyn's office who had welcomed her to New York warned her to be very cautious about her statements to the press. Neither Olivier nor Vivien was divorced, and the affair could have been damaging to their images with the prudish American public.

Finally, Vivien and Olivier were reunited at the Clover Field Airport in Los Angeles, where he went to pick her up. A couple of days earlier, the actor had a long talk with his American agent Myron Selznick, explaining that "a person" who could be professionally interesting to him and his brother David would soon arrive in Hollywood from England.

In the meantime, the *Gone with the Wind* cast was almost completed. David Selznick had also had a survey in which people voted for the actors they thought would be perfect for the different parts. The role of Rhett Butler was given to Clark Gable because he was the actor voted for by most of the almost two million Americans who answered the survey. For the part of Ashley Wilkes, Leslie Howard was almost unanimously voted for as the best choice. Although Howard had already played several "intellectual hero" or "dreamer poet" characters, he was not inclined to take the role. Melvyn Douglas, Ray Milland and Jeffrey Lynne were also considered, but Selznick thought that only Howard would be good as Ashley.

Finally, the producers persuaded Howard to accept. After the first costume rehearsal, though, Selznick momentarily regretted his choice, because Howard looked his age exactly: forty-five years old. In the opening scene of the film he should have been only twenty-seven years old. But the contract was already signed, and breaking it would have cost the producer a lot of money and caused the production to waste more time. For the role of Melanie Hamilton Wilkes, Selznick originally had Joan Fontaine in mind, but the actress, who aspired to play Scarlett, suggested her sister Olivia de Havilland, who was under contract with Warner Brothers. De Havilland was chosen for the part after only one screen test.

But the main problem was Scarlett. So far the most important actresses in Hollywood had been taken into consideration, and many of them had been screen tested. Furthermore, over one thousand unknown girls had been seen through a scouting search that lasted for more than two years. Selznick's press office, which was managed by Russell Bidwell, had launched a big advertising campaign for a quest for the ideal Scarlett. Every day they would receive thousands of letters from all over the country. The "Scarlett Letters," as they were called, usually contained photographs of women, often wearing an evening gown inspired by the novel and sometimes nothing at all. One morning a huge reproduction of the book *Gone with the Wind* was delivered to the front door of Selznick's house. As soon as he opened the door, a girl in a mini-skirt popped out of it exclaiming: "I am your Scarlett O'Hara!"

Selznick, though, was more inclined to use a famous face on the screen than an unknown one. Bette Davis, Miriam Hopkins, Claudette Colbert, Joan Crawford, Margaret Sullavan, Carol Lombard, Tallulah Bankhead, Norma Shearer, Paulette Goddard and Katharine Hepburn were all possible candidates. Hepburn was one of the most determined, and she insisted on being Scarlett. "This part was practically written for me," she told Selznick. "I am Scarlett O'Hara!" But the producer remained unconvinced, telling her, "I can't image Rhett Butler chasing you for ten years." "Well," she answered, "maybe other people's view of sex appeal is different from yours."[4]

Later, without false modesty, Bette Davis wrote in her autobiography about how perfect she would have been as Scarlett, and how during the quest she was always referred to as the best comparison.[5]

For the sake of pure amusement, Selznick invited all the Scarlett contenders to a big party at his brother's mountain house near Lake Arrowhead. The evening turned out to be a nightmare for all those who thought they were there because they had been chosen.

All the interior sets of Tara, like Twelve Oaks or the Atlanta Bazaar, had almost been completed inside stage 16 of Selznick's International Studios, but in order to build parts of the exterior such as the façades of some buildings, it was necessary to clean out leftover sets from old movies like *King Kong* or *David Copperfield*. It was therefore decided that the first scene to be filmed would be the "Burning of Atlanta," burning all the old sets to free the space.

The arrival of Vivien happened during this time of great uncertainty and desire to conclude the search for Scarlett since the film's budget was increasing daily. "I feel that our failure to find a new girl for Scarlett is the greatest failure of my entire career," wrote Selznick in one of his memos.[6]

Vivien was staying at the Beverly Hills Hotel, not too far from Olivier's residence, so that rumors of their adulterous relationship would not spread. On December 5, 1938, the famous Hollywood columnist Hedda Hopper wrote, "The cute English vamp Vivien Leigh is in our midst, but not doing a picture."

Vivien spent her first days in California sunbathing by the hotel swimming pool and sipping English tea, but her rest ceased with the meeting Olivier had arranged for her with his agent Myron Selznick.

There are two different versions about how and where the meeting that would change Vivien's career and life actually happened. The first took place in Myron's office, where Vivien arrived on time, and the agent, who was a horse-racing better, took her to the Santa Anita racetrack, a strange place for a business meeting, but a location very familiar to Selznick. There he introduced her to Nat Deverich, a former jockey who had many connections. He used to give the agent information, not only about horse races but also on studio executives who would bet on them.[7] Then Deverich introduced Vivien to Daniel O'Shea, an assistant of David Selznick's, asking him to include Vivien in the screen tests for Scarlett O'Hara. In exchange, Deverich gave O'Shea a tip on the horse races of that day.

According to the second version, though, Vivien met Myron the very first day she arrived in Los Angeles at the Beverly Hills Hotel. The agent knew that his brother David was still having difficulties in casting the part of Scarlett, and that the filming would have to start four days later. At that moment Paulette Goddard seemed to be the final choice, but she was handicapped by the ambiguous affair she was having with Charlie Chaplin, a relationship that prim Hollywood was unable to forgive.

As soon as Myron looked at Vivien, he knew he had to introduce her to his brother. He thought that the best moment would be the night of December 10, the day scheduled for the beginning of the shooting of the "Burning of Atlanta."

The agent invited Olivier and Vivien to dinner at Romanoff's, one of the trendiest restaurants at the time. During the meal Myron kept calling the set of *Gone with the Wind* to find out if his brother David was already there, knowing him to always be late. At 11 P.M., Myron arrived on the set with his guests. His brother David was descending from an observation tower with director George Cukor. It is not true, as was wrongly stated in a biography, that Vivien climbed the tower. First, it would have been very rude to interrupt the shooting, and, second, she suffered from vertigo.

"So there you are," said David angrily. "Where the hell have you been?" Myron merely grinned. "Hey Genius," he said woozily, taking Vivien by the arm, "meet your Scarlett O'Hara." With those words (genius was a sarcasm he often used with his brother)[8], Vivien was officially introduced to David Selznick.

She was wearing a mink coat, a Christmas gift from Olivier, a beige silk dress that emphasized her tiny waist, and a little black hat.

"Good evening, Mr. Selznick," she said politely, while the producer carefully observed her face on which the light of the "Burning of Atlanta" was reflecting. Years later Selznick said: "I took one look and knew that she was right."[9]

Vivien was very lucky, because a series of positive events turned to her favor: not only the good mood of the producer on that particular day, because the film had finally started with a scene of great visual impact, but also the belief that Selznick had in fateful events occurring at just the right moment.

So, without wasting further time, he suggested that she go to the director's office to read some lines from the script. Vivien was not intimidated when she saw all the different drafts of the screenplay piled up in Cukor's office, along with the sketches of the costumes by Walter Plunkett and the photographs of the location chosen for the outdoor scenes. Cukor asked her to take off her hat and gave her some sheets with lines of a dialogue between Scarlett and Ashley, whose part was read by him.

Although it was 1 A.M., Vivien started to feel more confident after delivering her lines several times. Cukor was very enthusiastic about her, and told her that she would be included in the last four finalists for the role, along with Paulette Goddard, Jean Arthur and Joan Bennett.

In a letter David Selznick wrote the day after to his wife Irene, who was at the Sherry Netherland Hotel in New York, he described that evening:

> Darling: ... Saturday night I was greatly exhilarated by the Fire Sequence. It was one of the biggest thrills I have had out of making pictures—first, because of the scene itself, and second, because of the frightening but exciting knowledge of *Gone with the Wind* was finally in work.
>
> Myron rolled in just exactly too late, arriving about a minute and a half after the last building had fallen and burned and after the shots were completed. With him were Larry Olivier and Vivien Leigh. Shhhhh: she's the Scarlett dark horse, and looks damned good. (Not for everybody's ears your own: it's narrowed down to Paulette, Jean Arthur, Joan Bennett, and Vivien Leigh.)[10]

Selznick also wrote to his general manager that the final choice for Scarlett would be made after the final tests scheduled that following Monday and Tuesday for the four candidates.

Once Vivien received the lines for the screen test from Myron, she did not waste a moment and memorized them with the help of Olivier. Vivien sent a telegram to Guthrie telling him she would not be able to be back in London on time for *Midsummer Night's Dream*. In addition,

she wrote a long letter to Leigh, in which she explained what was happening in her life. She was very excited, but at the same time she was also
worried. If she obtained the part, she would be forced to stay in the States
without seeing Suzanne for several months.

In the next five days Selznick shot more than thirty-seven tests of
the young actresses. He made several enlargements of some of the photographs of the candidates, and he would spend hours analyzing them and
having meetings with his assistants to discuss the pros and cons of each
of them.

In all of her tests, Vivien showed a great ability for perfectly imitating the Southern accent, even though Cukor asked her not to worry
about it because, if chosen, she would have a personal dialect coach to
help.

The first screen test was the scene in which black actress Hattie
McDaniel, playing Mammy, laced up Scarlett before the picnic at Twelve
Oaks. Vivien later remembered that the corset was still warm because it
had just been worn by another actress.

The last test was finally shot on December 21. Vivien was very tense
and she said a little prayer before she began filming. When Cukor saw
her becoming nervous, he told her a joke to break the ice. The test was
brilliant. On Christmas day the director invited Olivier and Vivien over
his house for a party. At the end of the night, Cukor took her aside and
in a serious tone of voice informed her that a choice had been finally
made. Immediately Vivien assumed the worst, sure that the part went to
another actress and that Cukor was there to comfort her. All of a sudden
the director exclaimed: "Well, I guess we're stuck with you."[11]

The quest for Scarlett was over. Vivien obtained a part that will leave
a mark on film history. She would play a role that took two years of
research, cost $92,000 and 90 screen tests of 1400 aspiring candidates.

Two days earlier Myron Selznick's office had requested a copy of the
contract Vivien had signed with Korda from London. The final decision
had been made on December 22, right after Vivien's last screen test, which
Irene Selznick approved with her husband after viewing it in their private screening room that same night.

The following weeks were not very easy for Vivien. She had to permanently break her contract with her British agent, Gliddon, who was
not happy about it and threatened legal action. Moreover, her contract
with Korda had to be modified because the producer could refuse to lend
Vivien to Selznick.

On New Year's Eve Vivien was invited by Myron Selznick to his
mountain house for a party he gave in honor of Korda, who was vaca-

tioning in California. At the party, the Hungarian producer told Vivien that playing Scarlett would be a mistake for her because she was not right for the role. Vivien desperately begged him not to give his opinion to Selznick, because she was afraid that he would change his mind.

The news that Vivien was chosen for *Gone with the Wind* was publicly announced only three weeks after Christmas. Vivien signed the contract without consulting Olivier, afraid that he would be upset because she would be professionally tied to Selznick for seven years. And in fact, Olivier was furious and ran to Selznick's office announcing that he would never allow Vivien to comply with the contract, because he was planning to marry her. He did not want to already be separated before the wedding, with him in England and her in California. Selznick's answer was very calm: "Larry, do you remember when I was head of RKO and I wanted to star Jill Esmond in *A Bill of Divorcement*?"

"Yes," Olivier replied.

"And you insisted that your wife give up the part and go back to England with you?"

"Yes."

"Larry, don't be a shit twice."[12]

So, Olivier had to give his approval and allowed Vivien to fulfill her contract.

In a following meeting, Selznick explained to Vivien and Olivier that the reason Paulette Goddard (who was the favorite choice before Vivien) was discarded was due to her affair with Charlie Chaplin. Nobody knew if the couple was legally married, and the American public was morally very sensitive to unorthodox relationships. He also illustrated why five days had to pass from the moment of the final decision to the time of official communication to her, since the production feared that the relationship with Olivier could be an obstacle if the public knew. Although Selznick recognized that it was true love, he could not forget that both were still married, and that each of them also had a child.

Even though their affair was common knowledge in England, it was not in the States. The possibility of a scandal and a sensational divorce would have ruined their careers and the opportunity of the film's success.

The producer added that Clark Gable and Carol Lombard were also having an affair, but because he was still married, they would both live in separate houses. Before making him sign the contract for the part of Rhett, the production house made Gable's wife Rhea sign several documents in which she would ask for a consensual divorce. Selznick warned Vivien and Olivier not to be seen alone in public, and to always be very discreet.[13]

Selznick chose his secretary, Sunny Alexander Lash, to be Vivien's personal assistant. He asked her to go and live with Vivien at 520 North Candem Drive, while Olivier kept his residence at the hotel. Sunny got along with Vivien immediately, and she would try to please her in every possible way. Often late at night she would go out to buy a pack of Player's, Vivien's favorite brand of cigarettes, and she would suddenly disappear when Olivier would come to visit Vivien. A cook, a butler, a personal maid and a gardener were hired, along with a twenty-four-hour guard who kept curious reporters and paparazzi away from the house.

Although the contractual formalities were quickly dealt with, Vivien's contract provided for an intricate agreement between Korda and Selznick according to which Vivien would play Scarlett for $1250 a week with the guarantee of at least two films a year in the following seven years for Selznick's studio production. Olivier maintained in his autobiography that Selznick took advantage of Vivien, offering her only $20,000 for a seven-year contract, saying, "I'd be the laughingstock of all my friends if I paid her any more, an unknown, a discovery, for such an opportunity."[14]

In an interview in 1944, the producer revealed that "Olivier tried in every possible way to kill the casting of Vivien as Scarlett O'Hara. He advanced every argument conceivable against it, and ... said that I wouldn't dream of going through with the idea of an English girl as a famous Southern heroine; that Vivien ... would be ridiculed in the role."[15] Selznick always thought that Olivier was possessed by a pure jealousy of Vivien because of the real possibility of her great triumph, and also because she was assured that if *Gone with the Wind* was a success, her contract would have to be revised.

With the possibility of spending several months in Hollywood, Vivien wrote to Leigh telling him that even if she was making this film, she would never abandoned her true love: theater. Her contract, in fact, included the opportunity for her to accept work in the theater from time to time.

Once the contract was signed, Susan Myrick, Selznick's technical adviser, informed Margaret Mitchell, the author of the book, of the casting decision regarding Scarlett before the news reached the press.

The author had decided not to be involved in the adaptation of her book into a screenplay, or in any casting decisions, but she was always kept closely updated by Myrick about the film's progress. In a letter dated January 11, 1939, Myrick describes Vivien to Mitchell as "charming, very beautiful with black hair and magnolia-petal skin."

After seeing Vivien's photograph, the author gave her full approval, considering it a very wise decision to use an actress almost unknown in the States, so that audiences would not confuse her with any of the previous characters she had played.

The choice of Vivien was hidden from the press for over three weeks, and except for a little tip-off from Ed Sullivan, a journalist from the New York Daily News, the news was held till the official day of its communication.

On January 13, when the news was disclosed to the American press, a statement of approval from Margaret Mitchell was printed.

Vivien was ecstatic, and on January 14 she sent a telegram to the author:

> DEAR MRS. MARSH [Mitchell's married name]: IF I CAN BUT FEEL THAT YOU ARE WITH ME ON THIS, THE MOST IMPORTANT AND TRYING TASK OF MY LIFE, I PLEDGE WITH ALL MY HEART I SHALL TRY TO MAKE SCARLETT O'HARA LIVE AS YOU DESCRIBED HER IN YOUR BRILLIANT BOOK.[16]

The biographical information that Selznick's press office sent out about Vivien was very inaccurate. They stated that her place of birth was India, that she was educated in Europe, and that her father was French and her mother Irish, as were Scarlett's parents. England was mentioned very briefly, and the presence of Olivier in her life never acknowledged. Vivien was simply described as the wife of a London barrister, and the mother of a little girl.

The only critique came from columnist Hedda Hopper from the Los Angeles Times. She regretted that after two years and interviews with millions of American women, Selznick "could not find one to suit him."[17] She accused him of insulting every American actress with his selection. When she saw *Gone with the Wind*, however, Hopper admitted in her column that she had been stupid to interfere with the casting and in attacking Vivien, who she predicted would be the star sensation of the '40s.[18]

On January 16, ten days before the scheduled day of filming, an official ceremony was organized, where Vivien, Leslie Howard and Olivia de Havilland signed their contracts in front of the flashes of hundreds of reporters. Vivien was soberly dressed, wearing a big black hat with a pendent and an off-white hatband. She was also wearing a pair of long, white gloves, because she was still very self-conscious about her big hands, and she was nervous about the fact that the photographers would be taking pictures of them while she signed the documents.

For the first half of that month, Vivien worked on her accent with the help of Susan Myrick and William Price (actress Maureen O'Hara's husband), who was very impressed with her ability to learn rapidly and by her open sensuality: "Vivien is a bawdy little thing and hot as a

Vivien starring as Scarlett O'Hara in *Gone with the Wind*, 1939.

firecracker and lovely to look at. Can't understand why Larrie Olivier when she could have anybody."[19]

Finally, filming resumed on January 26. The first scene shot was with Scarlett under her porch with the Tarleton twins, played by Fred Crane and George Reeves (who would later become famous as Superman in the TV show). That scene corresponded exactly to the opening scene in the book, but once it was filmed it did not satisfy Cukor or Selznick. It was re-shot many times over the following six months with different costume changes, so the first scene ended up being the very last one to be shot.

Vivien's extreme professionalism did not work well with Selznick's infamous pickiness and habit of focusing on every detail. The producer asked her to keep her look as natural as possible, especially her hair and eyebrows, which she should not shave under any circumstances. Selznick worried about Vivien's breast size. He complained that her breasts were not big enough to be revealed by some of the generously low-cut gowns created by Plunkett, who had researched the clothes of that historical period for more than two years.

The producer suggested that she wear fuller bras, so Vivien ordered her assistant to get them in different models. After she tried on at least a dozen in front of a mirror she exclaimed: "Fiddle-dee-dee, I'm not going to wear these silly props, when I have perfectly good ones of my own!" and she didn't. But the next time Selznick welcomed her to the set, he looked and said: "You see how much better you look now!"[20]

In some of the letters Vivien wrote to Gertrude and Leigh during the film's break, she mentioned how the script was constantly revised and how many screenwriters Selznick had hired and fired since he had bought the rights two years before. F. Scott Fitzgerald was one of them. He was fired from the film because he had dared to change Margaret Mitchell's prose. The script was modified until the last day of filming.

In a letter to her mother, Vivien informed her that director George Cukor had been fired without notice. The official reason was because he had been incapable of properly directing a big project like *Gone with the Wind*. Vivien was informed of the news while she was shooting the scene in the Atlanta Bazaar. She was wearing a black dress because Scarlett was mourning her first husband. Together with Olivia de Havilland "they rushed over to David Selznick's office, all in black, and pleaded and threatened and did everything in the world but he remained obdurate,"[21] as Cukor remembered.

Some said that the director was fired because he had acquired a reputation as a "woman's director," alluding to a homosexual sensitivity that had made Clark Gable complain. Gable maintained that Cukor preferred Vivien more in his close-ups.

"That's ridiculous absolute nonsense," said Cukor. "Some stupid press-agent said that I was a woman's director. It was bullshit. I used to say 'thank you very much' when they brought this up. Now I just mention the men I've worked with: Jack Barrymore, Spencer Tracy, Leslie Howard, everybody...."[22] It is nonsense to say that I was giving too much attention to Vivien and Olivia. It's the text that dictates where the emphasis should go. Gable didn't have a great deal of confidence in himself as an actor, although he was a great screen personality; maybe he thought that I didn't understand that.[23] When what's his name [Victor Fleming] took over, he didn't go any place. He didn't even go to the premiere."[24]

As Emanuel Levy states in Cukor's biography: "The director's friends suspected that Gable had other compelling reasons for wanting him off the film.

"Cukor knew of Gable's days as a hustler in the Hollywood gay circuit when the actor first arrived in Los Angeles. One of these sexual encounters was with William Haines, an actor who later become Cukor's friend and designer. Cukor's very presence may have reminded the macho

Gone with the Wind with Clark Gable, 1939.

actor of his dubious past. Cukor further irritated the actor by calling him 'dear' or 'darling' on the set, as was his habit with all stars, male or female."[25] This was apparently a custom too effeminate for Gable's virile tastes.

From her side, Vivien liked Cukor a lot from the beginning. Perhaps his theatrical background helped in the development of a special bond between them.

Cukor was replaced by Victor Fleming, who was completing the shooting of *The Wizard of Oz*, a film that Cukor had refused to take because it was based upon a children's book and, therefore, not considered prestigious enough.

Tensions between Fleming and Vivien arose immediately. During a rehearsal, the director blew up when Vivien kept resisting his instructions to put more bitchiness into the reading of her lines. "I can't be a bitch," she said. Fleming looked at her for a moment before furiously screaming: "Miss Leigh, you can stick this script up your royal British ass!" Then he threw the script away and left the set, complaining he was too nervous to go back to work.[26]

Vivien's décolleté problem also returned under Fleming's direction. She had lost weight since her first dress rehearsal and her breasts tended to spread sideways, concealing their fullness. Walter Plunkett had to tape them together tightly while Vivien cursed and complained that she could not breathe. One day when Olivier was on the set, he watched the painful procedure and joked: "And all the time I thought they were perfectly lovely!"[27] Olivia de Havilland remembers that Vivien "never lost her poise, despite the immense strain that she was under."[28]

A relationship based on mutual respect and a tinge of irony was established between Vivien and Hattie McDaniel, the actress who played Mammy. Typically at lunch time Vivien would walk over to Hattie and say "Mammy, may I go to lunch?" Hattie would reply in her Mammy manner, "Whea you going?" And they would laugh, remembering that they were not playing a scene.[29]

On the other hand, Vivien had a love-hate relationship with Gable. She detested kissing him, because he always had disgusting breath due to his false teeth and the whiskey he would drink before each take.

He later confessed that when obliged to kiss on screen he normally thought of a steak.[30]

From their first meeting things did not go right.

Clarence Bull, one of MGM's still photographers, remembered that when Vivien and Gable met for the very first time to pose together for some publicity shots, the crew had to wait for her over an hour, infuriat-

ing Gable. "Is this the way they do things over there?" he rasped, meaning England. "If it is, I don't want to make this picture with her." He later
added, "I still think I will walk out of this picture because of a dame like
that!"

"I quite agree, Mr. Gable," came a clear voice from a side of the set.
"If I were a man, I'd tell that Vivien Leigh to go straight back to England
and fuck herself."[31] It was Vivien, who had heard everything, but her joke
placated Gable's anger within five minutes.[32]

Although their relationship during the shooting was civilized, off
the set Vivien and Gable barely spoke to each other. Each was so involved
in their private love relationships that it would have been unthinkable to
imagine an affair between them, as the press had hoped.

Vivien always carried with her a copy of the novel, and she was
shocked when she heard that Fleming never read the book, and that he
was directing the film exclusively from the script. "I'd never have been
able to get through without the book and George Cukor," she said. "I'd
keep the book beside me and look up each scene as we filmed it to remind
me where I was supposed to be, and how I should be feeling until Selznick
shouted at me to throw the damned thing away. On Sundays, when we
didn't shoot, I'd steal over to George Cukor's and discuss with him the
bits we'd be working on the next week. It was probably terribly irregular,
but I couldn't have finished it without him."[33]

Only a couple of months later she learned that Olivia de Havilland
was doing the same thing by telephone.

Selznick was very apprehensive about the press discovering Vivien
and Olivier's affair, but his fear of a scandal was alleviated when Olivier
suddenly left for New York because he was cast in a leading role opposite Katharine Cornell in the play *No Time for Comedy* on Broadway, which
was also produced by Selznick's production company. Every day Vivien
became more nervous; she was to appear in almost every scene yet to be
filmed. Her daily routine was very stressful: all the outdoor scenes were
filmed at Lasky Mesa in San Fernando Valley and required her to wake
up at 2:30 A.M. to be ready on the set by 5:30 A.M. Crew members would
often tease her, telling her she had just three days of work to be finished
in one night.

According to Alexander Walker, she had only two days off each
month, which corresponded with her menstrual cycle. The tally of her
periods and those of the other female principals was kept by a studio aide
specially assigned to this delicate task. But Selznick saw a deeper malaise
in Vivien, one which no biological reason could easily explain.[34] She would
often quarrel with him, shout on the set and then suddenly burst into tears.

This behavior was attributed to fatigue and stress, but, as it would later appear, it would transform into serious pathologies.

In letters she wrote to Leigh, Vivien described her daily routine on the set and asked him again to grant her the divorce, informing him that Jill Esmond had finally decided to divorce Olivier.

Correspondence between Vivien and Olivier (recently acquired for a million pounds by the British Library of London) shows an ardent passion between the two lovers. Vivien would cry her eyes out with nostalgia every night for Larry, who was in New York. In a letter to Olivier, Sunny Alexander Lash wrote: "My heart ached for little Vivien. She cried last night after talking to you. Most every night and Sunday mornings are awful without you. She is a perfect little angel and tries to be so brave. But sometimes she just has to have a good cry."[35]

Olivier often took a fifteen-hour flight just to spend one day with Vivien. Once, due to a delay, he was unable to return on time to the theater for his performance, so Selznick allowed the lovers to meet halfway at the Hotel Meulbach in Kansas City. "Oh David, I'm so grateful," she said to him on her return. "Larry met me in the hotel lobby and we went upstairs and we fucked and we fucked and we fucked the whole weekend."[36]

After five months of shooting *Gone with the Wind*, the situation on the set was very tense. Fleming was exhausted and furious with Selznick's continuous interruptions. The director suffered a nervous breakdown and was replaced by Sam Wood, the director of *A Night at the Opera* with the Marx brothers, who acted like a puppet whose strings were pulled by Selznick.

On June 27, 1939, the last day of filming, Vivien, after the completion of her takes, walked to another rehearsal stage on the Selznick lot to have a screen test for *Rebecca*, based on Daphne du Maurier's novel. Olivier had been cast as the leading role for that film, which would have been directed by Alfred Hitchcock and produced by Selznick. It was a great opportunity for Vivien, because not only would she have worked with the love of her life, but she would also honor her contract with Selznick, which obliged her to act in two of his films within the next seven years.

Unfortunately, things did not go well. Her major problem was that having been Scarlett for almost six months, the character now overlaid her real personality. This created two different identities in harmony, while at the same time in conflict. This had disastrous effects on her acting style when she tried to become a completely different character like Rebecca. Years later when Vivien would play Blanche DuBois in *A Streetcar Named Desire*, a full immersion into a new character created serious mental problems because of her by-then schizophrenic and disturbed personality.

A big party was organized at stage lot 5 of the International Selznick Studios to celebrate the ending of *Gone with the Wind*. Right after this, Vivien packed her bags and flew to New York, even though Selznick told her that he would soon need her presence again. He had planned to reshoot the opening scene with Vivien and the Tarleton twins, but he also realized that Vivien needed to rest in order to regain her lost weight, natural beauty and youthful look fit for a sixteen-year-old Scarlett at the beginning of the story.

Vivien arrived in New York on time to assist with the last performance of *No Time for Comedy*. Since she could not stay at the same hotel as Olivier, or even worse, be seen sneaking in and out of the hotel, a mutual friend, actress Katharine Cornell, gave the lovers her country house at Sneden's Landing.[37]

Olivier could not even welcome her at Newark's airport, where reporters besieged "Scarlett" with flashbulbs.

In New York, Vivien got another chance for a second screen test for *Rebecca*, but this time she did not get an answer right away.

On July 11 the couple left on the *Isle de France* bound for England, where they arrived five days later. There the atmosphere was completely different from what they imagined: London was full of air-raid shelters, and sandbags and gas masks were being distributed because of a sudden forecast of war.

In America, people had talked to them about the state of emergency in Europe, but never of a real threat of war. The tense international situation ruined the short holiday the couple took to France. They also hoped to finally receive the news of the divorces granted from Leigh and Jill, and the news that Vivien got the part in *Rebecca*.

On August 17 they boarded a transatlantic liner accompanied by Gertrude, who had decided to take a little vacation and go along with them. She left little Suzanne with Leigh and Oake, the new nanny. After a day of cruising, Vivien and Olivier received a radiogram from Selznick, who explained to them why giving the lead role in *Rebecca* to Vivien would have been a mistake. According to the producer, although she was the perfect Scarlett she would not have made the right Lady de Winter. After all, Vivien had never showed any particular interest in the part until she had heard that Olivier was to be the star. Joan Fontaine was eventually chosen for the role.

Once back in California, Vivien and Olivier spent the first weekend of September at Catalina Island on a yacht that Douglas Fairbanks, Jr., rented for a group of British friends, including David Niven. On a sunny Sunday morning, while the boat was anchored in beautiful Emerald Bay, the guests heard a radio communication in which British Prime Minister Neville Chamberlain said that war had been declared on Germany. Even though they tried to joke about it, toasting to a sure and immediate British victory, all were worried about the news. Gertrude, who was on the yacht, asked to be taken back to shore, where she immediately called home to be sure that Suzanne was fine.

As soon they were able, Vivien and Olivier contacted their friend Duff Cooper at the Ministry of Information in London, who told them that the only thing that they could do was to stay in the States and help the British cause by behaving patriotically and collecting funds through charity events.

Olivier was envious of David Niven, a reserve officer in a Highland regiment, who was recalled back home. Suddenly, all the work commitments for *Rebecca* seemed trivial to him, while his desire to join the Army was more pressing. This sense of anxiety did not help his relationship with Joan Fontaine on the set. To get even for not getting the part, Vivien invited Fontaine and her husband Brian Aherne to a cocktail party on a Saturday night at their rented villa on Crescent Drive. As Fontaine describes that evening in her memoirs: "The maid showed us to the pool, where Brian and I waited alone in the garden for an hour. Eventually, Vivien and Larry sauntered, arm in arm, across the lawn from the house. They offered no apology. I don't know whether they'd deliberately given us the wrong hour; we left without finding out."[38]

Vivien resumed the shooting of the last takes of *Gone with the Wind* immediately, since Selznick was afraid to miss the opportunity in case she requested to go back to England, using the war as an excuse.

Vivien was still bound to the studio's contract, which committed her to shoot another film that year. She fervently hoped that the movie would be *Pride and Prejudice*, based on Jane Austen's novel, which was in pre-production with MGM under the direction of George Cukor. While Olivier was cast in the leading role, Greer Garson, who had worked with him on stage five years before, was preferred as the protagonist to Vivien, which greatly disappointed her. Instead, Vivien was cast in *Waterloo Bridge* opposite Robert Taylor, who had teamed up with her in *A Yank at Oxford* in 1938. The reason Vivien was not cast in *Pride and Prejudice* was that Selznick planned to earn more money by lending Vivien and Olivier to two different films, rather than shooting only one film starring both of them.

In October 1939, Gertrude decided to return to England, while

Vivien, who wanted to leave with her, was forced to be available for publicity for *Gone with the Wind* after enthusiastic audience reactions at pre-
views in Santa Barbara and Riverside.

News of the film's success spread quickly via radio and newspapers
before the movie played in the theatres. From that moment on, Vivien
was a star, and she was stuck with Scarlett's character forever.

Gone with the Wind's world premiere took place in Atlanta on
December 15, 1939.

Vivien was still taking piano lessons and working on her voice with
Dame May Whitty, who had helped her through the filming of *Gone with
the Wind*. She was doing this to prepare for a new production of Shakespeare's *Romeo and Juliet* she planned to play in and produce with Olivier
upon the completion of *Waterloo Bridge*.

On December 12, on board a chartered plane, Vivien and Olivier,
together with Selznick and Olivia de Havilland, landed in Atlanta. Simultaneously, another flight landed with Clark Gable and Carol Lombard.
Leslie Howard was not attending the event because he had returned to
England to participate in his country's war effort against Germany.

About 300,000 people, more than had participated in Atlanta's original battle, lined the seven-mile road that the stars took from the airport
to the Terrace Hotel, where they were lodged. Many in the crowd wore
their grandparents' best clothes from the Civil War era; aged veterans of
the war were paraded in their Confederate uniforms, while street musicians played "Dixie" on almost every corner.[39]

That night, the cast attended a ball staged at the actual Atlanta's
Bazaar, which had been shipped in sections from Hollywood at cost of
$10,000. Dressed in the original film costumes, Vivien, Clark Gable and
Olivia de Havilland made their entrance at the ball, where a crowd of
fans begging for autographs besieged them. The mayor of Atlanta was
very worried about gossip about Vivien and Larry, so in his speech he
mentioned that Olivier was also in Atlanta on his own business.

The premiere of *Gone with the Wind* was held at the Loew's Grand
Theatre, the façade of which had been transformed into a copy of Twelve
Oaks. The audience was extremely emotional during the almost four-
hour-long film, and at the end burst into a standing ovation. Shy Margaret Mitchell was called on stage, led by Carol Lombard, and she warmly
thanked everyone on behalf of "me and my poor Scarlett."

Vivien complained privately about the length of the film, comment-
ing with her usual colorful language that it was "hard on one's ass," but
she was satisfied with the final cut, overall.

Another party followed the screening, and the morning after, a

Gone with the Wind **premiere in Atlanta, December 12, 1939. Clark Gable, Carol Lombard, unidentified person, Vivien and David Selznick (right to left).**

farewell breakfast for everybody involved in the filmmaking was hosted by Margaret Mitchell at the Riding Club. Afterwards, a plane took the cast to Washington, D.C., where *Gone with the Wind* was presented the following day. The tour continued on to New York on the 18th, and concluded on December 27 in Los Angeles.

"Miss Leigh is so perfectly designed for the part by art and nature that any other actress in the role would be inconceivable."[40] Those were some of the praiseworthy words written by *New York Times* film critic Frank Nugent. It was the most flattering comment she ever received for her interpretation. A couple of weeks later, Vivien received the New York Critics Award as best actress of the year.

Vivien and Olivier again spent New Year's Eve at Myron Selznick's.

Chapter Seven

Romeo and Juliet

"Don't try to come between us, we've been together for
years. Nobody's coming between us. Don't you try!"
—Vivien Leigh to Jack Merivale

The filming of *Waterloo Bridge* had started and in her spare time,
Vivien was already studying Shakespeare's part of Juliet for her next play
and knitting balaclavas for the British troops.

Waterloo Bridge was the remake of a 1931 James Whale film based
on a play by Robert Sherwood. The character of Myra, played by Vivien,
required training in classical ballet, because the protagonist was a balle-
rina who becomes a prostitute and commits suicide after the officer with
whom she was in love, but who she believes to be dead, suddenly comes
back from the war. For the part, Vivien took ballet classes with the Ger-
man-Hungarian choreographer Ernest Matray.

Selznick had sent a memo to MGM, in which he gave precise instructions on how Vivien had to be treated on the set, requesting and obtaining the services of the best photography director available: Laslo Williger,
a true master of light. Vivien's black and white close-ups are the most
beautiful shots of her entire career, and her face radiates a dreamy, glow-
ing look completely different from her appearance in the Technicolor *Gone
with the Wind*. Filming lasted about four months and the only problems
that occurred on the set were caused by the use of artificial fog: "Everything, or nearly everything, was supposedly set in the fog, and the sound
stage was always full of the acrid smell of what the studio manufactured
for the effect. But the fog worked to our advantage too. We could suggest
a locale, and the fog would be so thick we didn't have to be too specific

Vivien and Robert Taylor in *Waterloo Bridge*, **1940.**

with our sets. There was a scene of Vivien walking on a bridge. All we did was built a part of the sidewalk and string some lights across it, then fill the set with fog, and we had our bridge."[1]

On January 29, 1940, Laurence Olivier divorced Jill Edsmond, who was granted custody of their son Tarquin. The following month Leigh Holman applied for a divorce, after another of Vivien's requests. She awarded him sole custody of Suzanne.

It took over six months before the divorce became final and allowed Vivien and Olivier to marry, even though it was no longer a secret in Hollywood that Scarlett O'Hara and the prince of the British theater were lovers.

Olivier had rented a villa in San Ysidro, next to actor Danny Kaye's, and although he was officially still sharing his residence with screenwriter Garson Kanin, the truth was that the writer was only occupying a guesthouse in the back yard. In actuality, Vivien was living with him.

At the end of the shooting of *Waterloo Bridge*, the cast threw a party in Vivien's honor. The film would become Vivien's favorite, and her acting was so moving that it seems that the prostitutes of Half Moon Street instantly moved their business over the Waterloo Bridge, which later became a must for any American soldier in London.[2]

On February 1940, Vivien participated in the Academy Awards ceremony. At that time the Oscars were awarded at a formal banquet at the Cocoanut Grove inside the Ambassador Hotel in Los Angeles. Vivien arrived with Olivier at 9:30 P.M. sharp. She was wearing a white ermine coat over an evening

Vivien as Myra Lester in *Waterloo Bridge*, 1940.

gown with a big aquamarine necklace. She was very nervous, and the press noticed that her lips were trembling.[3]

Comedian Bob Hope, who was the master of ceremonies, commented that the evening was more like a benefit for David Selznick, making reference to the 13 nominations that *Gone with the Wind* received.

Hattie McDaniel was the first to be awarded an Oscar for best supporting actress, becoming the first black actress in film history to win the award. For his part as Heathcliff in *Wuthering Heights*, Olivier was beat by Robert Donat in *Goodbye, Mr. Chips*, and not by Clark Gable as everybody expected.

Finally, at 1:15 A.M. Spencer Tracy handed Vivien her Oscar for best actress, confirming her win over Bette Davis's nomination for *Dark Victory*. "Vivien Leigh rightfully won, and I meant it when I told her that Scarlett was one of the greatest performances of all time. I'm not sure that she believed I was sincere, but Laurence Olivier did. Of course, he and I are the same kind of actor. But if *Victory* had been released any other year, I think unquestionably I would have won."[3]

Vivien's acceptance speech was very concise: "If I were to mention all those who've shown me such wonderful generosity through *Gone with the Wind* I should have to entertain you with an oration as long as *Gone with the Wind* itself." She then posed for photographers and later, when she arrived home, she gave the statuette to her secretary Sunny. She did not take it with her to London until 1950 because it was too heavy to carry, and she would often use it as a doorstop.[4]

Gone with the Wind opened in England in the spring of that year, and it ran continuously in movie theaters for four years. Vivien was declared by the British press to be the greatest star England ever gave Hollywood.[5] In May 1940, *Waterloo Bridge* opened in America. The film was a big success at the box-office and received enthusiastic reviews, affirming that Vivien's acting was also good in roles different from that of Scarlett O'Hara. *New York Times* critic Boswley Crowther stated: "Let there be no doubt about it. Vivien Leigh is as fine an actress as we have on the screen today."[6]

The idea of acting together again on stage in Shakespeare's *Romeo and Juliet* with Larry was suggested by a common friend, George Cukor. Olivier also wrote to Ralph Richardson asking his opinion and advice, and the actor replied that *Romeo and Juliet* seemed too extravagant in wartime. But Vivien and Olivier had already made a decision, investing about $60,000—all their savings from the making of *Gone with the Wind* and *Rebecca*—in the project.

Olivier had several new ideas on how to present the twenty-one

Vivien and her first Oscar as Best Actress for *Gone with the Wind*, February 1940.

scenes from Shakespeare's tragedy: each of them would be shown on a circular, rotating, mechanical stage. That way they would be freer to move naturally between scenes. The circular stage was built at the Vitagraph studios in New York and then shipped to California to tour the States with the company. Meanwhile, Olivier took lessons on musical composition and exercises in playing the piano because he decided to compose the music to accompany the play himself.

The actors for *Romeo and Juliet* were cast from the colony of British artists living in Hollywood. One of those was Jack Merivale, the stepson of Gladys Cooper, who had briefly appeared with Olivier in *Rebecca*. Merivale was invited to a party given by Vivien, and on that occasion Olivier offered to meet with him the following day to read some lines from the Shakespearian play. He considered him right for the part of Paris. But the reading did not go the way Olivier had hoped and Merivale suggested his half-brother John Buckmaster for the role. When Olivier heard that name he froze—apparently, Merivale didn't know that Buckmaster and Vivien had had an affair while she was married to Leigh.

"Oh yes?" said Olivier. "Vivien had said that, too ... but I don't know anything about his acting."[7]

In the end Merivale got the part of Balthasar, and the famous British stage actress Dame May Whitty was cast as Juliet's nurse. The rehearsals began at a Warner Bros. Radio Studio, a location the company offered because it had invested $10,000 in financing the show while Vivien was finishing *Waterloo Bridge* and Olivier was finishing *Pride and Prejudice*.

Olivier decided not to spend too much money in advertising, using only small advertisements printed in some local newspapers instead of posters and billboards.

Vivien worked very hard on the project, and to be more in the character of Juliet as a child, she often played with toys or bounced a ball against the wall while delivering one of Juliet's monologues. At twenty-six years old, Vivien was the youngest actress to ever play Juliet. It was, in fact, a tradition in the theater world that no actress would play that part until she was old enough to play Juliet's nanny, too.

The show had a planned tour of about twenty weeks, opening in San Francisco and then moving to Chicago, New York and Washington D.C. Olivia de Havilland, James Stewart and Margaret Sullavan attended the opening night. Within a few days, the show sold out for its entire run. Unfortunately, the night of the debut at the Theatre Geary in San Francisco, Olivier's athleticism created some trouble. The actor was thirty-two years old and not sixteen like Romeo in the play; when he tried to climb over the Capulets' garden wall, he shook it so much that it almost broke and scared the audience.

Vivien and Larry stayed at the Fairmont Hotel, which was constantly besieged by hundreds of fans. The couple realized the presence of fans was a problem because it limited their privacy every place they would tour. Reviews in San Francisco were mixed; critics did not appreciate Olivier's interpretation, but they all praised Vivien's beauty and acting.

After a special benefit performance to raise funds for the British troops, followed by a party, the company moved by train to Chicago. After a sixty-hour trip Vivien felt extremely fatigued, and she started showing the first symptoms of frail health. She had a high temperature almost every day.

Upon their arrival at Chicago's Union Square train station, she was welcomed by a thousand-person crowd holding a long banner that welcomed Scarlett O'Hara to the windy city. All the local newspapers and newsreels had, in fact, announced her show to the city. In a letter written to Leigh, Vivien stated that she found Chicago interesting only because of the Art Gallery with its fine Van Goghs and the lovely lakeside walk, but she found the rest of the city extremely boring. The rotating stage often malfunctioned, and the theater where the tragedy was performed had a capacity of 3500 and was used more for concerts than for plays. In fact, the press reported several acoustic problems in tepid reviews, disappointing the couple's expectations.

Despite this, Olivier and Vivien were sure that the response from the critics would be different in New York, where the audience was more intellectual and open to new ideas. But the debut on Broadway was a total disaster. Reviewers unanimously found *Romeo and Juliet* "pretentious" and Olivier's acting "arrogant," while they felt that Vivien was not artistically

Vivien and Olivier reading the script of *Romeo and Juliet*, 1940.

mature enough in her role. The fact that both Olivier and Vivien were popular movie stars helped at the box-office, but caused the snotty Broadway critics to turn up their noses because they believed that actors should pursue either a film or a theater career.

Some believe that the critics' fury toward the couple was related to their moralistic disapproval of those who have openly "lived in sin" while still married to others. They also may have been against Olivier for failing to follow the example of many colleagues and return to his country and fight.[8]

The following day, after the reviews were released, Olivier left Vivien with her secretary sobbing and went out to see what was happening at the box office of the Ziegfeld, where *Romeo and Juliet* was being performed every night. As he turned the corner, he was surprised to see a long line at that time of the morning, and quickly realized that they were all advance ticket-holders demanding a refund after reading the reviews. "Go ahead, give it to them," he yelled, distributing cash to the crowd himself.[9]

The failure forced Vivien and Olivier to cut expenses. They left the hotel suite and moved as guests into Katharine Cornell's house at Sneden's Landing on the Hudson River outside of New York. The number of performances was reduced to thirty-five, and when *Romeo and Juliet* closed, the total losses amounted to $100,000.

The couple was banned from the New York theater world. The only people to invite them out to dinner were the Lunts, who were the most famous American couple in the theater. They never mentioned or commented on the personal life of their British colleagues. "It was kindly calculated to keep us looking *persona grata*," commented Olivier, adding, "I have never known such a supreme example of beautiful manners. I would never know anyone within light-years of their generosity."[10]

"I don't call *Romeo and Juliet* a mistake. It was a failure but we learned a lot from it.... It was our entire savings and we lost. In the midst of it all we went to a war relief ball in New York and Noël Coward greeted us with 'Darling how brave of you to come.'"[11] It is these words that Vivien used to comment on her *Romeo and Juliet* experience in an interview released to the *Daily Express* in 1960.

Douglas Fairbanks, Jr., remembers the team spirit and the determination to reach certain goals shared by Vivien and Olivier during that period in New York: "It was a matter of classical animal passion for both. They seemed to be constantly impatient to get the trivialities of everyday life over so they could just rush madly back to bed. Or anywhere else handy and preferably variable. The possessor of delicate beauty and sharp intellect, Vivien was apparently extremely libidinous. Larry's own brand of prurience, though more disciplined, was no less keen.... During touring the United States in their own production of *Romeo and Juliet* ... Larry did something quite splendid. Quietly, in fact almost secretly, he rose very early every morning for the next few months. Not telling anyone but Viv, he went to a nearby airfield to learn to fly, even though he feared and detested flying. Eventually, after their none-too-successful tour, he and Viv did return to England, where Larry presented himself to the Royal Navy. He was shortly commissioned as sublieutenant and pilot-instructor in the Fleet Air Arm."[12]

One night some days after the closing of *Romeo and Juliet*, Vivien received a phone call from Jack Merivale. The actor was playing in a summer stock in upstate New York, and he started to worry when Vivien begged him to come over in a strange voice. Once Merivale arrived at Sneden's Landing, he found the couple already tipsy from martinis. After a little dinner, Olivier immersed himself in reading his flight manual, while Vivien proposed to her guest that they play Chinker Chess (her pet name for Chinese checkers), one of her favorite games. When Merivale won Vivien teased him a little, then suddenly became furious, accusing him of cheating and calling Olivier over to come and help her. She screamed at him: "Don't you try to come between us. We've been together for years. Nobody's coming between us. Don't you try!"[13] An embarrassed Merivale looked at Olivier and noticed that he sat unperturbed, reading his manual as if the scene was something normal.

Merivale was very saddened and offended by the episode, and the following day he left on an early train. The story upset him so profoundly that he could not sleep for days, thinking only of the fact that his friendship with Vivien was clearly compromised without understanding the real reason for her reaction.

Years later, when Merivale became Vivien's partner, it would be clear to him that those were the first signs of her mental instability which had started to show in sudden bursts of rage that look anyone close to her by surprise. When Merivale asked her for an explanation about the incident, Vivien told him that she could not remember it at all, but that if what he was saying was true, the only justification was that she had probably seen him as a threat to her relationship with Olivier.[14]

Chapter Eight

Times of War, Times of Love

"My dear Vivien, Emma was vulgar."

*"My dear Alex, you wouldn't have given me
a contract if I'd been vulgar."*

—Alex Korda and Vivien Leigh on the set of *Lady Hamilton*

An unexpected phone call from Korda in London interrupted the period of Vivien and Olivier's dire straits. The producer told them that he was leaving for Hollywood, where he planned to make a movie as demanded by Winston Churchill. Vivien and Olivier had been cast as the leading actors, and the film would tell the sad love story of Horace Nelson and Emma Hamilton. Korda's idea was to use the story of Lord Nelson to remind the audience of the efforts that England was making to fight against Hitler. He planned to use Nelson's speeches and some of his dialogue to attack the American politics of isolationism.

Although the project seemed interesting, both Vivien and Olivier were eager to go back home. However, the British ambassador in Washington informed them that all British citizens over thirty-one years of age had to stay in the United States. The reasoning was that England didn't need men, but planes, supplies and weapons, so it was therefore useful to keep raising funds.

Vivien felt that she was not right for the part of Lady Hamilton, but Korda, who was very shrewd, explained to her that the film would not only be seen as a contribution to the war, but that in only six weeks of work they would recover from their shaky financial situation. In addition, they would be given the opportunity to have their own children evacuated to the States until the war was over.

Olivier was, in fact, very worried about Tarquin, who recently had fallen ill with meningitis, and Vivien was also thinking of Suzanne. Leigh Holman decided to send Suzanne to stay with Ernest's sister, Florence Thompson, in Canada until the end of the war. So Vivien left for Vancouver to look for a good school for her daughter. While there she was impressed with the striking beauty of the city.

Accompanied by her grandmother Gertrude, Suzanne arrived in Canada after a long and dangerous journey. It was a pure coincidence that she was on board the same ship as Jill Esmond, little Tarquin and a nanny, but Mrs. Olivier refused to talk to the mother of the future bride of her ex-husband. Soon after, the grandmother and granddaughter met with Vivien in Toronto.

All of Vivien's thoughts were on Korda's film, which was in preproduction and appeared to Vivien to be a form of positive war propaganda. Upon her return from Canada in August, after a brief holiday at Martha's Vineyard, she reluctantly returned to California. In a letter to Leigh, Vivien wrote: "Hollywood is more odious each time and I loathe it heartily."[1] While there she was voted as having the most beautiful face on the screen and also organized a fundraiser for the Red Cross.

On August 28, 1940, Vivien and Olivier were finally free to marry. In order to keep their intention a secret from the press, Vivien asked her friend Benita Colman to buy the wedding bands. The marriage took place at the Colmans' ranch in Santa Barbara, where the local county clerk maintained the secrecy of the occasion by hiding the printed marriage license from the public.

Screenwriter Garson Kanin, who had been Olivier's "house-mate," was chosen as his best man. Without notice, Kanin was called while he was in a meeting with Katharine Hepburn in the MGM offices. He asked Hepburn if she wanted to go with him to a wedding, where she would be a bridesmaid. Hepburn accepted without asking whose wedding it was.

After a turbulent trip in the car, during which the bride and groom had a furious fight because Olivier did not have directions and got lost several times, the group eventually reached the San Ysidro ranch late at night.

On August 31, 1940, a few minutes after midnight, in front of a municipal judge, Laurence Olivier and Vivien Leigh were pronounced husband and wife. "The service was cut so short by the judge," recalled Vivien, "that all we did was to say the I'do's. I wanted to say I love, honor and obey, and I kept complaining that the judge was cutting my best lines, but all he said was 'I now pronounce you man and wife. Bingo.' Bingo indeed!... After a while we put the radio on to listen to the news to hear if there was anything about the wedding. There was nothing. Having kept the wedding such a secret we were absolutely furious about it that no one should know about it, so we kept switching on the radio every hour and hoping that news was out, and then finally it was and we were all happy and we all relaxed."

Altogether, Vivien said she received three wedding bands from Olivier: "I'd lost the first when I was in the West End watching *Les Enfants du Paradis*. I put my hand up to rub my eye and the ring slipped off. Then Larry gave me another which I wear now, although it is chased and what I really wanted was plain gold band. So finally Larry gave me a third which I keep locked up in my jewelry box. Inside it he put an inscription—and that inscription reads: 'This is the last one you'll get. I hope.'"[2]

Vivien woke her mother in the middle of the night with a phone call to give her the news before she heard it from the press, and the following day the newlyweds left on a short honeymoon on the Colmans' yacht, cruising off the coast of Catalina island.

The trip was short because *Lady Hamilton* was already in production (the film was known to American audiences as *That Hamilton Woman*). Korda was personally working on the script with Walter Reisch and R.C. Sherriff, and the trio made daily changes to it. Shooting began on September 18, 1940, and was completed in only five weeks because of its tight budget. Korda had paid Vivien and Olivier half of their salary in advance because he knew of their financial troubles.

The set design included a huge terrace overlooking the bay of Naples and the interior of the luxurious villa of Lord Hamilton, created by Vincet Korda, Alexander's brother, who worked night and day to complete it on time. He also built a scale model of an entire British fleet of eighteenth-century naval vessels for the recreation of the Battle of Trafalgar. Only the decks of the ships were built to real size, with a machine that moved them back and forth to reproduce the movement of a ship at sea.

As the simulated decks were tilted, Korda noticed that Vivien suffered from seasickness. "Vivien," he said, while she turned paler with each roll of the deck, "you know in Victorian times women were supposed to lie back and think of England when their husbands wanted sex. I want you to stand up and think of England."[3] Vivien tried to do so with the help of Dramamine but several of her main scenes had to be shot again and

Vivien and Olivier in *Lady Hamilton*, 1940.

again because she would suddenly cry out in the middle of a kiss, "Oh God, I'm going to be sick!"

Lady Hamilton tells the story of how Emma Hart, the beautiful but plebeian wife of Lord Hamilton, the British ambassador to Naples, became the miserable mistress of the admiral of the British fleet, Lord Horace Nelson. Her husband's death left her alone and poor, and her lover's death brought her back to the bottom of the social ladder. The story is told with flashbacks in the beginning and at the end of the film, where Emma herself explains how she was ruined by prostitution and alcohol.

To emphasize the moral and social decline of her character, Vivien used a lower tone of voice and the director of photography, Rudolph Mate, created a believable outcast by playing with lights and shades on her face.

As Vivien remembered: "I had to wear a rubber mask, we could only afford to cover the upper half of my face so that I was always photographed at a certain angle."[4]

Lady Hamilton was shot in chronological sequence, which helped Vivien to give a better, more moving portrait of her character and to better identify with the part. Korda had only one criticism of her acting style: "My dear Vivien," he said, "Emma was vulgar" and Vivien snapped back, "My dear Alex, you wouldn't have given me a contract if I'd been vulgar."[5]

Henry Wilcoxon, who played the role of Captain Thomas Hardy, Nelson's right-hand man, wrote in his autobiography: "Whenever the call sheet said we (Vivien and I) would be working together the next morning, she'd send a note around to my dressing room to meet her for tea after wardrobe. We'd sit and talk while she went through make-up and hair.... I, in turn, found her a funny and delightfully feminine creature.... I never had an affair with Viv at any time. Good God, Larry was an old friend of mine, and I was newly and happy married, myself. But in Viv's case, if circumstances had been different, I definitely would have made an exception to my rule regarding on-stage romances! To this day I have always felt that I would have been a better match for Vivien than Larry was. Our personalities and our senses of humor meshed far better. I mean, Larry was always taking himself so seriously in those days."[6]

Lady Hamilton was an instant big hit, despite reviews that were not very favorable. Churchill was so enthusiastic that he watched it several times and was moved to tears each time. "My father used to show it in the private cinema whenever we had important guests until we, the family, all knew it by heart," said Sarah Churchill. "He never tired of seeing it and it was through this film and his admiration for the Oliviers that they later become friends."[7]

Lady Hamilton was the first foreign film to be distributed in Russia during the war. People would stand in long lines to see it, trying to escape from their problems by watching the tragic love story set during a war that was less violent than the one they were living. It became the highest-grossing film that year.

Americans criticized the movie because they considered it too pro-England and thought it contained a clear accusation concerning the politics of neutrality that the U.S. had maintained toward the war in Europe. Upon the request of the American censors, two scenes had to be added later: precisely two dialogues in which the two lovers repent their adulterous conduct. Those two sequences were then cut in a later version of the film.

Once *Lady Hamilton* was completed, Vivien went to Vancouver to visit Suzanne. Although she tried to travel incognito, she was recognized everywhere. The relatives who were hosting her in Vancouver naively tried to dissuade journalists, stating that too much publicity could put the daughter of such a celebrity in danger of being kidnapped. The final outcome was the opposite of what they expected, and the local press printed articles on a possible kidnapping threat made against Vivien Leigh's daughter.[8] The news made the cover of the *News Herald* of Vancouver, forcing the Reverend Mother of the convent school where Suzanne was studying to fear for the safety of the other students. In addition, the fact that Vivien was now publicly divorced and married to another man became another reason for the religious school to dismiss Suzanne, and the child was eventually transferred to another school.

When *Lady Hamilton* was finished, Vivien and Olivier thought that they would go back to the theater since the Broadway Theatre Guild had requested that they act in George Bernard Shaw's play *Caesar and Cleopatra*.

The idea was put aside, because the desire to go back home to

Vivien as Emma Hart Hamilton in *Lady Hamilton*, **1940.**

England grew stronger every day. Although Vivien knew she was still tied to the seven-year contract with Selznick, she thought that the war was a priority at that moment and that leaving was the best thing to do. First she flew to Atlanta for a second premiere of *Gone with the Wind* followed by a benefit event for the British war relief. After that she and Olivier threw a good-bye party for all of his friends.

Two days after Christmas 1940, the Oliviers boarded a ship to Lisbon. The journey was very long and tiresome and after many days of cruising, the five-hour flight they took from Portugal to London ended with a scary emergency landing in Bristol, due to an air-raid. They found an unheated room in a little hotel in Bristol where their stay was very unpleasant because of the continuous air raids and the cold temperature that forced them to go to bed fully clothed, making it very difficult to sleep.

Finally, they arrived at Durham Cottage in London. They found it in an awful state because the ceilings were partially cracked from the bombing, but fortunately there was no damage done to the antique pieces inside since neighbors had protected all the windows with large pieces of wood.

Vivien heard that her old house in Little Stanhope Street, where she had lived with Leigh, was completely destroyed, and that her ex-husband was serving at a naval base.

Vivien and Olivier met some of their old friends, many of whom were wearing military uniforms, which made Larry extremely upset because he had failed a medical examination for active military service due to a ruptured eardrum.

Their long state of inactivity in London drove Olivier to accept a cameo role in *The 49th Parallel*, and after participating in a brief tour of air bases with Vivien, he did a scene from *Henry V*.

The euphoria of being at home was quickly replaced by a sense of not belonging. Olivier became a flight instructor in Lee on Salent. Vivien decide to moved closer to him, with her new cat Tissy. She first rented a house in Plymouth and later, when Olivier was transferred to the Royal Air station, in Worthydown in Headbourne close to the aviation field.

It was a very unhappy period for Vivien, who spent most of her time alone gardening, reading or playing with the cat, but she always felt the desire to go back to work.

Binkie Beaumont was one of the few friends close to her in those moments of deep solitude. He would visit her when Olivier was away and he would call her every day. He realized that Vivien needed to go back to work, but he was unable to help her because she had to have Selznick's approval before accepting any stage engagement. "It's that fucking seven-year contract," she shouted to him one day, using her favorite adjective at a time when it still carried considerable force and shock value. This was one aspect of her character which he did not like: to hear obscene language from a woman, particularly a lady of Vivien's quality.[9]

In the end, it was Olivier who suggested that Vivien accept George Bernard Shaw's play *The Doctor's Dilemma*. Before the war Vivien had studied the play for a radio broadcast. She had been dubious of imitating the vulgar Cockney accent but decided to try. At the last moment, however, the script had been replaced by another of Shaw's plays, *Pygmalion*. Then the sudden departure of Olivier for Hollywood to make *Wuthering Heights* left the Shaw project incomplete.

Beaumont was an old friend of Shaw's and visited him one day to propose the project. The playwright gave his permission enthusiastically, but affirmed that he would not be interested in becoming involved in the rehearsals because he was too old and tired. "The part is unusually difficult to bring to life," Shaw said. "Jennifer Dubeat is the sort of woman I really dislike. Perhaps you'll warn the young lady of this."[10]

In August 1941, with Selznick's approval, Vivien started the rehearsals for *The Doctor's Dilemma*. It was an expensive, five-act production with many costume and set design changes. Once Vivien's presence in the play was confirmed, it was very easy to collect the money to produce the play and to cast the best actors. The six-month tour opened at the sold-out Manchester Opera House, where the audience was curious to see Scarlett O'Hara on stage. Oswald Frewen and Leigh Holman attended the performance, and her former husband noticed that Vivien delivered her lines unusually slowly in order to give more maturity to her character.

In the meantime, Vivien decided that no matter where she was, during the weekend she would travel to see Olivier. The tour was very stressful because of the state of the war: traveling by train was incredibly slow, and the hotels where the company would stay often did not have hot water or heat so the actors got little rest. The winter of 1941 was one of the coldest in England, and during those long train trips Vivien would wear a raincoat and wrap a long scarf around her head. She read all the works of Dickens, who was her favorite author after Shakespeare.

Despite all the precautions she took, Vivien often fell ill and a couple of times she had to be replaced by her understudy.

Chapter Nine

Cleopatra

"I'd rather be an Edith Evans any day than a Garbo"
—Vivien Leigh

In Edinburgh, photographer Cecil Beaton saw a performance of *The Doctor's Dilemma*. In his diaries he wrote: "Vivien is almost incredibly lovely.... She wants to do Shaw's *Caesar and Cleopatra* next. She is madly in love with her husband—who adores her—& is convinced he is a much greater person than herself. Her former husband dotes upon & adores her still.... The adulation of her beauty leaves her cold."[1] Beaton also praised the lavish Victorian costumes that Vivien wore. He photographed her in her dressing room wearing one of these beautiful dresses and a hat with a veil. That photograph became Olivier's favorite.

On March 4, 1942, *The Doctor's Dilemma* opened at the Haymarket Theatre in London, where it ran for over thirteen months, a record for one of Shaw's plays. The entire city was covered with posters of Vivien advertising the show. The reviews were discordant; the real dilemma was whether such an extraordinary beautiful woman could also be a talented actress. The issue often created opposing opinions, which would haunt her for the rest of her stage career.

During the running of *The Doctor's Dilemma*, Vivien had many partners on stage: Cyril Cusak was replaced by Peter Gleneville, and later by John Gielgud, who had to learn his part in only one week and remembered, "We began an acquaintanceship which slowly ripened into a deep friendship and affection.... Although she seemed so astonishingly resilient, she often suffered ill health and fits of great depression, but she made light of the fact and rarely admitted to it or talked about it to other people. Her courage in the face of personal unhappiness was touching and remarkable."[2]

Although Vivien accepted *The Doctor's Dilemma* because she was tired of being inactive, the real reason behind her acceptance of the part was that the idea of acting on stage as the queen of Egypt in Shaw's *Caesar and Cleopatra* really appealed to her. She set out to try to prove to the playwright that she was right for the part. But during those thirteen months at the Haymarket Theatre, Bernard Shaw never went to see the show, even though he was aware of the incredible success Vivien was having.

Meantime, Shaw granted permission to producer and director Gabriel Pascal to make *The Doctor's Dilemma* into a film. Pascal had already adapted Shaw's *Pygmalion* for the big screen in 1938. Vivien was interested in the project, but the director cast Greer Garson in the leading role, which infuriated Shaw because he had given his permission to ensure that Vivien would play Jennifer Dubeat.

Vivien obtained a meeting with Shaw through the help of Binkie Beaumont, who accompanied her. Before seeing Vivien, the playwright asked Pascal Vivien's age, and the producer answered "in her twenties." Vivien would be thirty a couple of months later. Pascal had also described her as slender and petite. The director had now decided to make a film from Shaw's *Caesar and Cleopatra* starring Vivien as the queen of Egypt, but this time only with the playwright's approval.

Meeting Shaw was a success for Vivien, who never mentioned her project idea; however, from the moment she walked into Shaw's living room she acted like a Persian cat, simultaneously sweet and determined. At the end of the visit, Shaw suggested that she should play Cleopatra. Pretending to be humble, Vivien asked him if he really thought she was ready for such a difficult role. The playwright told her that it did not matter how good she was, because Cleopatra was a foolproof part. "You are the Mrs. Pat Campbell of the age," added Shaw, paying her a great compliment. Pat Campbell had been Shaw's love interest fifty years earlier, but was also an actress known for her ability to obtain every role she wanted.

Throughout the 474 performances of *The Doctor's Dilemma*, Vivien also met the director of the National Gallery, Sir Kenneth Clark, whose office was very close to the Haymarket Theatre. Often during his breaks he would have tea with Vivien, conversing with her about theater and art: "She is not only intelligent but she has class," commented Clark on Vivien.

When the show closed Vivien was again restless to work. She also terribly missed Olivier, who was always busy working as a flight instructor. She told Beaumont of her desire to learn how to drive an ambulance, to enroll as an auxiliary policewoman or to do fire-watching on the roof of the Haymarket in the hopes of feeling more useful. The manager gently discouraged her: she was too valuable to risk her life participating in such dangerous activities. "Your war work is just what you are doing," Beaumont said. "You're giving pleasure to the public, cheering up the servicemen on leave, keeping people happy."[3]

But Vivien did eventually arrange to take a first-aid course.

In April 1942, Vivien participated in a benefit play in *The School for Scandal* along with veteran actor Cyril Maude, who was celebrating his 80th birthday. Years later Vivien and Olivier would tour that play in Australia. The show was organized as a charity event to benefit the Actors' Benevolent Fund and the press defined Vivien as being "fresh as a rosebud."

Again at Beaumont's suggestion, Vivien accepted a part in a tour called *Spring Party* to entertain the British troops stationed in North Africa. After dismissing the idea of playing a scene from *Romeo and Juliet*, Vivien chose to read two dramatic recitations: Lewis Carroll's poem *You Are Old, Father William* and a satirical song while wearing a copy of a costume from *Gone with the Wind* satirizing Scarlett O'Hara. The show was produced by John Gielgud, and besides Vivien the company included veteran musical actress Beatrice Lillie and two British comedians.

The show toured for three months in North Africa, from Gibraltar to Cairo, in excruciatingly hot weather. The stages where *Spring Party* was performed were often made from whatever was available, anything from simple sand dunes in the desert to a Roman amphitheater in Leptis Magna, near Tripoli.

The show attracted many high-ranking military officials, including General Montgomery, General Eisenhower and King George VI, who attended a performance at the Royal Command in a remote location in Tunisia. On that occasion Vivien added something to the repertoire under the king's personal request: his favorite poem, *The White Cliffs of Dover* by Alice Duer Miller.

Despite the sultry weather, the mosquitoes and the long distance away from Olivier, Vivien extended her presence on the tour for three weeks due to the great success she achieved and the requests from other military bases. But her health suffered from the fatigue caused by the tour. She lost almost fifteen pounds, and she was continuously afflicted by whooping cough, which she did not try to cure.

Once back in London, Vivien found Olivier preparing to star in the film *Henry V*. She was interested in being part of the project and playing the part of Princess Katherine.

She thought that her fluency in French would perfectly complement the period costumes, whose sketches drawn by Roger Furse she greatly admired. In addition, the love scenes between her and Olivier would add more realism to the play. But Selznick's refusal via telegram was categorical: "ABSOLUTELY UNDER NO CONDITIONS WILL YOU PERFORM MEDIOCRE PART IN HENRY V. YOU ARE STILL CONTRACTUALLY OBLIGED TO SELZNICK. REMEMBER? SO STOP. DAVID."[4] Renée Asherson was then cast in the part.

Beaumont tried to explain to the American producer that the role of Princess Katherine, even though small, was the best female supporting part in the tragedy. Although Selznick was known to be a man of culture with knowledge of European literature, like so many American producers, he was obsessed with grandeur. Only big was beautiful, and he did not understand that a small part could also be a very good part.[5] Instead, Selznick offered Vivien the lead role in a new version of *Jane Eyre* based on the Charlotte Brontë novel. His idea was to cast Suzanne for the role of Jane as a child. Vivien was against the idea that her daughter would have to interrupt her studies in Canada to be an actress.

To distract Vivien from the disappointment of not working with Olivier, Beaumont took her out to lunch to tell her of a strange idea he had in mind. "What dear Larry ought to do is to film all the Katherine scenes with you after he's finished filming them with Renée Asherson. The scenes can be kept in a vault until your seven-year contract has finished and they can be slotted in to the film," proposed Beaumont.

"Rather hard on her," said Vivien. "I don't think she would like that."

"Not so hard. She'll get the premiere and she'll be in it for the first few years. Better than nothing. So there would be two versions of the film and they can both be shown. It's never happened before and it'll cause a sensation. The cinemas can show both versions on alternate days: just think of the publicity."[6]

Vivien was happy about it, especially the thought of Selznick's reaction. However, after a consultation with the film company's legal department, it proved too difficult to achieve. So Vivien never played Katherine to Olivier's Henry, and Beaumont never stopped regretting the loss.

Meanwhile, the *Caesar and Cleopatra* project stayed on hold until 1944, not only due to Selznick's veto, but also because Pascal had been unable to find the right actor to cast as Caesar. Later, he decided to go to the States to see if he would be able to find the ideal actor there.

So, Vivien went back to her domestic life and waited for a definite date to begin filming, while Olivier was on the set of *Henry V* at the studios in Denham. David Niven and his wife Primula asked her to be the godmother at the christening of their new-born son David, Jr., Vivien gladly accepted and as a present gave them a silver drinking mug that she had found in a flea market while hunting for rare antiquarian pieces.

Vivien never liked to be home alone, especially at night, so she would constantly invite friends over. These were often personalities from the entertainment business who would spend long weekends with her playing cards or chatting into the night. Some of these guests began to notice strange behavior. During the Easter holidays, Vivien was invited to a party where she received some beautifully painted Easter eggs as a gift from the host. Vivien enthusiastically thanked the giver for the gift, saying she would treasure them forever. The following day during breakfast, Robert Helpmann, who was a guest at the Olivier's along with the Lunts, asked her what she would do with those lovely eggs. Vivien replied, "You're eating them now." Years later when somebody else asked her why she had cooked them, she answered, obviously annoyed, "Well it was during the war when there were no eggs available."[7]

In the beginning of 1944, the Oliviers started looking for a new house in the countryside. Leigh Holman, who still had a very good relationship with Vivien, had just moved to Woodlands and the Oliviers had spent a lovely weekend in his new house. They admired the property so much that they decided to buy something similar. They looked at many properties without finding anything attractive, and shortly after they had to postpone their search because the filming of *Caesar and Cleopatra* was scheduled to begin.

Her contractual problems were partially solved when Selznick accepted an offer of 50,000 pounds to let Vivien appear in the film, but the initial excitement that Vivien had shown at the beginning was now completely gone. She was still feeling fatigued by the African tour, and the effects of dehydration

Vivien as Cleopatra in *Caesar and Cleopatra*, 1944.

from several shows in the desert had given her a wan face. Her voice was also growing faint.

Cameras began to roll at Denham's studios on June 12, 1944, and a few days later the Allies invaded Normandy.

Claude Rains was cast by Pascal as Caesar, even though Shaw had insisted up until the last moment to cast John Gielgud who, in his opinion, would have been the perfect successor to John Forbes Robertson, who had played the Roman Emperor in a previous version. When Shaw visited the set, he prophetically said, "I pity poor Rank [Arthur Rank was partially producing the movie]. The film will cost a million."[8] In fact, the movie cost about 1.3 million, because Pascal wanted to respect even the smallest historical detail; he even requested that many loads of sand be shipped directly from the Sahara for the desert scenes.

Shaw did not allow any alteration of the original dialogue without his permission. When he saw Claude Rains, he decided that it would not be proper for him, as Caesar, to be called "thin and stringy." The playwright wrote a note to Vivien saying, "Your Julius Caesar is not rather thin and stringy (I have just seen him); so will you say instead, 'You are hundreds of years old; but you have a nice voice'.... I think this is the only personal remark that needs altering; but if there is anything let me know. G.B.S."[9]

Vivien replied that she could make the original line believable with her voice intonation. Shaw was very annoyed and answered immediately,

> No. Rains is not stringy, and would strongly resent any deliberate attempt to make him appear so. Besides, 'you are hundreds of years old' is a much better line, as it goes with the childishness of Cleopatra in the first half of the play. I never change a line except for the better. Don't be an idiot. G.B.S.
> Why don't you put your address in your letters.[10]

Filming *Caesar and Cleopatra* was very difficult due to the unfavorable meteorological conditions. Vivien would often freeze in her luxurious but light costumes. She would always rush into her dressing room where she had a small electric heater, but it was not enough to protect her increasingly delicate health.

The shooting was often interrupted by air raids that required the studios to be immediately evacuated, causing tiresome delays. One day on the Pharos set (Alexandria of Egypt port), a bomb blew up 150 yards from Pascal's office. Although it shattered all of the windows, it did not injure anyone.

Construction materials on the set and fabric for the extras' costumes were in short supply; towels were used to costume thousands of actors who played soldiers or common people. Some of these extras, like Roger Moore, Joan Collins, Jean Simmons and Kay Kendall, later became famous. Stewart Granger, who was playing Apollodorus, had some problems identifying with the character since Shaw requested that he act more effeminately. This was a very difficult request for an actor with the reputation of a playboy. At that time, although married to Elspeth March, Granger was having an affair with Deborah Kerr. One day he was astounded to learn that everybody on the set knew about it when Vivien became exasperated and told him to concentrate on his work rather than on Deborah Kerr.[11] A few days later, filming of the movie began and Vivien realized that she was pregnant. She had been pregnant by Olivier before, in September 1942, but she miscarried after only a couple of weeks. Her intolerance and her fits of hysteria were justified by her pregnancy, and Pascal tried to do his best to ensure that all the scenes with Vivien were filmed first.

Vivien wrote to Leigh: "I'm to have a baby.... Everyone keeps asking me how I suppose they are going to make me look like a 16 year Cleopatra.... I think it is a very good thing really because they'll just have to hurry up with the film."

During a take of an action scene in which Cleopatra runs up some stairs after a slave to whip him and then jumps over a platform to proclaim herself queen, Vivien slipped on the shiny marble floor and fell to the ground. After she was carried to her dressing room, a doctor was called to see if she had any fractures. The physician ordered her an X-ray and a few days of rest, but during the first week of September she was rushed to the emergency room of the London Clinic, where she had her second miscarriage.

"There will be plenty more where that one came from," she commented, but the disappointment and the grief was intense, because she thought that having a child with Olivier would strengthen the relationship.[12] With a splinter of ice in his soul, Olivier examined the fetus. Astounded by the perfection of its form, the only comment he made to his son Tarquin was, "It had a penis and would have been a little boy."[13]

Vivien returned to the set to complete the film the day after she was dismissed from the clinic. She had recovered physically, but not psychologically. She was overcome by a very bad mood that slowly transformed into a grave depression with frequent fits of hysteria. Stewart Granger remembers: "She never forgave Pascal for this and from then on was constantly trying to have him replaced by another director, but without success."[14]

The infamous scene in *Caesar and Cleopatra* (1944) where Vivien had the fall that later caused her miscarriage.

While she was playing in an important scene re-enacting a banquet that Cleopatra gives in honor of Caesar, Vivien's facial expressions suddenly changed and her voice became harsh. She did not follow her lines but, instead, started to scold her dresser for some omissions in her costume. She raised her eyebrows and showed all of her unjustified rage. Filming was suspended and Vivien was escorted into her dressing room while she was protesting that she was perfectly fine. She had suffered a short hysterical fit, surprising all the bystanders. The following day she wrote an apologetic note to the director and to all her colleagues.

At the time, Vivien's mental illness was underestimated; everybody justified her strange and irrational behavior with excuses connected to her pregnancy or to the depression she suffered after the loss of the baby. But her still partially treatable symptoms would come back in cycles, and within a few months they would transform into violent attacks that would accompany her until death.

Olivier did not understand the reason for Vivien's crazy manners, and he attributed them to the strain of work and to stress rather than considering them serious. One night while they were home alone having dinner and chatting pleasantly, however, her mood suddenly changed in a terrifying manner. She became as intolerant as an animal in a cage and then her voice changed, becoming very unpleasant, and when Olivier tried to calm her, she turned on him verbally and then physically. For the first time, Olivier saw Vivien as a complete stranger.

After a long hour of terrible screams and acts of violence accompanied by the tossing of objects everywhere, Vivien started to sob hysterically and would not allow Olivier to come near her. When the attack of hysteria was over, Vivien could not remember what she had done or said, but she refused to see a doctor. She too justified the episode as a symptom of the stress she had recently suffered.

Chapter Ten

Lady Olivier

"Acting is difficult, that's what makes it so interesting."
—Vivien Leigh

Somebody sent Vivien a copy of Thornton Wilder's *The Skin of Our Teeth*. The year before, the play had been a big success on Broadway in a production directed by Elia Kazan and starring actors Tallulah Bankhead and Montgomery Clift. *The Skin of Our Teeth* told the story, in an allegoric form, of a family trying to survive over the course of 5000 years.

Vivien loved the play and she particularly liked the character of Sabina, a very feminine woman who was capable of handling all of life's difficulties with great irony. She felt it was a part that would give her the opportunity to explore her acting qualities as a comedian. Vivien convinced Olivier to acquire the British rights and to direct the play, but her enthusiasm over starting a project that was so exciting for both of them was interrupted when David Selznick claimed his contract with her. He wrote her a letter in which he stated that she already was granted twelve weeks' stay in England, but now it was time to come back to Hollywood to be available for one of his films.

Vivien opposed, and Selznick applied for a legal injunction. During the judgment Vivien was represented by Sir Valentine Holms, who maintained that as a married woman who was not working at the moment, she was under obligation to the national service regulation due to the country's state of war. The judge ruled in her favor, stating that Vivien was better employed in a theater than in a munitions factory, and the case was closed.

Vivien was freed from Selznick's contract, but she was still tied to

Alexander Korda, who was now head of the British MGM. The producer had bought from Myron Selznick the rights to three films with the intention of having Vivien star in them. But she was only interested in working in *The Skin of Our Teeth* and refused any offers related to films. Korda was about to take her to court, but because he had plans to retire soon, and in the name of his old friendship with the Oliviers, he decided not to sue Vivien, replacing her instead with Deborah Kerr.[1]

On January 13, 1945, in a letter to her friend Alan Dent, Vivien wrote, "I don't think I have ever been more excited on the eve of any venture—or more nervous."[2] She had started rehearsing *The Skin of Our Teeth* during the trial against Selznick. In order to study the part of Sabina deeply, she began going to cabarets and burlesques in London, and used all the techniques she learned observing veteran comedienne Beatrice Lillie during the tour of *Spring Party* in North Africa.

In April 1945, Vivien, under the direction of Olivier, debuted in Edinburgh with *The Skin of Our Teeth*. Although the show puzzled the audience with its allegory, which was often difficult to interpret, the reviews were all positive and Vivien's interpretation was praised. "In the face of all critical prejudice, Vivien had now established herself as a stage actress and a star of the brightest mettle," commented Olivier in his memoirs.[3] Friends and colleagues will remember Vivien's stint as Sabina as one of the best roles she ever played, and her greatest achievement as a comedian. The first praise came from the author, whose only criticism was that Vivien's voice seemed not to reach the right tone in some scenes; however, overall he considered her acting brilliant.

The show also ran for a while in Blackpole. One day while she was in her dressing room, Vivien received a visit from Jack Merivale, who was serving nearby in the Royal Canadian Air Force. The last meeting they had together had ended abruptly years earlier after one of Vivien's hysterical fits. Merivale had forgiven her, and he nervously went backstage to congratulate her. He had recently married the actress Jan Sterling and had planned to go back to work in the theater once his duty in the Canadian Air Force was over. Vivien was very happy to see him, and at the end of the meeting they promised to keep in touch.

The next day the company was scheduled to move to London for its opening in the West End, but after 78 performances Vivien looked very tired, pale and sick. Since her debut in Edinburgh, she was continuously coughing, especially when she was in smoky and noisy places, which seemed to aggravate her state. Finally, she had two doctors visit her and they both made the same diagnosis: tubercular infection in her right lung. She was ordered to rest completely, to immediately schedule recovery in a sanatorium in Switzerland or Scotland, and to totally abstain from smoking and alcohol.

So *The Skin of Our Teeth* had to close its performances by the end of July, while Olivier was touring with the Old Vic Company in Germany. He was notified by a friend about Vivien's health condition only a few days later, when she finally decided to check into the University College Hospital for a six-week treatment.

Doctors had ordered her to rest for at least six months, but the always stubborn Vivien refused to be cured in a sanatorium. She considered it to be comparable to a mental institution and preferred instead to have a short holiday in Scotland with Olivier.

At the end of September, when the war was almost over, the Oliviers moved into their new country house in the countryside near Buckinghamshire, where after a long search, they had purchased property: Notley Abbey. It was a historic residence on a large estate nearly seventy acres. It was founded during Henry II's reign to be used as an abbey and then as a hospice for the Augustinian order. Later, under Henry VIII, Notley Abbey was purchased by a protestant family. Over the centuries it had been transformed in a private residence with twenty-two rooms, including a servant's quarters, a refectory barn, a pigsty and a henhouse. The Oliviers acquired the property with the fishing rights for the stretch of the River Thames that ran through it, using all their savings to repair and furnish the estate.

Vivien was extremely proud of owning that piece of English history, and after returning from her trip to Scotland, even though she was still recovering, she concentrated all her efforts on furnishing the main part of the house. This consisted of several living rooms and Olivier's study. Notley Abbey needed major, radical improvements: water pipes were old, and there was no kitchen or any modern bathrooms. Within a short time the Oliviers transformed their place into a very comfortable property and made Notley Abbey their principal residence. It was their own retreat and a place where many celebrities from show business, as well as the art and the literary world, were hosted over the years by what was considered "the most beautiful couple of the British theater."

"The Oliviers would be synonymous with wit, beauty, taste, audaciousness, power and even semi-royal status."[4] Every guest would find Notley Abbey to be a luxurious accommodation. They slept in silk sheets, found that their toilet paper matched the color of the bathroom tiles and that they could have lunch or dinner ready at anytime of the day or night with impeccable and superb hospitality.

According to biographer Alexander Walker: "The Oliviers set the

Vivien in a portrait from the '40s. (Ken Galente collection)

seal of a style of life with the same romantic richness as the Duke and the Duchess of Windsor.... What they lack in family ancestry, they made up for in the aristocratic nature of their talents."[5]

Vivien spent her first four months at Notley Abbey completely resting, and was assisted by a twenty-four hour nurse. Most of her life took place in her L-shaped bedroom, which was located on the second floor of the house with a large fireplace and an original four-poster bed from *Gone with the Wind*. While resting, Vivien worked every day on the refurbishing of Notley; she refused to have even one seed planted by her gardeners without her supervision. Slowly, along with the help of Vivien's friend and decorator Sybil Colefax, the property assumed a different look.

Every week a specialist would visit her to check the stages of her convalescence from the tuberculosis; Vivien had quit smoking and drinking and she had all her meals served on a tray in bed or while sitting in her armchair. Meanwhile, Olivier was rehearsing Sophocles' *Oedipus Rex* and Sheridan's *The Critic* on opposite days at the Old Vic.

Finally, Vivien seemed to have recovered from tuberculosis—though the doctors told her that she would always be at risk of relapsing—and she was then able to accompany Olivier to New York, where he was scheduled to play on Broadway in *Henry V*, *Oedipus Rex* and *Uncle Vanya*.

At the time, Olivier was more interested in making movies because it was more lucrative than acting in plays. Due to the enormous expenses he had incurred in refurbishing Notley Abbey, economics were a concern. But Selznick, punishing him for what had happened with Vivien in court, had threatened everyone who wanted to hire Olivier with the possibility of never working with his production company again. Therefore, the actor was banned for two years from all Hollywood sets. During her stay in New York, Vivien met writer Somerset Maugham. The author was impressed by her tremendous erudition, beauty and perfect French.[6]

Her sojourn in the States was disturbed by two accidents related to airplanes. The first happened when Olivier, who was receiving an honorary degree at Tufts University near Boston, missed his return flight, which Vivien and her friend Jerry Dale had already boarded. Vivien became very tense because she detested flying, especially without Olivier by her side. A couple of weeks later, while on board a flight that was to take them back to London, one of the two engines caught fire and the plane had an emergency landing in Willimantic, Connecticut, scaring all of the passengers. The Oliviers arrived in London two days later.

Vivien had decided that because of all the expenses they had from refurbishing Notley Abbey, it was time to go back to work and resume the running of *The Skin of Our Teeth*. She was still dedicating a lot of her time to gardening, often with the help of Dicky, Olivier's brother, with whom she bought some pedigree cows to add to a market garden they had established together. Each cow was named after one of the characters Vivien had played on the stage or screen: Emma, Cleopatra, Juliet, Sabina but no Scarlett, because it was the only part originally played by her.

In September 1946, *Caesar and Cleopatra* was released in the States. Vivien refused to see it, waiting five years before finally watching it due to the sad memories it brought to mind. She was urged to do so by the fact that she had decided to play Cleopatra again, this time on stage opposite Olivier as Caesar.

The new run of *The Skin of Our Teeth* had a different cast from the original, and the play ran for 109 performances at the Piccadilly Theatre. Although her health was still very frail, Vivien appeared in almost every performance, missing only one matinee and one evening show. During that fall, a curious episode happened. An Oxford missionary student and a former member of the Old Vic who had been expelled from the university because of some strange, undisclosed behavior waited at Notley Abbey for Vivien. When she returned from the theater, he attempted to kiss her while she was coming out of her car. That gesture cost him a punch in the nose from Olivier and a sentence of six months in prison.[7]

Vivien was offered a role in a new film version of *Cyrano de Bergerac*, a project that had been very dear to her for a long time, but one she had hoped to do with Olivier, who was about to direct and act in Shakespeare's *Hamlet*. Although Olivier was forty years old and not young enough to play the Prince of Denmark, filming *Hamlet* was a challenge that was too important to give up just because of his age, especially since it could easily be disguised by a good make-up artist. On the other hand, Vivien was visibly too old to play Ophelia and too proud to play Hamlet's mother. Instead, the producers cast nineteen-year-old Jean Simmons as Ophelia.

Around Christmas time Vivien had another serious manic-depressive attack, apparently provoked by Suzanne's refusal to spend the holidays with her. Olivier tried in vain to convince Vivien to see a psychiatrist, but opted for the alternative—a short vacation in the warm Italian weather. At Notley Abbey, Vivien would often wear a fur coat and gloves to stay warm, causing Olivier to worry that the house was too cold and that it could affect his wife's fragile health.

They stayed at the Hotel Miramare in Santa Margherita Ligure on the Italian Riviera and occupied a five-room suite. Olivier had, in fact, convinced *Hamlet*'s Italian producer Filippo Del Giudice to include the Italian vacation in the budget of the film. In Santa Margherita the Oliviers were joined by Del Giudice, who would spend most of the day with Larry talking about the *Hamlet* production, while Vivien would sun herself on the terrace of her suite. They also went on a short excursion to Florence to visit art critic Bernard Berenson, who had invited them to his villa "I Tatti."

When they returned to England, Korda, who knew how eager Vivien was to go back to work, offered her the leading role in *Anna Karenina*, which was based on the famous book by Russian author Leo Tolstoy. Anna's story seemed very similar in certain aspects to Vivien's: a woman leaves her husband and child because she is in love with another man. Vivien immediately accepted the part without reading the script, and Korda scheduled the making of the film a couple of months after Olivier had started *Hamlet*.

During that time, the speculation of Olivier's sexual infidelity crept into Vivien's mind. It was an obsession that would haunt her throughout the marriage. She was constantly imagining that Olivier was having affairs. In a letter recently found in Olivier's correspondence at the British Library in London, Vivien wrote to a friend, "Goddam Larry is fucking his Ophelia—I'm losing him to a bloody child [Jean Simmons]. I was barely out of my teens when Larry started fucking me." Over and over again in this material, Vivien cannot wait to have him back to herself.[8]

She began shooting *Anna Karenina* at the Shepperton Studios in May 1947 under the direction of Julien Duvivier, a French director who had made *Pepe Le Moko* with Jean Gabin. Duvivier emphasized the historical accuracy of the story and chose Cecil Beaton as the costumer. Ralph Richardson had been cast as Karin, Anna's husband. The actor was an old friend of Olivier's and his friendship with Vivien grew while they worked together.

Vivien and Ralph Richardson in Alexander Korda's production of *Anna Karenina,* **1947.**

To more closely identify with her character, Vivien again read Tolstoy's novel, even though in the script Anna's suicide is highlighted to add more dramatic force to the tragic ending.

Only two weeks before the filming began, Vivien went to Paris with Beaton for a costume fitting. She found all her corsets too tight and uncomfortable, and had Beaton remake them in record time. Later they realized that Vivien had previously worn them upside down. During her time in Paris, Vivien received a phone call from an excited Olivier. He announced that the Queen was going to knight him, but Vivien's reaction was extremely cold—most likely because of professional jealousy.

While she was studying Anna, Vivien began to deeply ponder her own personal life and compare it to the events in the life of her character. She would get terribly depressed when thinking about the way she had left Leigh and Suzanne for Olivier.

The hot summer did not cooperate, as the cast was pretending to be in Moscow during a snowy winter. Vivien would sweat under her beautiful but heavy scene costumes, making it very difficult to film. Her fatigue would intensify her nervousness, and Gertrude was often on the set trying to relax her. She had also developed a sort of phobia about her appearance. Once after she complained several times to Beaton about a pair of tight gloves, the exasperated costume designer told her, "It is because your hands are too big!" This touched upon one of her weakest spots.

Originally, Korda had wanted to cast Olivier as Vronsky, Anna's lover, but the actor was busy with *Hamlet*; therefore, the promising new actor Kieron Moore was chosen. Unfortunately, his presence in front of the camera was not charismatic enough when compared to Richardson and Vivien. In a letter addressed to his friend Greta Garbo, Beaton wrote, "I think *Anna* will be a good film. It is well directed. The leading lady is not Anna—she is not you—but she is sympathetic and has great character and style. Vronsky is a disaster."[9]

While Korda was in California on business, a grave tension developed between Vivien and the director, who was also not an easy person to deal with. The troupe refused to go on working, and Korda had to return to the set to calm down the situation.

On July 8, 1947, Vivien, wearing a simple black dress and a brimmed black hat, accompanied Olivier to Buckingham Palace for his investiture ceremony. For that occasion the set of *Anna Karenina* was closed for a day. She seemed almost annoyed by it because, in her opinion, it was a ridiculous and anachronistic tradition.

Olivier would be the youngest actor to ever receive the title of Sir from the British monarchy.

From that moment on Vivien became Lady Olivier, but the noble title was not enough to make the cloud of unhappiness and dissatisfaction, which now covered her life, disappear.[10] In her mind, her obsessive devotion to Larry was no longer being returned by him. He was restless, bored, easily irritated, and the strength of Vivien's feelings toward him now seemed more and more hysterical to him. She was jealous and suffocating rather than loving and exciting. He wanted more freedom, and she was terrified that if she gave it to him she would lose him.[11]

An occasion to spend even more time together arrived when the Old Vic planned a tour of Australia.

Vivien had completed *Anna Karenina*, which had cost almost $3 million to make, even though it bombed at the box-office and was snubbed by critics, who inevitably compared it to Garbo's unforgettable 1935 interpretation. Only Richardson's acting was praised in the reviews, while Vivien's was considered too cold and distant. The failure increased her depression. She sadly confided to Richardson's wife Mu: "I know Anna, I was inside her. I know everything about her, and yet they say I can't do it."[12]

On the contrary, *Hamlet* was a big success. The entire Royal family, including Princess Elizabeth and her new husband, Prince Philip, turned

out for the premiere. With this film Olivier reached tremendous popularity and universal prestige. *Hamlet* won several awards including an
Oscar for best actor the following year.

Before their tour to Australia, Vivien and Olivier spent a month on
the French Riviera with their children, renting a villa that belonged to
Leigh's brother. During that vacation, Suzanne shared her plans to study
acting with her mother. Vivien wasn't happy but managed to control herself, reacting in the same way that Leigh had reacted to her when she took
up acting. She did not say anything, thinking that Suzanne would give
up once the first obstacle presented itself.

On February 15, 1948, after a thorough medical check-up, the
Oliviers left for their 10-month Australian tour. The night before the trip
Danny Kaye threw a good-bye party at Notley Abbey, inviting 70 peo-
ple.

Following Olivier's advice, the Old Vic's final choices for the three
plays for the Australian tour were *The School for Scandal*, *Richard III* and
The Skin of Our Teeth. The tour was partially sponsored by the British
Council, which wanted to show a gesture of unity for the Commonwealth
after the war. They designated a part of the profits to help the shaky financial situation of the Old Vic. The company also planned to scout new
young talent for possible international growth of the theatrical company
in the Commonwealth. It was the first time that a major English company had visited the Australian continent. All the shows had been
rehearsed at the Haymarket Theatre in London before leaving.

Besides Olivier and Vivien, the company also included Peter Cushing, George Relp and his wife Marcia Swinburne. Cecil Beaton created
the costumes and stage designs, which were all supervised and approved
by Vivien.

The long trip by ship was an opportunity for the members of the
company not only to become better acquainted but also to continue their
rehearsals every morning before lunch and every afternoon before tea-time
in the dining room. Olivier adopted a patriarchal attitude toward the
company, while Vivien behaved kindly toward everybody, soon receiving
the nickname "Angel." Although Vivien stated in many interviews she had
always detested gossip, the truth was that she adored it, and she proved
it during this trip. She simply hated the fact that something was happening
in the company that she was not aware of, and she was jealous of any pretty
woman in the company.[13] Vivien was also extremely picky about her
clothes; every night she had to fold her clothes perfectly, wrapping her
underwear in tissue paper, as she was taught in the convent as a child. If
the tissue paper was not fresh, it had to be ironed until it looked new. One

morning, while her personal maid was ironing her underwear and the tissue paper, two boys in the company who were intrigued with the strange practice decided to play a joke. They crumpled up some tissues and filled the breasts of one slip. Vivien overreacted to the infantile joke and became very aggravated.

Arriving at Fremantle, Vivien, wearing a brown wool French suit, was welcomed with a huge bouquet of flowers by a big crowd of Scarlett O'Hara's Australian fans. From that moment until the end of the entire trip, the Oliviers were treated like royalty: the king and the queen of the British theater. The tour included a lot of press conferences, interviews and social functions at universities, hospitals and civic receptions where Olivier would often invite people to send food to England, where food rationing was still in progress.

In Camberra, Vivien met Prime Minister Ben Chifley, who allowed her to visit the Parliament once she arrived in Melbourne.

In Perth *The School for Scandal* had extraordinary success, not only because of the acting, but also because the costumes and the set design deeply impressed the audience and local reviewers.

The theater in Perth had only two dressing rooms, and one was assigned to Vivien and one to Olivier. Vivien thought that this was not fair to the rest of the company, so she offered hers to the other actors, choosing to change her costumes behind a screen in the theater wings.

The following stop on the tour was Adelaide, where they had sold out every evening of the two-week schedule, alternating *Richard III* and *The Skin of Our Teeth*.

In April they reached Melbourne, where Vivien was so capable of coping with the very stressful task of balancing work and frequent social occasions that the press nicknamed her "Miss Vitamin B."[14] But the fast change of weather, especially the cold climate of Hobart in Tasmania, gave her a sudden case of bronchitis and a very high fever, which forced her to stay in bed for five days and cancel her performances. Because of the biting cold she had to wear her mink coat during scenes of *The Skin of Our Teeth*.

After Tasmania the Old Vic Company took a short vacation on the Surfer's Paradise coast nearby Brisbane. Olivier remembers in his memoirs that Vivien kept a certain distance from him for inexplicable reasons.[15] In fact, the relationship had slowly transformed into one based on a professional managerial rapport, which replaced the intimacy and passion.

In Sydney, *The Skin of Our Teeth* debuted during a frigid, cold night and ran for more than sixty performances, reaching more than 120 thousand spectators. While there, Olivier had a bad knee accident and had to return to the stage of *Richard III* with crutches.

After eight months, some of the actors started to feel homesick, especially Vivien after she received a letter that her beloved Siamese cat New Boy had been run over. She cried all day and her swollen face was noticeable under her heavy make-up on stage that night.[16]

During their stay in Sydney, the Oliviers heard about a promising young Australian actor named Peter Finch, who was having great success playing Argan in Moliere's *The Imaginary Invalid*. They went especially to see him perform at a glass factory. It was, in fact, customary in Australia at the time to have local theatrical companies perform during lunch breaks to entertain the workers.

The couple was very impressed by the actor's performance. "If you ever come to England, get in touch. You're good." With those words Olivier suddenly changed Finch's life, as his former wife remembers: "He had met the greatest actor in the world and he had met the woman who was to be his greatest passion, his mistress and very nearly the death of him."[17] Finch left for London three month later, becoming the first non-British actor Olivier hired into the Old Vic Company.

After the last performance of *The School for Scandal* in Brisbane, the tour resumed in New Zealand. On the flight to Auckland Vivien felt horribly sick. She could only take short breaths and needed an oxygen mask. By now everyone was eager to go back home, and the tour was reduced to only five weeks.

In Wellington, Olivier was in physical pain and had surgery on his knee for the Sydney injury. The operation was successful. The performance also continued to have huge success, winning all the records that the country had to offer at the box-office.

In Christchurch two young costume makers witnessed a furious and violent fight between Olivier and Vivien in their eighteenth-century clothes. They were insulting and slapping each other and Vivien burst into tears before going on stage to lessen the tension. The argument had been caused by Vivien's continuous flirting with the young blond actor Dan Cunningham, who was always around her, provoking Olivier's jealousy.[18]

On October 17, 1948, the Old Vic Company finally boarded in Wellington to go back to England.

During the crossing, Vivien started to rehearse *Antigone*, which was the play scheduled to replace *The Skin of Our Teeth* in the trilogy to be performed at the New Theatre in London once they arrived. *Antigone* was a play written by Jean Anouilh, in which the main character personified the ruin of France, a woman chosen by the gods to destroy the country. On board the *Corinthic*, Vivien started to work on her tone of voice, attempting to lower it in order to give her character more solemnity. The vocal lessons continued in London with the help of George Cunelli, an old Italian tenor. In a short amount of time Vivien achieved amazing results, which would contribute to the success of the play.

While they were still in Australia, Cecil Beaton informed Vivien about a new show in New York that had just opened on Broadway to great reviews, *A Streetcar Named Desire*, with a leading role that seemed perfect for her. So Vivien had asked Cecil Tennant to bring her a copy of the play when the agent later visited the company. She started reading the text during her free time on the tour, finishing it while on board the *Corinthic*.

The character of Blanche DuBois particularly impressed Vivien, probably as much as Scarlett O'Hara had done years before. It was a completely different part from all the roles she had played thus far, and the part slowly created a new obsession in her.

The three Old Vic productions were also a success in London. People would stand in line for hours to buy a ticket, even for standing room places to see one of the plays. At the opening night, the New Theatre's foyer was crowed with celebrities, including David Niven, Ralph Richardson, Margot Fonteyn and Danny Kaye.

As the critic and old friend of the couple Alan Dent maintained, "The Oliviers had reached such a point of fame that they could do no wrong in the eyes of their public."[19]

Resuming *The School for Scandal* in London marked the end of their artistic collaboration and friendship with Cecil Beaton. The Oliviers were offended by the designer's total disinterest in the occasion of their debut in London. When Beaton went to see a performance of the play, neither Vivien nor Olivier spoke to him. Apparently, Vivien had also become jealous when she found a photograph of Garbo in Beaton's bedroom, feeling that he preferred the Swedish actress to her.

Suddenly, one night that spring, while sitting at a table in her small winter-garden of a porch at Durham Cottage, Vivien said to Olivier, "I don't love you anymore. There is no one else or anything like that: I mean I still love you but in a different way; sort of, well, like a brother."[20] It was like a cold shower to Olivier, even though he had noticed some changes in Vivien's behavior during the Australian tour, during which, according to many, they had stopped being physically intimate.

According to biographer Donald Spoto, although the Oliviers had made many attempts to rekindle the passion of their marriage during the summer of 1949, their relationship was only based on the past and on what they had in common with their professions. Vivien had complained too much about her physical dissatisfaction with Olivier as a lover, and at the same time she had started to suspect her husband's sexual ambivalence, not only because of his strange behavior with Peter Finch but also because of the numerous visits and attention he showed toward Danny Kaye, who would spend a lot of time with him when the American actor would come to London.[21]

It is not clear when Vivien began her affair with Peter Finch, who had arrived from Australia as Olivier suggested and was quickly cast in *Daphne Laureola* opposite Edith Evans. But it was during the same time that Vivien was living her own life, which was more detached from Olivier. They maintained only a professional dependency but no physical contact.

Chapter Eleven

Blanche DuBois

"Why are you so fucking polite?"
—Marlon Brando to Vivien Leigh

In those days, Irene Selznick, who had recently divorced David Selznick, was the only female producer on Broadway. Binkie Beaumont convinced her to cast Vivien as Blanche DuBois for the British production of the play that had just won the Pulitzer Prize. Irene Selznick wanted Elia Kazan to direct the play, because he had directed the original version of *A Streetcar Named Desire* in the States, but Beaumont warned her that Vivien would not accept the part if Oliver were not the director.

Tennessee Williams had never seen Vivien on stage and had severe doubts that she could play the part. He flew in from a holiday in Rome to spend a week in London to see Vivien acting as Lady Anne in *Richard III*, as Lady Teazle in *The School for Scandal* and as Antigone in the new version by Anouilh.

Williams was not a theater-goer, admitting candidly that it bored him. He enjoyed writing plays but he did not enjoy watching them. He further admitted that he had no interest in the classics and could not even understand them.[1] The fact that *Antigone* had been updated with modern and more comprehensible language convinced him to watch the show. In a letter to his friend, writer Donald Windham, Williams wrote, "Vivien Leigh is not really good in *Antigone* but I have the feeling, now, that she might make a good Blanche, more from her off-stage personality than what she does in the repertory, though she is quite good in *The School for Scandal*. She has great charm."[2]

Beaumont had notified Vivien when Irene Selznick and Tennessee

107

Williams were to be in the theater, knowing that the final casting decision for Blanche would depend on what they saw of her acting. After
those three informal auditions, Williams gave Vivien his blessing, while
Selznick chose Olivier as the director.

At a party thrown by Beaumont, Williams and Olivier talked all
night about possible changes or cuts to the text. In Olivier's opinion, the
play was good but too long, but Williams firmly refused to consider any
variations or cuts to the original. Nevertheless, the playwright was thrilled
that such a prestigious figure as Olivier would be directing one of his
plays.

The problem of cutting was the single cause of long discussions between
Olivier, who refused to imitate Kazan, who had directed the original version, and Irene Selznick, who along with Williams did not want any
changes. The anti-cut crusade continued when Kazan arrived in England.
The American director had previously sent a warm message to Olivier
giving him permission to use all of his ideas for the British production,
but he stressed the importance of not cutting any material. In his opinion, these changes would spoil the entire structure of the play.

Although Olivier surrendered to it, the battle was not completely
over. Lord Chamberlain, the director of the British board of censorship,
approved the play with the exception of the sixth scene in which Blanche
describes the suicide of her husband after she finds him with another
man. The word "degenerate," as an euphemism for homosexual, had to be
removed whether the audience understood the reference or not. In 1949
any explicit expression related to any type of "sexual perversion" was considered loathsome and inadmissible, but a vague, unspecific allusion could
be accepted by the censorship board. So the scene was eventually changed.

New problems arose regarding Vivien's interpretation once Irene
Selznick began assisting with the rehearsals. The producer thought that
her approach to the character of Blanche was wrong, unfaithful to the original play, and that it had nothing in common with Jessica Tandy's brilliant performance on Broadway. What was clear was that the play implied,
without being specific, that Blanche was a prostitute. Vivien believed the
opposite and felt that the play could be interpreted in multiple ways. Irene
tried to convince her that Tennessee Williams and Jessica Tandy made
it clear that Blanche was an immoral woman, but Vivien insisted that she
couldn't copy another actress no matter how good or faithful her performance to the play. She had to be allowed to do it her own way.[3]

The great publicity that preceded the debut of *A Streetcar Named
Desire* was generated by the topics of the play: insanity, nymphomania and
rape. At six months until the scheduled date of the beginning of the show,

the 1200-seat Aldwych Theatre received requests for 10,000 tickets in advance. After great success in Manchester, the line in London to purchase one of the 200 non-reserved seats in the balcony started three days before the opening of the box-office.

The night of the debut, Vivien entered the stage with bleached hair, and her pale face was covered with cheap make-up and flooded with a bright light, shocking the audience incredibly. Vivien seemed old, despairing and tired. She was completely stressed about her heavy make-up, and the nervous tone of her raspy voice due to her gin-drinking showed a faded beauty. She triumphed, though, because of her expressive ability and demonstrated a new maturity in her acting.[4]

Vivien as Blanche DuBois in *A Streetcar Named Desire,* **1951.**

Blanche was so deeply inside Vivien's soul and mind that the character would remain a part of her for the rest of her life. Off stage Vivien would speak using the same type of voice she used for Blanche. Later, during her frequent manic-depressive attacks, Vivien would truly believe that she was Blanche.

At the end of the performance Vivien received a long, standing ovation; she had made *A Streetcar Named Desire* a triumph.

"Everyone said I was mad to try it," Vivien stated in an interview. "They are often saying I am mad to try things. But Blanche is such a real part, the truth about a woman with everything stripped away. She is a tragic figure and I understand her."[5]

The reviews were unanimously enthusiastic and they praised her acting: "It was the most exhausting performance of her career and probably her highest stage achievement," said the *Daily Express.*[6] On the other hand, there were several tabloids that denounced the play from another prospective: "Obscene pornography ... disgustingly squalid ...

vicious." All of these adjectives only helped to lengthen the line at the box-office.

During the day Vivien would wear a black wig that she would take off before going on stage to reveal her blonde hair. Because of her health problems, she successfully requested that all the ashtrays in the theater be removed, and that the audience be allowed to smoke only in the lobby of the theater.

For the duration of the 326 performances of *A Streetcar Named Desire* Vivien's behavior appeared to be very strange. A recurring symptom of her manic-depression was an increase in her sexual drive, and at that time, sedation was the only treatment available for that pathology. In a way, Vivien had developed her own antidepressant by enhancing her sexual activity. This was effective, but it later became compulsive.[7] One night she was stopped in the streets of Soho by a policeman because she was screaming out parts of her dialogue from *A Streetcar Named Desire* along with a young actor with whom she had spent the night. Olivier tried to hide the episode by threatening to ruin the career of the young actor.

Often at night after the show Vivien would dismiss her driver and would walk alone through the red-light district near the West End, frequently stopping to chat to the prostitutes. She admitted that she felt a kind of empathy between them and the character of Blanche that according to her brought her close to madness. Vivien also found out that some of the girls were her fans, and that they had seen the play in the company of their customers. The Australian actor Bonear Colleano, who played Stanley Kowalski, remembered that Vivien would often imitate the way those prostitutes talked and would laugh about them.[8]

Vivien's nightly walks would end in sexual encounters with the taxi drivers who would take her home. She had also begun an affair with Peter Finch. By now Olivier was not only incapable of satisfying the insatiable sexual requests of his wife but also of controlling her crises.

Upon Vivien's request, Irene Selznick returned to London to see the show. The producer completely changed her initial opinion about Vivien's portrayal of Blanche, and considered her the only possible candidate for the film version of *A Streetcar Named Desire*, forgetting about Jessica Tandy or Uta Hagen, who had played Blanche in the States.

The film rights had been sold to Charles Feldman, one of the most important producers in Hollywood. He had been invited to the premiere of the play in London by Binkie Beaumont and had been mesmerized by Vivien's performance. As a result, chose her over Olivia de Havilland for the role of Blanche on the screen.

The success of *A Streetcar Named Desire* was now international. In

Paris the play was directed by Jean Coucteau and starred Arletty and Jean Marais. In Italy it was directed by Luchino Visconti and starred Marcello Mastroianni and Vittorio Gassman. For a while there was talk of possibly exchanging theaters for a week of performances between the British company and the French one, but the project never took place.

After the last performance, Vivien hosted a good-bye party at Notley Abbey and left for the States alone. Before going to Hollywood, she stayed for a while in New Town, Connecticut, at Kazan's, to discuss details of the film. The director had previously explained to producer Jack Warner that Vivien had recently recovered from tuberculosis and requested that he send Lucinda Ballard, the costume designer for the film, to London in order to spare Vivien a tiresome trip. Vivien had become a very close friend of Ballard, whose southern accent inspired the accent Vivien used for Blanche.

Kazan had a lot of problems with censorship even before the casting of the actors began. Censors had ordered many cuts and changes to the script, especially with regard to its profanities and sexual innuendos.

In order to give a Production Code certificate, the American censors insisted that the homosexuality that resulted in Blanche's husband committing suicide had to be completely removed, and the conversation that alluded to it had to be rewritten. They only allowed Blanche to say: "He wasn't like other people." After Kazan's firm insistence, the only scene that was not censored was Blanche being raped by her brother-in-law Stanley.

Vivien's salary was settled at $100,000, the highest amount ever paid to a British actress in America. Jack Warner did not complain because he was sure of Vivien's widespread popularity, as well as the publicity that would be created in the contrast between the sophisticated English actress and Marlon Brando, who was cast as Stanley Kowalski. "Beauty and the beast," "the lady and the tiger" were some of the phrases used by press agents to launch *A Streetcar Named Desire.*

Cameras were set to film in the beginning of August for approximately 36 days. Vivien arrived in Hollywood after a long trip by train, with only one stopover in Wisconsin to visit Alfred Lunt and Lynn Fontanne. She confided to Fontanne (who years before had been one of the few people in the theater business to be by her side after the *Romeo and Juliet* tour fiasco) her obsessive jealousy toward Olivier. Both women agreed that they would much prefer their husbands to have homosexual rather then heterosexual affairs, and neither felt able to cope with the threat to their ego that another woman would pose.[9] Vivien did not yet know that she would soon deeply regret such a confession.

Marlon Brando arrived on the set four days after Vivien. The two stars met in Jack Warner's office, where Vivien showed up wearing a blonde wig and a costume scene (this time she wore a specially made wig from London so that she could maintain her natural hair color off the set), while Brando was wearing a t-shirt and jeans and had dyed his hair black. At a press conference followed that meeting, Vivien, tired of being called "Lady Olivier" by journalists, suddenly said to a reporter, "Her Ladyship is fucking bored with such formality and prefers to be known as Miss Vivien Leigh!" The film's producer laughed nervously beside her.[10]

But on the set Vivien's British language correctness was still very formal, irritating Brando enormously, who in a moment of rage said to her, "Why are you so fucking polite? Why do you have to say good morning to everyone?" And Vivien answered, "I believe in good manners at all times."[11]

Another time Brando asked her: "Why do you always wear scent?" "Because I like to smell nice, don't you?" replied Vivien. "Me? I just wash. In fact I don't even get in the tub, I just throw a gob of spit in the air and run under it."[12] Vivien laughed and she shortly began to appreciate Brando's sense of humor. He would often tease her by imitating Olivier and referring to him as "Henry the Fifth Larry."

"Brando was rather strange at first. I thought he was terribly affected.... I got to understand him much better as we went on with the filming. He is such a good actor and when he wants to he can speak excellent English without mumbling. He is the only man I ever met who can imitate Larry accurately. Larry is awfully difficult to imitate, Brando used to do speeches from *Henry V* and I closed my eyes and it could have been Larry."[13]

Brando recalls Vivien with a different tone:

> In many ways she *was* Blanche. She was memorably beautiful, one of the greatest beauties of the screen, but she was also vulnerable, and her own life had been very much like that of Tennessee's wounded butterfly.... Like Blanche she slept with almost everybody and was beginning to dissolve mentally and to fray at the ends physically. I might have given her a tumble if it hadn't been for Larry Olivier. I'm sure he knew she was playing around, but like a lot of husbands I've known, he pretended not to see it, and I liked him too much to invade his chicken coop.[14]

Brando's statements were confirmed in some letters he wrote to a friend at the time of the filming, in which he graphically described what a "great ass and tits" Vivien had. "It was all vulgar, infantile stuff, and what Marlon went on about was wanting to fuck Leigh so badly that his teeth ached, but her husband was there all the time, as a guard dog."[15]

On August 14, the filming of *A Streetcar Named Desire* began on a set that was an identical copy of the Broadway version. The first problems arose between Vivien and Kazan regarding the approach of how to play Blanche. The director was one of the founders of the Actor's Studio and insisted that his actors use "the Method," an acting technique based on the complete identification of the actor with the character. For Vivien, it was difficult to change her approach to the part, and she thought that she would reach the same results Kazan wanted by exclusively following the advice and directives she had received on stage from Olivier.

"I requested that Vivien do something we'd done with Jessie (Jessica Tandy) in New York, and she came out with: 'When Larry and I did the play in London...' and went on to tell us all what she and Larry had done.... As Vivien spoke, I became aware of the other actors looking at me.... 'But you are not making the film with Larry in London now, Vivien,' I said. 'You are making it here with us.' Then as gently as I could, I insisted on my way."[16]

Two weeks of great tension had to pass before Vivien slowly forgot her artificial mannerisms and followed Kazan's instructions, finally recognizing the fact that he was just "photographing the play."

According to Kazan, "She had a small talent, but the greatest determination to excel of any actress I've known,"[17] adding, "Vivien was a lovely, beautiful woman, but I don't think she was right for the part. When I look at it now, I think Julie Harris or Geraldine Page should have done it."[18]

Although Vivien felt a bit ostracized by the rest of the cast in the beginning, since they had originally starred in the play in the States together, she was soon able to get into the hearts of everybody except Karl Malden, who could not stand her. "Unlike Jessica [Tandy] who was as gracious and well-grounded a human being as you could hope to meet, Vivien was more like Blanche herself. She had a more tenuous relationship with reality," MaMalden wrote. He continued:

> I remember that when we finished shooting, Vivien and Olivier invited Mona and me to a party. Although Mona and I are chronically early, we happened to arrive late because we were unfamiliar with Los Angeles and had gotten lost. Everyone was already seated around their tables. I was called over to a table and left Mona stranded for a moment. She finally ended up sitting on a swing by the pool all by herself. Who should come along but John Buckmaster, an English actor, and Vivien Leigh. They sat down on either side of Mona. Mona told me later about how they literally, and figuratively, talked over her head. Vivien and Buckmaster traded bizarre non sequiturs as Mona sat there, utterly baffled. Never once did they acknowledge

that another person was even there, let alone sitting between them. Vivien didn't have to be polite, or even civil; after all, she was Scarlett O'Hara.

Several months later, we read in the paper that Buckmaster had been spotted running down Fifth Avenue stark naked, brandishing a knife. Mona was actually relieved by the news; it assured her she had not been the crazy one sitting on that swing after all.[19]

Vivien was living with Olivier in a villa in Burbank close to the studios. Olivier was making *Carrie* opposite Jennifer Jones, and David Selznick's new wife was producing the film. Suzanne was there too, spending her summer vacation in California visiting her mother before starting acting school in London at the RADA. For the first time in years mother and daughter lived under the same roof, but the familiar quiet was often disturbed by violent fights between Vivien and Olivier when they both came back home late at night exhausted after having spent an entire day on the set. Olivier was very preoccupied with Vivien's health. She would sleep very little and constantly had Blanche on her mind. On her side, Vivien started to suspect that Olivier was having an affair with Danny Kaye.

As biographer Donald Spoto tells in his biography of Olivier, "At first Vivien had merely thought Kaye rude, since he arrived at their house unannounced at odd hours, without invitation or permission. But Olivier was also spending long, late hours with him." Suddenly the gossip spread, first in Hollywood, and then everywhere else. According to Spoto it "was no secret to Vivien, nor did Olivier deny it. For Olivier, the affair with Kaye revealed more about his need for affection from those he admired than for sex itself, about which he was, for the most of his life, remarkably diffident. She had always been the aggressor, demanding sex, facilitating it and taking control; yet for him it remained something perfunctory and to it he never brought his fullest passion.

"Kaye was not simply amusing, but vibrantly intelligent; not merely encouraging and admiring of Olivier, but also quick-witted, original and capable of discussing the fine points of art, literature and music history. Unlike Olivier, Kaye had an understanding with his wife, the composer Sylvia Fine, for by this time Kaye led a quite independent sexual life."[20]

They even traveled alone to the Caribbean together to visit the openly gay playwright Noel Coward at his Jamaica home, and there were stories of a costume party in which Kaye performed in drag. Even Kaye's sexless screen image made Vivien start to work up a real dislike for him.[21]

Out of respect for Olivier Vivien did not say anything, but the fact was distressing to her frail mental state, especially while she was under the strain of being Blanche. Perhaps Olivier's homosexual affair became a way to justify her strong sexual appetite to herself. She would fulfill this with frequent and fleeting encounters, and her alcohol abuse would shock those who knew her. Her actions were in total contrast to her way of being, but in total synchrony with the character of Blanche. Perhaps this explains her statement in an interview: "I could not wait to get to the studio every morning and I hated to leave every night."[22]

The Oliviers' marriage became more miserable by the day. Nevertheless, the couple, who had been away from Hollywood for ten years, tried to keep up appearances when invited to parties or other social events.

Kaye had organized a glamorous party in the Crystal Room of the Beverly Hills Hotel as an official welcome back to Hollywood for the couple. Many stars were invited, from Errol Flynn to Lana Turner, from Montgomery Clift (big fan of Olivier's) to Ginger Rogers. An unknown Marilyn Monroe also attended the bash as the date of a William Morris agent. At the party Vivien and Olivier met Lauren Bacall and Humphrey Bogart, both of whom became very good friends during Vivien's stay in Hollywood.

The filming of *A Streetcar Named Desire* concluded at the end of October. Vivien was very satisfied with her job, saying, "It took three months to make the film and I loved every second."[23] She felt that the movie was superior to any of the stage productions because the camera was able to bring the characters so close to the audience and to highlight nuances in the expressions on the actors' faces. It could also reveal subtleties of feeling that were lost in their passage over the footlights.[24]

Vivien had to go to New Orleans for three days, where Kazan shot Blanche's arrival at the old train station. She materialized out of a cloud of smoke from an old locomotive, an idea that the director "stole" from a description in the book *Anna Karenina*.[25]

Once *A Streetcar Named Desire* was completed, the film continued to have problems with censorship. Joseph Breen, who was responsible for the Bureau of Censorship, demanded formal respect of the moral code and asked Kazan to remove any allusion the director had left to homosexuality, despite what they had previously decided. In addition, the character of Stanley Kowalski had to be punished for committing the rape and for the abandonment of his wife. Kazan had to make twelve cuts, and the opening night at Radio City Music Hall in New York had to be cancelled because the League of Decency threaten to ban the film if those changes were not made, stating that all Catholics who would see *A Streetcar Named Desire* would commit a sin.

Finally, after a final cut, the film was approved by censorship and it

A dramatic scene from *A Streetcar Named Desire*, 1951

opened in Los Angeles. The following year *A Streetcar Named Desire* received twelve Academy Award nominations, establishing once and for all that Vivien was in the Hollywood star system. It also made Brando a real movie star, and his white t-shirt and blue jeans became the uniform for teen-agers all over the world.

Chapter Twelve

Fire and Air

> *"I am fire and air; my other elements I give to baser life."*
> —Cleopatra in Shakespeare's *Antony and Cleopatra* 5.2.288

Once Olivier finished *Carrie*, he decided to go back to London. Vivien, however, seemed too nervous to face a long trip by plane. Spencer Tracy, who was a very good friend of Olivier's, advised him to put Vivien under a period of abstinence from alcohol and suggested that a boat trip home would be the right time to start.

Because no transatlantic liner was available at the time, the Oliviers and five other passengers boarded a slow cargo boat, which carried 10,000 cans of sardines and 40,000 cotton bales and was traveling from San Francisco to Europe via the Panama Canal. Vivien spent the five weeks on board, mainly reading Fitzgerald and pondering what plays to present at the next Festival of Britain. As Olivier commented, the journey was not exactly a honeymoon.

Finally, on December 18, 1950, the Oliviers arrived home. They had not yet chosen a worthy production for the festival, so they decided to spend a few days in Paris with the hope of finding inspiration.

Vivien seemed interested in James Barrie's *Mary Rose* and Shakespeare's *Othello*, but the idea of alternating Shaw's *Caesar and Cleopatra* and Shakespeare's *Antony and Cleopatra* prevailed over other projects. Part of the excitement was created not only from the idea of acting in a comedy and a tragedy based on the same subject, but also in playing a character already familiar to her.

Tickets for the twenty-six-week performance of the two Cleopatras sold out in less than a week.

To identify deeply with her character, Vivien read all the biographies written on the queen of Egypt. She also decided not to change any lines of the original texts, and she chose different make-up for the two plays. In Shaw's play, in which she portrayed Cleopatra at age sixteen, she emphasized the higher parts of her cheeks with rouge and covered her lips with pale lipstick. In Shakespeare's tragedy, in which Cleopatra is thirty-nine years old, she painted her jaw line with shadow to make her face look slimmer and more interesting. In addition, Vivien worked with Maestro George Cunelli to lower her tone of voice as Shakespeare's Cleopatra, and to raise it to a higher pitch for Shaw's Cleopatra.

She would complain to costume designer Audrey Cruddas that her neck was too long, her hands too big and her voice too high. Cruddas used precious materials for Vivien's costumes, and had her wear rings and bracelets to distract attention from her so-called "paws." She also sewed some sponges inside the armholes of her dresses to avoid perspiration stains.

Rehearsals began in a very serene environment as Jill Bennet remembers: "Vivien worked intensely hard, with passionate determination to get things right. She also created a happy atmosphere, everybody in the company loved her, she was friendly and kind.... It is curious to remember her rehearsing. She wore such formal clothes; slender highheeled shoes, jewelry, even a hat."[1]

The stage for the show was built with a rotating mechanism; one side had a Roman background and the other had an Egyptian background. The opening night at the St. James Theater, Olivier gave Vivien a gold necklace with a ruby pendant as a lucky charm.

Reviews were all positive, except for one written by the young critic Kenneth Tynan, who tore apart Vivien's interpretation in both plays. He also insinuated that Olivier's reputation as an artist was at risk since he often favored his wife in the shows to his own disadvantage. The review, which deeply depressed Vivien, caused a great fuss in the theater industry.

Although the cruel article was written, as Tynan later admitted, as an attention-seeking device using Vivien as a scapegoat, the critic stood behind it, believing in what he had said.[2] On the other hand, friends like John Gielgud remembered: "She gave her finest classical performance, she succeeded in lowering her whole register from the natural pitch she was using as the little girl Cleopatra in Shaw's play—a remarkable feat that few actresses could have sustained as successfully as she did."[3]

During the four months that the shows ran at the St. James Theatre, little accidents occurred. One night in Shaw's play, in a scene where

Cleopatra had to slap Ftateeta, the nurse (played by Elspeth March), who was wearing a fake nose, the smack was so close to her face that the nose flew into the air. Vivien caught it with her left hand and returned it to Elspeth. The audience did not notice anything because Elspeth was quick in covering her face with her hand before going off-stage to put it back on.[4]

Another time during the performance of *Antony and Cleopatra*, the mechanism which changed one set to the next malfunctioned. When Cleopatra and her attendants made their entrance onto the scene, instead of finding themselves in the Egyptian Court they found themselves among the columns of Rome. Vivien stayed cool while she delivered her lines until the next change of scenes. Once she returned back-stage, the stage-hand came over to her, drenched in sweat and ready to apologize. She put her hand on his arm and laughed, quoting Rhett Butler in *Gone with the Wind*: "Darling, I don't give a damn."[5]

But frequent signs of disagreement between the Oliviers were noticed

Vivien, Olivier and Joan Crawford at a dinner in New York during the running of the two Cleopatras at the Ziegfeld Theater, 1951.

by the other actors. Often, Vivien would suddenly burst into a rage against her husband in front of everybody, such as the time he accidentally stained one of her costumes with fake blood, provoking an uncontrollable, violent attack, or when Olivier, at the end of a performance during the final applause, forgot to bow and smile at her. She ran to her dressing room and slammed the door furiously. Despite all the fighting, Olivier always remained her idol. Her professional admiration for him was so high that she would describe him to other people as a real genius.

Winston Churchill, who was still a fan of Vivien's after seeing a performance, invited the Oliviers to dinner to celebrate Larry's birthday. The statesman gave Vivien a painting he had made as a gift. It was a picture Vivien had admired some time before at his house. The amateurish oil painting represented a still life of two white roses in a crystal vase, and it became one of Vivien's favorites, which she hung in her bedroom.[6]

In June, while at a party given by John Mills, Vivien expressed her interest in playing the leading role in *Tender Is the Night* based on F. Scott Fitzgerald's novel. She had recently read and enjoyed it, but Selznick had already cast his wife Jennifer Jones in the part.

On June 25, in honor of the *Night of a Hundred Stars*, an annual benefit show organized as a tribute to the late comedian Sid Field, the performances of the two Cleopatras were suspended to allow a hundred stars from the entertainment industry to perform sketches on stage. Olivier, Danny Kaye and Vivien played in a funny vignette as "terrible triplets" and received a warm applause from the audience.

In September 1951, when the running of the two Cleopatras was over, the Oliviers took a long vacation and cruised the Mediterranean on Alexander Korda's yacht. They boarded in Piraeus and toured the Greek islands, Istanbul and Italy, before flying from Rome to Nice. During the holiday Vivien developed a behavior that Olivier had never noticed before, "a funny little childlike clinging need for protection,"[7] a sort of infantile regression.

The mental instability of his wife did not worry him until they arrived in New York, where they were scheduled to continue the performances of the two Cleopatras at the Ziegfeld. On board the transatlantic *Mauritania* the Oliviers had brought the original British company from England, along with the complete stage design that weighed almost twenty-seven tons.

All the shows quickly sold out, and it became not only a hit at the box-office but also with reviewers.

Brooks Atkinson of the *New York Times* wrote, "There has not been an *Antony and Cleopatra* to compare with this in New York in the last quar-

Vivien and *New York Times* critic Bosley Crowther at the New York Film Critics presentation of *A Streetcar Named Desire*, 1952.

ter of a century; and there have not been many productions of any Shakespearean play that have approached this exalted quality.... Miss Leigh's Cleopatra is superb."[8]

Vivien declared that she preferred Shakespeare's Cleopatra because it was more interesting and offered a fuller character.[9]

On opening night the American audience and critics did not notice that Vivien was very nervous, not only because she had a cold and laryngitis but also because she was afraid that the rotating stage would malfunction, as it already had to be maneuvered by two technicians. And among the audience were the Lunts, David Selznick and the omnipresent Danny Kaye.

Off-stage Vivien always appeared extremely tense, and Olivier would often find her at home crying in bed in a distressed state. Apparently nobody or nothing could help her. Some actors from the cast noticed that before going on stage Vivien would tremble like a leaf, but her acting would never be affected by the personal distress she suffered from her manic-depressive crises. She would be able to hide these from the public.

The situation did not change when in March 1952 Vivien won her second Academy Award for *A Streetcar Named Desire*. Greer Garson accepted the Oscar on her behalf while Vivien was in New York, too busy with her performances and too nervous to be able to travel.

Chapter Thirteen

Peter Finch

"I have a husband and I have lovers.
Like Sarah Bernhardt."
—Vivien Leigh

Before the end of the season, Vivien's mental condition had deteriorated, and Olivier finally realized the gravity of the situation and turned to a specialist. "She was in a pitiful state,"[1] as Irene Selznick remembered after a performance of *Antony and Cleopatra*.

But sessions with a psychiatrist were a complete a waste of time; Vivien was terrified that a paparazzo would photograph her while coming in or out of the doctor's office. At this time she also developed a mistrust of men and thought that both acquaintances and strangers were always trying to seduce her and that she would not be able to resist them.[2]

Again, Olivier thought that a vacation would be helpful for Vivien and accepted Noël Coward's invitation to visit him in Jamaica. The trip was useless, and when they returned the situation did not change. Vivien would continuously cry and often would not say a word for days. Other times she might suddenly leave the house and not come back until the next day, spending the night with strangers.

To avoid Vivien's crazy behavior, Olivier egotistically found escape in his work, accepting a part in the play *The Beggar's Opera*. He also suggested that Vivien accept a proposal that just arrived from Hollywood. Although Vivien was reluctant to star in *Elephant Walk* because the part was not interesting, it offered her a handsome salary.

The film was planned to be shot in Ceylon, so Vivien would have had the opportunity to return to places very similar to the area in which she was born, and according to Olivier this could be helpful in calming her down.

Paramount Pictures had acquired the rights to Robert Standish's novel before casting the lead actor. The production company had Olivier in mind, but he was already committed to Peter Brook's film *The Beggar's Opera*. With great enthusiasm Vivien proposed Peter Finch to Paramount for the lead role, making it clear that she was not attached to him merely out of professional admiration or friendship but by something more. At two A.M. Vivien hurried to the house of Peter and Tamara Finch in a state of hysterical euphoria, offering him the role in the film. Vivien convinced Finch in less than an hour that accepting the part in *Elephant Walk* would be a great opportunity. Then they talked about the script until dawn.

They left for Ceylon after only one week's time. The last words spoken by Olivier to Finch at the airport before they boarded the plane were: "Take care of her, Finch," knowing that Vivien had a fear of flying. Smiling, Finch assured him, "Don't worry, I will."[3] When their plane arrived at its destination, Vivien and Finch were enchanted with its natural beauty and by the local culture, which evoked many memories of her Indian childhood.

Elephant Walk tells the story of a young British woman married to the owner of a tea plantation, who takes his bride to his residence in Ceylon called Elephant Walk, because it was built in the middle of what used to be a trail used by pachyderms. The woman, played by Vivien, is unable to adjust herself to the new life and new people and ends up having an affair with her husband's employer.

Vivien's bizarre behavior revealed itself several days after their arrival. One morning soon after they began shooting, while Vivien was being made up, a young Singhalese native who was employed to call the actors onto the set when they were needed came in to see if she was ready. As he stared at her in admiration of her beauty, she suddenly began trembling. When he left the make-up artist asked her what was wrong. "I'm sorry," said Vivien, "I'm … I'm so frightened of black eyes. I've always been frightened of black eyes."

"But my eyes are black and you're not frightened of me," said the make-up man reassuringly.

"No your eyes are *not* black," said Vivien firmly. "They're dark brown. I mean black—Indian black."[4]

John von Kotze, the main Technicolor technician on the set, remembered Vivien's strength and energy, but also her eccentric ideas. "She would get us—about six of us together—to come into the jungle, build a campfire and sing songs around it. On the equator that is not what you enjoy doing. Peter always went along with her schemes."

Often the troupe would have dinner in the restaurant of an old elegant hotel in Colombo. The dining-room had a cupola for a ceiling, and many English used to eat there dressed very formally and would often behave very rudely to the local people. As von Kotze remembers, Vivien made a strange proposal one day: "'Let's get those ice-cream bombes they have for dessert and let's take them up to the cupola and at a signal we'll drop them down on those enormous fans that are spinning around and let's see what happens.' Peter was absolutely delighted with the idea and it was only at the last minute we were able to persuade him to dissuade Vivien from this outrageous scheme."[5]

The troupe did not pay too much attention to Vivien's eccentricities because she compensated for them with her extreme kindness toward everybody. One night George, von Kotze's assistant, arrived late to the hotel room he was sharing with him. He was extremely upset because Vivien had stopped him in the aisle of the hotel and tried to "vamp" him (as he called it). George was sixty-four, bald and fat, and he adored Vivien, but he was shocked and had run away from her. The following day when von Kotze saw Vivien, it was obvious that she did not remember the incident.[6]

Soon after that, everybody noticed that Vivien's face was increasingly pale and emaciated, so an additional shooting schedule was announced to the cameramen and crew: all the dialogue scenes with Vivien in them were to be shot twice—once with her and once without her, with just with the set and the background. The reason was that director William Dieterle had noticed Vivien's rapidly changing moods, from simply being tense and crying to severe depression, so he thought of it as merely a safety precaution. Paramount could foresee that Vivien would not make it to the end of the shooting.

The situation worsened, and Olivier's presence was required on the set. The production crew erroneously thought he could relax Vivien. Larry arrived quickly in Ceylon from London, but the tension on the set increased and Olivier left after a week feeling impotent and leaving Vivien in an even worse state.

Finch was feeling guilty because of the affair he was having with Vivien; he had betrayed his mentor, his idol and his boss. In Ceylon he met an entirely different Vivien for the first time. Away from Olivier, Peter was exposed to her complete personality; she was more herself, more determined, more independent and more beautiful. "I find Vivien totally fascinating," he told von Kotze.

When Finch noticed strange things in Vivien's behavior, he would ask her the reason for them. Her last follies were that she could not act if the director looked at her, and she always wanted to wear the costume wig only halfway on her head and refused to move it. When Finch asked her about these things, though, she was always evasive and blamed it on the heat and the humid climate that would not let her sleep.

Finch knew that Vivien had suffered from tuberculosis and that she was subject to occasional outbursts of rage, but when he advised her to consult a doctor she refused.

Once Olivier left the situation deteriorated: Vivien would follow Finch everywhere, calling him *Larry*. She also started having hallucinations that were obviously not caused by exhaustion. Production decided to remove her from the set and fly her to Hollywood for a few weeks of rest before resuming work at the Paramount studios.

Finch was forced to go with her, and as soon the plane took off, Vivien unfastened her seat belt, stood up and started screaming that one of the wings was on fire and that the plane had to land immediately. With the help of the flight attendants Finch tried to calm her, but she responded with verbal and physical violence. She became hysterical, beating the plane windows with her fists and fighting to get out. Then she started to strip her clothes off, scratching at everyone who tried to stop her. They finally managed to sedate her, but the shock was so strong that at that moment Finch also developed a fear of flying.

Once they landed in Los Angeles, Vivien was hosted at Finch's by his wife Tamara and their little daughter, who arrived from London the following day. Vivien welcomed Tamara wearing a gold and scarlet sari and telling her that Peter was at the studios, explaining that she would have to stay as a guest for a few days. "You have got to get yourself into a sari immediately. I've laid one out for you and I'll come up with you to show how you drape it."

"Why?" Finch's wife asked.

"Because at seven-thirty, seventy people are coming. I'm giving a party for you," replied Vivien

Tamara, exhausted from her trip, had to run upstairs to prepare herself for the evening, but once she was ready Vivien announced that she felt too ill and too unhappy to entertain her guests and that she was going to bed. So on her first night in Hollywood, Tamara and Finch had to entertain seventy guests, among them Stewart Granger, David Niven and George Cukor, all of whom were complete strangers to her.[7]

During those terrible days at the Finches', Vivien revealed her long-time affair with Peter to Tamara during one of her attacks. At first the woman thought that Vivien was raving, because she would often call Peter *Larry*, confusing the two men. In addition, Vivien would suddenly quote

A Streetcar Named Desire in a southern sing-song voice. Tamara realized the gravity of the situation when she discovered that it was not possible to leave Vivien by herself even for a moment. As had happened several times in the past, Vivien would leave the house and go to John Buck-master's, who was also mentally disturbed. They would both be found naked on the floor staring at each other to "exorcise the devil."

None of Vivien's friends had the courage to explain to Tamara the seriousness of her illness, one that Finch himself did not fully understand. It was obvious that the stress she went through in Ceylon and her heavy drinking could not be the sole cause of her behavior.

Finally, Sylvia Fine, Danny Kaye's wife, explained Vivien's illness to Tamara, giving her a book on psychiatric pathologies, which confirmed that Vivien was suffering from symptoms of manic-depressive attacks.

On her tenth day at the Finches' Vivien, apparently feeling better, decided to go to the studios and visit the set of *Elephant Walk*. She told Finch that she felt fine, and that she would move into Spencer Tracy's house, which the actor had left at her disposal while he was out of town. But at the studios a few hours later, Vivien collapsed on the set and was taken to her dressing room, where she became worse, transforming her-self into Blanche DuBois.

David Niven was immediately called to drive her home. Once there he called Olivier who was on vacation on the island of Ischia, in Italy. It took three days before the actor could arrive in Los Angeles.

What happened during the following forty-eight hours was remem-bered by Stewart Granger, who Niven had called for help.

> David took her back to the house she had rented, and then he called me and the two of us spent most of a day and one whole night try-ing to get her to swallow a couple of pills that would sedate her enough to allow a couple of nurses to come and take her into a clinic. Vivien was fiery and very cunning and absolutely determined not to be taken away by people in white coats, and she brilliantly managed to get an entire bottle of pills one by one into the swimming pool, so that in the end it's five o'clock in the morning and we still haven't got the pills down her, and Vivien is now watching all-night televi-sion stark naked, and David says let's make breakfast and slip the pills inside the scrambled eggs, so we cook this enormous breakfast and then Vivien says she's on a diet so to avoid suspicion David has to eat the eggs, and of course passes straight out on the sofa. So then I'm left alone with her and in the end I had to hold her down on the bed while the nurse stuck the needle in her arm to sedate her, and Vivien just looked up at me very calmly and said, "I thought you were my friends."
>
> While the nurse tried to calm her down she said to her, "I know

who you are. You're Scarlett O'Hara, aren't you?" And Vivien screamed "No, I'm not Scarlett O'Hara, my name is Blanche DuBois."[8]

Once Olivier arrived in London from Ischia, he asked his friend Cecil Tennant to go with him to Los Angeles to see Vivien. The flight to California had a stopover in New York, where the two friends spent the night at the Sherry Netherland Hotel, where Danny Kaye had a suite.

The following day the trip continued on to Los Angeles, where Sylvia Kaye picked them up at the airport after she alerted her psychiatrist, Dr. Martin Grotjohn. The specialist advised Olivier that Vivien had to immediately go back to England and submit to intense treatment.

The meeting between Olivier and Vivien was described by the actor as the worst encounter of his life. "When I arrived at this house I was told I would find her outside on an upstairs balcony; stepping gently onto this, I saw her. She was leaning with her elbows upon the railing and her face in her hands. I called her softly and she looked up at me. It was as if her eyes were misted over, all gray-green-blue; only the tiniest pinprick of a pupil was discernible. I said, 'Hello, darling,' and when she spoke to me it was in the tone of halting, dreamlike amazement that people in the theater use for mad scenes when they can't think anything better. My instinctive reaction was that she was putting on it ... she said 'I'm in love.' I asked very gently, 'Who with, darling?' Then—approaching the Most High—'Pe-ter ... Fi-i-inch.' Where the hell was he, by the way, I wondered."[9]

Vivien had to leave the country immediately because if mental illness was officially diagnosed she incurred the risk of being confined to a mental institution, and bringing her back to Europe would be a problem. With Olivier's approval, Vivien received a strong dose of sedatives for the long trip back home. Unfortunately, it was impossible to avoid the press and a reporter photographed Vivien while she was boarding the plane on a stretcher.

The flight from Los Angeles to New York was smooth; Cecil Tennant was exhausted not only from the stressful situation but also because he had to negotiate up until the very last moment with Paramount executives about breaking Vivien's contract.

Elizabeth Taylor was called to substitute for Vivien in *Elephant Walk*.

"Vivien Leigh was my heroine," she said to those who noted a striking similarity between the two brunette beauties.[10] The long shots filmed on location with Vivien were used in the film, while all the dialogue and the close-ups had to be shot again with Taylor.

Vivien's physical constitution was so strong that she got up in spite of the heavy sedation and the next thing Olivier knew she was sitting next to him.

Tennant was afraid of a sudden crisis and invited her to play cards in order to distract her until the plane landed.

At the airport, while waiting for the connection to London, Olivier met Danny Kaye. As soon Vivien saw her husband with Kaye, she reacted in a violent way, screaming terrible insults and allegations about their homosexual relationship.

Olivier explained that Vivien was terrified of needles. When the time came to put her on the plane again the nurse appeared with an unusually large needle and a hefty container filled with liquid, and Vivien made an attempt to escape. So, along with Danny Kaye, they tried to hold her down while she was scratching, biting and screaming "appalling abuses at both of us, with particular attention to my erotic impulses."[11] Finally, Vivien was sedated and carried on board.

As soon she arrived in England the following day she was admitted to Netherne Hospital in Coulsdon. She was at Surrey, a medical center that specialized in mental illnesses, where she remained for a week and received shock treatments. Dr. Freudenberg's diagnosis was very clear: "evident manic-depressive condition which develops a marked increase in libido and indiscriminate sexual activity."[12]

An exhausted Olivier decided to go back to Ischia in order to relax rather than being at Vivien's bedside when she woke up. Everybody noticed that Olivier consciously avoided further responsibilities and left his wife alone, but the actor later admitted that he felt very guilty about his conduct.

On April 11, 1953, Vivien was transferred to the University College Hospital, where she stayed for eight days before returning to Notley Abbey. During her time in the hospital, thieves broke into both of the Oliviers' houses in London and in the countryside on different days, stealing Vivien's jewelry, fur coats and the Oscar she received for *A Streetcar Named Desire*.

Noël Coward was one of the few friends who visited her several times while she was at the hospital, and when he could he would call her to check on her health and send her flowers with little notes. Later, he went often to see her at Notley Abbey during her convalescence. "She solemnly promised to be good in future and not carry like a mad adolescent of the twenties," wrote the playwright in his diary. Coward also had a long conversation with Olivier, who had opened himself up to him by revealing that the marriage had been sinking since 1948.[13]

Chapter Fourteen

Stage Door

> *"I only saw Vivien Leigh once in my life in person.*
> *I got into the elevator of the Ritz-Carlton Hotel*
> *in Boston and she was there. And I got goose*
> *pimples. I got off on the wrong floor, like a fool.*
> *The goose pimples remained for ten minutes."*
> —Walter Matthau

Nineteen fifty-three was the year of Queen Elizabeth's coronation; Vivien was recovering slowly and she watched Leigh, who was wearing his military uniform, march in the Royal parade down St. James Street. Ernest and Gertrude were by her side.

In honor of Queen Elizabeth, Vivien and Olivier decided to play in a new comedy by Terence Rattigan, *The Sleeping Prince*. The playwright was reluctant to have the Oliviers star in his play because, in his opinion, the characters he had created did not suit two stars like them. The leading role of the Grand Duke was in fact described as an unattractive man completely the opposite of Richard III, one of the most sensual characters roles Olivier had recently played, and Vivien, who was polished and sophisticated, hardly looked able to play a Cinderella role with a Brooklyn accent. However, Olivier's persistent requests were finally met with Rattigan's consent to act in and direct *The Sleeping Prince*.

The official announcement was given at a party thrown by Binkie Beaumont, where the press seemed more interested in Vivien's recent admission into the hospital than the future project. Vivien managed it well, explaining that her stay at the hospital was a result of stress caused by too much work.

In September 1953, the show began touring with great success in Brighton, Edinburgh and Manchester. Many of Olivier's fans could not wait for his London debut and traveled to see the play.

On November 5, Vivien's fortieth birthday, *The Sleeping Prince* opened in London at the Phoenix Theatre. Rattigan noticed that Olivier had lowered his performance because his biggest worry was about "Puss" (his nickname for Vivien) and her performance. "Tell me, Terry, how are they liking Puss?" asked Olivier.

"Very much," said Rattigan.

Olivier shook his head. "I don't think so. I don't think so at all. I don't think she's going over as well as she should be."[1]

Vivien was wearing a strawberry-blonde wig, and she spoke with a Southern accent, imitating Katharine Hepburn's mannerisms to some degree.

Although most of the reviews were positive, they unanimously agreed that Olivier's talent was wasted in a light comedy such as *The Sleeping Prince*. Theatergoers, including Queen Elizabeth and Princess Margaret, were very pleased with the performances, and they crowded the sold-out theater every night.

Peter Finch, who was back in London with his wife Tamara, attended a performance of *The Sleeping Prince*. Afterwards they went backstage to congratulate the Oliviers. The couple first visited Vivien's dressing room, where Finch kissed her and greeted her quickly before paying his respects to the rest of the company, leaving his wife alone with Vivien. What Tamara saw was a normal and beautiful woman completely different from the woman who had spent those terrible days at her house in Los Angeles. "I feel very sorry for you," said Vivien suddenly, while other people were coming into her dressing room, and she introduced Tamara as "the most courageous girl I know." Those ambiguous words were interpreted by Finch's wife to be a warning for her to keep being courageous in the future. In fact, Vivien was still as attracted to Peter as Peter was to Vivien.[2] "Once you had slept with Vivien, you don't care about anybody else," stated Finch. The two lovers would often meet in a studio that their common friend and actress Lady Rachel Redgrave would lend them for their sexual encounters.[3] Later, Tamara Finch would say to a friend, "I couldn't fight Vivien. It would have been like trying to fight the Queen of England."[4]

Part of 1954 was uneventful. Vivien saw a charity play called *The Frog*, saw Marlene Dietrich in concert, and participated again in the annual *Night of a Hundred Stars* with Olivier and other colleagues. Kirk Douglas was among the present, and he remembers Vivien's strange behavior in his autobiography, describing a curious episode: "In a restaurant one day with a group, including director Terence Young, she turned to Olivier and said, 'Larry, why don't you fuck me anymore?' Then she started coming on to me, very seductive, with Olivier sitting right there. At first, I didn't believe it. I felt uncomfortable. She was behaving like Blanche DuBois in *A Streetcar Named Desire*—sexual, bizarre."[5]

In honor of the RADA and in tribute to Dame Sybil Thorndike's career, Vivien played for one night in a scene from *The School for Scandal* opposite Alec Guinness and James Donald.

The Sleeping Prince closed on July 3, 1954; Vivien had missed only one performance in the eight months it ran, when she accidentally broke her wrist. She covered the cast with a scarf made of feathers that matched the color of her stage costume. During the summer the Oliviers picked Italy as their destination for a holiday. They went on Lake Garda and later they stayed in Portofino with Rex Harrison and his wife Lilly Palmer in their villa. "It is heavenly here & I'd like always to be on holiday," wrote Vivien to Leigh, with whom she was always in touch.[6]

Rex Harrison's marriage was already on the rocks when he met actress Kay Kendall, who was vacationing in Portofino, as well. Kendall later became very close friends with Vivien and Harrison's second wife before dying a few years later of a terminal disease.

Once she returned from her holiday in September, Vivien began filming *The Deep Blue Sea*. It was the story of the wife of a high court judge, who falls madly in love with a frivolous and unstable former RAF pilot. For him she loses her dignity and her financial stability. The film was a psychological melodrama based on a play written by Terence Rattigan. The screenplay had been completely modified by director Anatole Litvak, who stubbornly thought that he was making necessary improvements.

Kenneth Moore, who was the lead opposite Vivien, hated the script, but because the play had had a lot of success, he accepted the offer to star in the film.

The Deep Blue Sea was produced by Alexander Korda, who had personally insisted that Litvak cast Vivien in the lead role instead of Marlene Dietrich, even though everybody agreed that she was not right to play the part of a dull, unattractive woman. As co-star Moira Lister remembers, Litvak was a very difficult director:

"He had this theory that you have to destroy somebody first to get a good performance out of them and he used to—systematically, every day—destroy Vivien until he got her to cry and said 'Right. Now you're in a mood to do the scene. We'll do the scene.' He was really very harsh with her."[7]

Vivien and Kenneth Moore in Anatole Litvak's *The Deep Blue Sea.*

At the Shepperton Studios on another set, Olivier was starring in *Richard III* opposite Claire Bloom, a young actress who had been made into a star by Charlie Chaplin's *Limelight* in 1952. Vivien and Olivier would have lunch in Olivier's office, where they would talk about their next project together: the Shakespeare festival at Stratford-upon-Avon. They decided to play *Twelfth Night*, *Macbeth* and *Titus Andronicus*. Although the salary was very limited compared to the money they would earn for a film (only 60 pounds a week versus the 50,000 pounds Vivien was getting for *The Deep Blue Sea*), the prestige was incommensurable. During breaks from *The Deep Blue Sea*, Vivien would study the part of Lady Macbeth with the help of Emlyn Williams, who was playing her husband in the movie.

The Deep Blue Sea was presented at the Venice Film Festival as a part of a British retrospective, with a tepid reception that continued at the box office. When the Oliviers publicly announced their program at the Stratford-upon-Avon festival, about 600 theatergoers bought their tickets on the first week and the shows sold out for the entire season.

John Gielgud was the director of *Twelfth Night*, which opened on April 12, 1955. The show ran for two months and was followed by *Macbeth* and *Titus Andronicus*. During the month of August, Vivien alternated acting in the three plays. However, because the season lasted for over 33 weeks the Oliviers decided to move to a place closer to the theater. Instead of staying in a hotel they rented a house in Avoncliffe in the county of Alveston.

Working with Gielgud was not easy because the director had a confused approach toward the play, and many of the actors often chose to rehearse when he was not around and chose not to follow his instructions. On Olivier and Gielgud's suggestion, Vivien tried to look and act more masculine, as the character of Viola appears as a man in almost the entire play.

Prince Ranieri of Monaco attended the premiere of *Twelfth Night*, and although the reviews were all favorable, Vivien was not convinced as to the strength of her own performance, saying to Gielgud, "I know you thought I was awful."

"Why didn't you cry?" he asked. "All my leading ladies cry."

"I did, but not until I got home."[8]

Vivien had a romantic quality and a boyish charm, which were perfect for that type of character, but her voice was lacking in lyrical power and her personality in comic vitality.

At the same time Vivien was also playing the role of Lady Macbeth, who was a more complex character, and she was secretly being coached by Peter Finch. Between shows he would often spend his weekends at Notley Abbey, and would often be seen holding hands with Vivien, who had one of his pictures in her dressing room.

Olivier had a completely detached attitude toward the situation, and Vivien had become a total stranger to intimacy with him. Their relationship was purely professional at this point.

Olivier was incapable of satisfying Vivien's sexual desires, and he could only calm her down momentarily, while the younger Finch was full of energy and always ready to fulfill every one of Vivien's insatiable requests.

Olivier rarely expressed feelings of jealousy toward Finch; he actually was grateful to him for taking care of Vivien when he was not able to. So when the two lovers were at home, Olivier would lock himself into his study to work, read or to make plans for his professional future. This reaction often upset Vivien, who would have preferred her husband to make a scene because it would have proved that he was still interested in her, but it never happened.

Vivien tried to run away twice with Finch with the hope that Olivier would stop her. But they were vain attempts: the first time she boarded a train to France she had a panic attack at the thought of permanently leaving her husband so she pulled the emergency brake to stop the train. The second time she arrived at the airport, and after a long wait before boarding due to a flight delay, she changed her mind and went back home.

Macbeth aroused very discordant opinions in the reviewers. Ivor Brown, one of the most important critics of the British Theater, wrote an interesting piece naming Vivien one of the best actresses in the last twenty years for her memorable performances in roles such as the two Cleopatras and now Lady Macbeth.[9] On the contrary, terrible Tynan, after praising Olivier in his review, dismissed Vivien's acting with few nasty words: "Vivien Leigh's Lady Macbeth is more niminy-piminy than thundery-blundery, more viper than anaconda, but still competent in its small way."[10] Afterwards, Tynan regretted his reviews and his bitter words against Vivien, admitting that it was one of the biggest errors in judgment he ever made.[11] But the remark was enough to provoke a new crisis in Vivien, as Olivier remembered.[12]

Olivier, along with Gielgud and Glen Byam Shaw, the director of *Macbeth*, stated in several interviews how extraordinary Vivien had been in that part, and film director Orson Welles was also so impressed that he wanted to cast her in the movie version that eventually was never made.

Although mild symptoms of tuberculosis appeared, Vivien continued living a frenetic life; when she was not working, she would entertain guests or wildly attend all the social events to which she was invited, being deprived of precious sleep and rest time.

The third play presented by the Oliviers at the festival in Stratford was *Titus Andronicus*, which was considered the bloodiest of all the Shakespearian tragedies. Young Peter Brook was the director and created a totally original production in which all the violent acts were not shown directly to the audience, but only suggested through the use of red ribbons and light effects. It was the first time that *Titus Andronicus* was presented in Shakespeare's native village and only the third staging in England.

Vivien played Lavinia perfectly, even though she did not say a word because her character had her tongue and hands mutilated. Her acting only required miming and the use of facial expressions. Many noticed a certain aloofness in Vivien's performance, which showed her disturbed mental state for the first time. She was unable to mask it with her typical discipline.

Anthony Quayle, who was part of the cast, remembered and is still shocked by the insults that the Oliviers would utter to each other while delivering their lines: "'You shit, you shit' ... while Larry would continue to spout the most marvelous poetry and then at the end of it whisper,

'Fuck you, fuck you' ... I remember Vivien appearing with a swollen eye one day, saying she'd been bitten by a mosquito. Someone had hit her, I thought."[13]

Maxine Audeley also told biographer Hugo Vickers:

> Vivien started to go a bit mad during *Titus*. She started to go strange in the spring and through the summer months, and by the autumn she seemed to have recovered. Not only did she behave violently to everybody, probably worse to the people she loved and who were closest to her, but she physically swelled up.... Her whole body, particularly round the neck and face and shoulders. That would last two days and then she would go back to normal again.[14]

At the end of the season in December Vivien visited her friend Ginette Spanier in Paris and invited Finch to join her. Olivier was fed-up with his wife's irresponsible escapes, and he was afraid that her affair with Finch would be disclosed by the press and harm his career. His public image was strictly tied to Vivien's and her behavior was not proper for the image of "Lady Olivier." So when Vivien and Finch returned to Notley Abbey he invited his wife's lover in for a conversation behind closed doors in his library.

> Peter and Olivier looked at each other. Then they looked down at their glasses. Neither of them said a word. After a long pause they start quoting Shakespeare, almost in a grotesque way, and then looked into each other's eyes and started laughing and crying tears drunk with whiskey.
> At three A.M. the great double doors of the library were flung open. There in a nightdress stood Vivien, like Lady Macbeth, magnificent. Proud, threatening. "Well?" she said, viewing with some bitterness the shambles of the library and the two disheveled actors gaping foolishly at her. "Which one of you is coming to bed with me?" Her words were greeted with shrieks of laughter ... and before she knew it, she was laughing as hard as they were. Sitting in the library the three of them laughed till dawn.[15]

On January 23, 1956, Alexander Korda died from a heart attack at 62 years of age. His sudden passing deeply shocked Vivien, since the producer had played a key role in her career and success. Many celebrities like Charlie Chaplin, Claire Bloom and Ralph Richardson participated in his funeral.

Meanwhile, another cut to Vivien's past was made by Olivier, who put Durham Cottage on the market. It was in fact, no longer big enough for Vivien, one cook, one maid and two secretaries.

Chapter Fifteen

Madness, Madness, Madness

"It was a glimpse into the anguished world of Vivien's mental imbalance, a glimpse into the kind of hell that the Oliviers' life together must have become."
—Claire Bloom

While playing Shakespeare, Olivier received a proposal to direct and play in the film version of *The Sleeping Prince*. Milton Green, an American photographer and close friend of Marilyn Monroe's, had recently bought the play rights from Terence Rattigan. Green, in partnership with Monroe, had opened a production company and he wanted to produce the film with Marilyn playing the part that Vivien had played on stage.

There are two versions of Vivien's reaction when she learned the news. According to many people, she was the first to suggest Monroe for the role after she watched her performance in *How to Marry a Millionaire* and told Olivier how perfect she would be to play the part if the play one day became a film.[1] According to a second version, Olivier hid the news from Vivien for a while, because he was afraid she might react in anger at the idea that a younger actress had been chosen instead of her. So he decided to wait until he knew that Vivien had been cast in Noël Coward's new play, *South Sea Bubble*.[2]

South Sea Bubble's rehearsals began right away and the show toured briefly before opening at the Lyric Theatre in London. The comedy received great acclaim even though the text was weak, but Vivien's pres-

137

ence was a big magnet at the theater box-office, and the show ran for 276 performances.

During the summer of 1956, while she was busy with *South Sea Bubble*, Vivien, who was now 42 years old, got pregnant. Suzanne, Tarquin and Olivier were the first to learn the news. Vivien was very excited and started to interview prospective nannies for the baby, whose name, if it had been a girl, would have been Katharine. But Olivier seemed much more excited about the idea of the arrival of Marilyn, with whom he was scheduled to start filming *The Sleeping Prince*, which was renamed *The Prince and the Showgirl* for the screen.

A couple of months earlier Olivier had met with Milton Green and Marilyn in New York to discuss the details of the film. Contrary to Marilyn, Olivier did not remember a previous encounter with her that had occurred many years before at Danny Kaye's party.

On July 14, 1956, Vivien and Olivier welcomed Marilyn and her husband, playwright Arthur Miller, at Heathrow airport. The meeting at the airport was immortalized by many photographs that show Marilyn looking adoringly at Miller, while Vivien seems less thrilled to have to pose next to a woman twelve years younger than herself, all too aware of the fact that the camera would only magnify their age difference.[3]

After Marilyn's 27 suitcases were loaded on several cars, the Oliviers escorted the Millers to the residence that they had rented for them in Egham. Vivien and Olivier also gave a welcome party in honor of the famous American couple at Terence Rattigan's in Ascot. A journalist asked Olivier his opinion of Marilyn. "She has an extraordinary gift of being able to suggest one moment that she is the naughtiest little thing and the next that she's perfectly innocent," he said.

Larry had a terrible crush on Marilyn, but Oswald Frewen observed in his diaries that Larry said that Marilyn Monroe had "the brain of a *poussin* & one dress for day & evening; black & cut low."[4]

While in London Marilyn saw a performance of *South Sea Bubble* and personally congratulated Vivien backstage at the end of the show. Vivien's personal opinion of Marilyn was not very high. She considered her rather vulgar and more than a little obtuse. She enjoyed telling an anecdote she had been told of Marilyn visiting Arthur Miller's family home, where she had matzo balls served up so often at the meal table that she finally asked innocently, "Isn't there any other part of the matzo we can eat?"[5]

Noël Coward did not see Vivien's pregnancy announcement as a happy event. The playwright was upset that he did not learn of the news until Vivien was already four months pregnant. She decided to leave *South*

Sea Bubble at the peak of its success, making it difficult to find a perfect substitute.

Many maliciously thought that because Vivien was ill with tuberculosis she could not have children any longer, and that her pregnancy was only the fruit of her hysterical fantasy and a scheme to get people to talk about her, taking away all the attention from Marilyn. But on August 12, 1956, the day after her last performance of *South Sea Bubble*, Vivien was five months pregnant, but still not yet visible. She had suffered a miscarriage at Notley Abbey. All her friends showed their support even though the grief did not cause her the crisis that everybody had feared it would.

According to some witnesses, Vivien only had herself to blame for the event; she had behaved irresponsibly in the first months of her pregnancy, partaking in exhausting rehearsals for the *Night of a Hundred Stars*, in which she had danced wildly and sung with Olivier and the actor John Mills.

Larry was also worried that Vivien would have a crisis due to the great media coverage of the news of her miscarriage. Dr. Conachy, who had been treating Vivien since 1949, realized all the possible risks that Vivien could be exposed to right away, especially during her manic-depressive crises which were aggravated by her tuberculosis. By this time he had diagnosed her as schizophrenic. The physician advised Olivier to be aware of the possible public exposure that Vivien could incur when her libido increased uncontrollably. His first advice was to help her to quit drinking, because he was certain that alcohol sharpened the depression phase.

Suddenly, parties became an occasion of great nervousness for Olivier, because he did not understand whether Vivien's euphoria and cheerfulness were normal or whether they were first signs of a manic attack.

It was a very difficult time for Larry, who had to deal with Marilyn's problems on top of Vivien's serious health condition. She was always late and she never cared about all the other people waiting for her on the set of *The Prince and the Showgirl*, nor did she care about the money wasted due to her disrespectful behavior. Olivier had been warned from the first moment he went to New York not to get upset with her, because Marilyn was easily subjected to nervous breakdowns which made her incapable of working for weeks, risking a total shut-down of the set. Olivier's patience was enormous; only once, exhausted by her behavior, did he rail at her: "Why can't you get here on time, for fuck's sake?"

"Oh" said Marilyn, wide-eyed, "do you have that word here in England, too?"[6]

He was finally rewarded with the sudden departure of Vivien for Rex

Vivien in her bedroom of her new home at 54 Eaton Square in London, 1956.

Harrison's villa in Portofino, where she took a short holiday with Binkie Beaumont. When Miller and Monroe finally returned to New York, Olivier organized a trip to Spain with Vivien, to recover from the exhaustion caused by attending to Monroe's whims and the making of the film.

One month after the end of *The Prince and the Showgirl*, Marilyn's marriage to Miller was already on the rocks.

Although many problems still afflicted the Oliviers' marriage, on their return trip from Spain they bought a big apartment at 54 Eaton Square in the elegant neighborhood of Belgravia. Vivien decorated the new apartment, hanging her collection of paintings, which now included prestigious artists such as Degas and Poussin. Eaton Square became her permanent residence in London during the week and she would spend her weekends at Notley Abbey.

During that time, as Vivien was always interested in new productions, she asked Olivier to take her to see John Osborn's *Look Back in Anger* at the Royal Court Theatre. Olivier was very impressed by the dramatic fierceness of the play and asked the author if he would consider writing something for him to play. Osborn was already working on his next project which he started to adapt, keeping Olivier in mind for the lead role. Months later the result was a play called *The Entertainer*.

When Vivien read it, she was immediately interested in playing the part of the wife if Larry would accept the role of Archie Rice. Olivier loved the part, but he also thought that Vivien was not right for the role she wanted to play. She was too beautiful and, therefore, would have wear a mask to look ordinary and unattractive. The producers agreed with Olivier's opinion and decided not to cast Vivien in the play. Although she was disappointed, Vivien would attend the rehearsals every day. Olivier had cast a young actress named Joan Plowright for the part of his daughter. Although both Vivien and Osborn did not approve of his choice, Larry insisted in having her because, in his opinion, Plowright's acting style represented the new generation of actors necessary for this kind of play.

Vivien's constant presence at the theater made Olivier terribly nervous. She would interfere with Tony Richardson's direction, making things extremely difficult for the entire company. Finally, after an argument with George Devine, the artistic director of the theater banned her from the theater on the morning of the dress rehearsal.

Olivier had an agreement with the producers of *The Entertainer* to star in a limited engagement of performances because he and Vivien had agreed to be a part of the *Shakespeare Memorial Tour* throughout Europe and present *Titus Andronicus*.

The Oliviers had also refused to film a Hollywood version of Rattigan's *Separate Tables* because they did not find the script as interesting as the original play.

As soon as the run of *The Entertainer* was over, the "terrifying" experience of the *Shakespeare Memorial Tour* began. The original company, including Maxine Audley, Ian Holmes and Anthony Quayle, met up in May to leave by train (at Olivier's insistence because he was fearful of what flying might do to Vivien) to Paris, Venice, Belgrade, Zagreb, Vienna, Warsaw and London.

Titus Andronicus was a big success in Paris. It played at the Theatre Sarah Bernhardt, where Vivien was also made a Chevalier of the Legion of Honor. She was moved to tears while she read her thank you speech for receiving such a high honor from the Minister of Cultural Relations, Roger Seydoux. Olivier had already been nominated *Commandeur* years earlier.

While in Paris, Vivien spent most of her free time at the French designer Balmain's atelier, where they had created a plastic dummy, reproduced to her exact measurements, so they could fit her for her wardrobe in her absence. She wore one of the exclusive haute-couture designs at a party given in honor of the company by Paul Luis Weiller. Many French celebrities like Maurice Chevalier, Charles Boyer, Jean Marais and Jean Pierre Aumont were also in attendance.

In Venice the Oliviers were joined by Suzanne and Gertrude, who had to return to England unexpectedly because Ernest had to have emergency surgery for an ulcer.

It was the first time that Vivien and Larry performed in Italy, and Olivier gave a short opening speech in Italian. Although the show received a warm reception from the Italian critics, director Peter Brook was not pleased with the performance of the company because, in his opinion, it lacked conviction. A party was thrown for the company and Olivier and Vivien received some prestigious honors from the mayor of the city of Venice.[7]

From Italy, the tour continued on to Belgrade by way of the Orient Express, crossing the borderline in Trieste. The *Shakespeare Memorial Tour* was the first theatrical company to cross the Iron Curtain. Yugoslavian president Tito organized a party to celebrate the event. All the members of the company were warned to be careful in expressing their opinions and, in particular, in discussing anything related to politics.

Everywhere in the streets people recognized Vivien, screaming *Scarlett! Scarlett!* and begging for an autograph or a handshake. It was a sort of collective hysteria from a people who were not used to seeing a movie star in person.

It was June and it was very hot; Vivien had already shown some mild signs of intolerance during a previous train trip. This announced the arrival of a new attack of schizophrenia. The symptoms she had this time were so serious that Cecil Tennant and Binkie Beaumont had to fly to Yugoslavia to help Olivier.

One afternoon Vivien disappeared. Alarmed, the entire company searched for her in all the museums, art galleries and any other places she was likely to have gone. Vivien was found in a park sitting alone on a bench crying. The next day, in a rush of euphoria, she threw off her clothes in a public garden. Fortunately, it was very early in the morning and few people noticed her act of madness.[8]

But her manic-depressive attack reached its worst peak during the long train ride between Belgrade and Warsaw, where she paced the corridor shouting abusive phrases and profanities. When Olivier tried to lock her in a compartment, Vivien smashed a window with a beauty case in an attempt to escape. Then her rage exploded against Maxine Audley, because in her mind Audley was always getting a dressing room that was larger than hers. First, she attacked her verbally, then she chased her into the ladies room, where Audley had gone to hide.

Vivien violently banged on the door shouting: "Get out, bitch! Get out!"

When she came out of the toilet Audley was bombarded with pieces of bread that Vivien had taken from the dining car. Finally, after 16 hours of such behavior, Vivien collapsed into an exhausted sleep.

Vivien's psychotic behavior shocked all the members of the company, but after that they become more protective toward her. Olivier, on the other hand, become completely fed-up. Reaching his limit of tolerance during this trip, he made the decision to leave Vivien once and for all. Vivien's madness was now common knowledge, and this was enough for him to break off the marriage for good.

Peter Brook suggested that Vivien see a specialist while in Vienna, but the sedatives the doctor prescribed did not have any effect on her, and the crisis continued to escalate. Finally, once she arrived in London, Vivien returned to Dr. Conachy, who was able to calm her down with a new therapy. Vivien was then able to perform for a month at the Stall Theater, where *Titus Andronicus* was presented as the conclusion of the *Shakespeare Memorial Tour.*

As if he did not have enough to contend with, Olivier had also returned home to the news that the West End district would soon lose the St. James Theater, one of its more prestigious historical buildings. The theater, which had staged the most important British productions, including some of Olivier's, was going to be demolished even though Rattigan's *Separate Tables* was still successfully playing inside.

The London County Council had given their permission for the 122-year-old theater to be torn down. They reasoned that it had only 800 seats and that it was a fire hazard, which needed at least 250,000 pounds to be completely restored. Although theatergoers throughout England rallied in solidarity and used the press to make sure that St. James was not demolished, nobody acted drastically enough to prevent the demolition.

In the beginning Olivier did not agree with the idea of preserving the theater, although Vivien had often financed some of his plays there in the past. But he was convinced by Vivien's fierce decision to join a march along Fleet Street with signs and bells in an attempt to awaken the public to participate in the campaign to preserve St. James Theatre. During the march Vivien was followed at a distance by her Rolls Royce—license plate VLO1—driven by her personal chauffeur, until the protest ended near Westminster Cathedral because people had generally ignored the cause.

That same evening the House of Lords discussed the problem. During the meeting it was pointed out that all the theaters built during the

Georgian era had disappeared and only two were left, including St. James. The debate lasted over an hour, but it just delayed the scheduled time of the demolition until the Parliament made its final decision.

The morning after, all the newspapers carried the news, but Vivien was not satisfied and was invited by her friend Lord Bessbourg to assist in the next debate about the St. James at the House of Lords.

Wearing a black and green dress with a white hat, Vivien sat in the guest box in the public gallery. After Lord Blackford terminated his speech in favor of the destruction of the theater, Vivien stood up and declared in a firm and clear voice, "My Lords, I wish to protest about the St. James's Theatre being demolished."[9] No woman in the history of the House of Lords had ever spoken except the Queen during her formal speeches. She was escorted away with the words "Now you have to go," and she replied, "Certainly—I have to get to the theatre." After she left, the House of Lords deliberated about extra financial support for the arts, but the majority still approved the demolition of the theater.

When the press heard the news of Vivien's protest at the House of Lords, many journalists waited for her at the theater to interview her regarding what had happened. Vivien declared that she regretted being too impulsive, but she would continue to fully support the cause. The news covered the front pages of all the morning papers.

A couple of days later a second march was organized. This time, Richard Attenborough, Peter Cushing, Edith Evans, Michael Redgrave and others from the entertainment industry joined Vivien and Olivier, who were marching at the front of the line. In a letter to Winston Churchill, Vivien asked for his support as a parliamentarian and offered him 500 pounds, but he disapproved of Vivien's subversive methods.

On December 27, 1957, the St. James closed, and even though Vivien fought until the last day and obtained a meeting with the Minister of Housing, Henry Brooke, she could not prevent its demolition six months later. The only consolation was the approval of legislation, proposed by Brooke, to the effect that if a London theater was torn down, a new one had to be built in its place.

Titus Andronicus closed on August 3. It was the last time Vivien and Olivier worked together. Their home situation became more unbearable every day due to the return of Vivien's attacks. Gertrude remembered one such episode: during a violent, verbal fight between the couple, Vivien suddenly physically assaulted Olivier, preventing him from sleeping and hitting him with a wet towel in the face. Larry locked himself up in another room, while Vivien tried to break the door down. Eventually, Olivier lost control and violently punched her, causing her to hit her head against a sharp corner. The following day Vivien did not remember anything about what had happened.

Because her physician suggested she not work, Vivien went on holiday with Suzanne and Leigh. They first stopped in San Virgilio on the Lake of Garda and then they went to Greece. The local press continuously inquired as to the reason Vivien was taking the trip with her former husband. Her answer was that the trip had been organized for their daughter, who had not spent a vacation with both parents in a long time. Leigh had to go back to London earlier than scheduled, and mother and daughter continued their trip to the South of France.

To discourage rumors of an approaching divorce, Olivier, for the sake of appearances, went to the airport to pick up Vivien and Suzanne. However, once they left the terminal, the couple headed in opposite directions.

While Vivien was on vacation, Olivier was busy touring the country with *The Entertainer* and had begun an affair with Joan Plowright, the talented young actress cast in the role of his daughter, who was married to actor Roger Gage.

In November, a lonely Vivien decided to surprise Olivier by visiting him in Glasgow, where the company was performing, with the intention of celebrating her forty-fourth birthday with him. There was a general embarrassment among the company because everybody was well aware of the affair between Olivier and Plowright, and they tried to pretend that they did not know anything. When Vivien heard the story, she was more disappointed by the fact that Olivier did not tell her personally than by the betrayal itself.

The year 1957 concluded with a trip to Ireland with Ernest. Father and daughter revisited all the places they had visited when Vivien had been an adolescent. On December 6 Suzanne married Robin Farrington, an insurance broker.

Vivien and Leigh organized the wedding reception at the High Park Hotel, and Olivier participated just to show that he was still with Vivien, although he had moved out of Eaton Square's apartment and rented another place by himself.

In February 1958 Vivien received an offer to play Paola in Jean Giraudoux's *Duel of Angels*, which was planned to be staged at the Apollo Theatre and translated by Christopher Fry. The duel in the play was between two beautiful women; hot tempered and heartless Paola and the quiet and virtuous Lucile, who would be driven to suicide by Paola.

Vivien liked the play a lot. As critic Cecil Wilson would write: "[*Duel of Angels*] is battle between vice and virtue, contested in a strange but immaculately written mixture of mythical tragedy and Victorian melodrama with a tang of French bedroom farce, all rather overloaded with philosophy."[10]

Vivien demanded that the direction of the play be given to Jean-Louis Barrault, who had directed the original version, *Pour Lucrece*.

Claire Bloom was cast opposite Vivien and she remembers Vivien's rigid self-control and her obsessive need for order and organization.

> Vivien was in her mid-forties, and I was twenty-seven. A gap in age that, in an actress less generous than Vivien might have given rise to jealousy and dislike. In spite of my brief affair with her husband some five years earlier [while filming *Richard III*]—which was tacitly understood but never mentioned—there was never any tension or rivalry between us: Vivien never showed me anything save the greatest kindness and affection.[11]

Photographer Angus McBean's version is slightly different.

> I had taken what I thought was a very good set of pictures and shown them to the two ladies. To my dismay I discovered that nearly half were rejected with their corners torn. Someone jokingly suggested that clearly Claire had rejected all the pictures where Vivien looked more beautiful than herself and Vivien had discarded all those where Claire looked younger—so it was a wonder that I had any left at all for the displays. However, luckily for me, one early critic of the play wrote that Vivien was "breathtakingly beautiful," and I was able to persuade her later to pass quite a few more photographs.[12]

The magnificent costumes created by Christian Dior and the elegant set designs contributed to the great success of the play.

After eight months Claire Bloom left the show to take part in a film, as was specified in her contract. Bloom was replaced by Ann Todd, who Vivien immediately detested without a reason.

Symptoms of schizophrenia returned often during that period, but Vivien was now able to detect the early signs, submit herself to electroshock sessions, and be ready and on stage the same night. The only visible problem was the burn marks on her temples, which she would cover with make-up and by changing her hairstyle.

But sometimes a crisis would suddenly present itself, as Bloom remembers:

> I was asleep in my bed at about three in the morning when the telephone rang, and half asleep as I was, I recognized Vivien's voice, and the desperation behind it. Vivien had canceled her performance that night, and her understudy had performed her role; this was already serious, for Vivien, an obsessively responsible actress, would never

have been "off" for any trivial reason. "Would you come over at once," she cried, she was "quite alone"; she went on to say that she had put the lavender bath salts I had given her in her bath and had tried to drown herself, holding her head under the lilac-colored water. Thoroughly alarmed, I threw on some clothes, and took a taxi to her home on Eaton Square. When I reached the apartment I found that, far from Vivien being alone, a lively party was in progress. She opened the door herself, and I saw that her lovely face was puffy and swollen, almost unrecognizable. One record player was blaring away at one end of the room, and another one at the other. Vivien had been drinking, and so had most of her guests; they were all people I had never seen before. Her doctor was trying to calm her and get her to go into the bedroom for a sedative injection. I waited, but knew there was no way I could be of any help. I went home extremely disturbed and worried. It was a glimpse into the anguished world of Vivien's mental imbalance, a glimpse into the kind of hell that the Oliviers' life must have become.[13]

Lauren Bacall, who had just moved to London after the death of her husband Humphrey Bogart, had a similar impression of Vivien.

On arrival in London I learned she was heading toward another breakdown—still playing *Duel of Angels* eight times a week, but having gained a great deal of weight.... Larry asked me to lunch at the Ivy. He was honest, simple, and terribly sweet.... He was going to California to be in a film and would not come back for long time, and when he did, it wouldn't be to Vivien. The marriage had been heaven the first ten years—hell, the second. Now it was over. But she needed her friends—he wanted me to stand firm and close to her. He felt such concern for her, such pain at the ending of all. But he knew he would not survive if he did not get away.

He took me to see her play, in which she was wonderful and beautiful, overweight or not. Backstage she greeted us with champagne and non-stop talk, then we left for the party.... [Later] we were dragged to Connaught or somewhere for scrambled eggs by Vivien, who was possessed of a maniac energy and total inability to sleep— all symptoms. Watching her and Larry that night, it was hard to believe they were the same people whose life had once seemed so idyllic.[14]

Her friendship with Bacall became very important for Vivien. They and Kay Kendall, the third wife of Rex Harrison, had formed an inseparable trio. At that time, Kendall was in London because Harrison was playing in *My Fair Lady*, and she was not yet aware of the terminal illness that would soon kill her. The three actresses spent a lot of their free time at parties, shows and social occasions, all activities that were carefully covered by the society news.

French actress Jeanne Moreau was a guest for a weekend at Notley Abbey. During lunch there was a conversation about the possibility of working together on a film with Olivier. Suddenly, Vivien's mood changed, and speaking in the same tone of her character Paola from *Duel of Angels*, accurately polite in her words but mercilessly cutting with her intonation, she said: "Oh, you speak English well enough, do you, to play with Larry? And you think you look young enough to play the part, do you?"[15] It was a sadly embarrassing episode for all the guests, but Moreau realized that Vivien was unwell and patiently did not respond to her attack.

On Vivien's forty-fifth birthday, Olivier gave her a blue Rolls Royce she had admired at a car show, and on November 7 the Oliviers participated in a ball honoring Lauren Bacall. It was the last social occasion they attended together. Afterwards, Olivier left for the States to star in *Spartacus*, and each day he would write long love letters to Joan

With her daughter Suzanne on her wedding day, December 6, 1957.

Plowright, while Vivien was finishing her run of *Duel of Angels*. She was interested in playing Evita Peron in a play about the life of the former Argentinean First Lady, but the project did not materialize until the '70s, when it became a successful musical.

On December 4, 1958, Suzanne had a baby, Neville Leigh Farrington, making Vivien a grandmother and Gertrude a great-grandmother. The following day Vivien organized a party at the Hotel Savoy to celebrate Gertrude's seventieth birthday and the birth of Neville. The newspaper headlines declared, "Scarlett O'Hara Now Grandma," and Vivien

"Scarlett O'Hara Now Grandma." **Vivien, Robin, Suzanne, and baby Neville, December 8, 1958.**

commented, "It's divine. I have been a godmother loads of times, but being a grandmother is better than anything."[16]

Although she was always surrounded by friends, Vivien was feeling very lonely, and she was missing Olivier's habitual presence. He had returned from the States and was playing in Shakespeare's *Coriolanus*, and Vivien did not miss the debut.

In August of the same year, Vivien decided, as agreed by Olivier, to sell Notley Abbey and posted an ad in the magazine *Country Life*.[17] The interest in the property was enormous and the estate was quickly sold. Vivien felt very melancholy after yet another place with so many memories now belonged in the past. To forget the sadness she accepted a role in Noël Coward's new comedy, *Look After Lulu*.

The play was originally a farce written by Georges Feydeau called *Occupe-toi d'Amélie*, which Coward had adapted to his own style, thinking that Vivien would be perfect for the lead and a magnet at the box-office.

During the break in rehearsals, Vivien would often meet with her old friend Godfrey Winn. Winn was a writer and a journalist who had met Vivien before the war and slowly had become a sort of confidant. He had often spent weekends at Notley, and other times Vivien had visited his house in Sussex.

After a short tour, *Look After Lulu* opened at the Royal Court Theater in London. The reviews were horrible and especially critical of the text, which was considered boring and predictable, while Vivien was considered too beautiful and wasted for such a show. Despite the critics, the play topped at the box office.

While Vivien was playing in *Look After Lulu*, a German tabloid published an article, with photographs, on her split with Olivier and the fact that they did not live together anymore. Vivien showed the magazine to Coward; she was worried that the news would soon spread in the British press. A few day later, reporters started to inquire about her personal life with Olivier, who tried to remove the suspicions and further gossip by being photographed with Vivien in her dressing room.

The *Daily Mail* contacted Gertrude to inquire about the real status her daughter's marriage. Her response was that Vivien's marital difficulties were not serious, the same answer Olivier had previously given to an editor of the *Daily Sketch*, mentioning the uncertainty of the future.[18] Among these personal difficulties Vivien had to cope with the premature death of 31-year-old Kay Kendall, who died from myeloid leukemia at the London Clinic. Vivien went with Noël Coward to the funeral and to the memorial, where she paid homage to her friend by reading some words written by their mutual friend Terence Rattigan.

Vivien had accepted a role for a TV network version of *The Skin of Our Teeth*. Although she was in perfect physical shape, she disliked the result and in an interview with the *Daily Mail* she called it a total failure. To celebrate the closing of *Look After Lulu*, Vivien bought some presents for all the members of the company, but her happiness was dimmed by the sudden news that Ernest needed a delicate surgical operation, which was never performed because he died before it could take place.

Chapter Sixteen

Jack Merivale

"Leigh taught me how to live, your father
how to love, and Jack how to be alone."
—Vivien Leigh to Tarquin Olivier

To recover from the loss of Ernest, Vivien visited Noël Coward in Les Avents in Switzerland. But her privacy was still violated by the local press. After Christmas, Vivien took Gertrude to Ireland to scatter her father's ashes in the River May, as he had wished.

Once back in London, Vivien left for New York, where she would begin the tour of *Duel of Angels*. The American production of the play was directed by Robert Helpmann, and Mary Ure co-starred with Vivien; however, the rest of the company had to be made up of only Americans because the American Equity wouldn't allow any more actors to be imported from England. So Vivien cast actor Jack Merivale for the role of her husband.

Although he was born in Canada, Merivale was exempt from the Equity's restriction. After the war he had played in secondary roles and had divorced his wife, always having had a special affection for Vivien, who he had not seen in two years.

During the rehearsals of *Duel of Angels*, Merivale acted very reserved with Vivien. On a Sunday morning he went to one of the bars at the Hotel Plaza for a drink and was picked up by a man. To save himself from the explicit advances of the stranger, Merivale left and went across the street to the bar of the Sherry Netherland Hotel, where Vivien was having lunch with Helpmann. The director invited him to their table, and from that time the intimacy between him and Vivien was restored.

After that Merivale would often go to pick her up at her apartment at the Hampshire House on Central Park South to walk her to the theater. In the beginning Merivale did not expect anything other than friendship from Vivien, mostly because she would obsessively mention Olivier in her conversations, using him as a term of comparison and displaying his photographs at home and in her dressing-room. Merivale's marriage had gone adrift because someone else had come between him and his wife, so as a rule, he said, "it was one of my principles never to interfere in anyone else's married life."[1]

Vivien and Jack were friends before they become lovers, but their friendship evolved into something deeper while the company was in New Haven, Connecticut, before the Broadway debut. There Jack revealed his feelings and gave Vivien a little medallion of St. Genesius made by Cartier with her name engraved followed by three exclamation points as a present. Vivien loved the gift so much that she had it pinned insider her Dior costume. Later, she gave him a matching medallion with the date of the first night of the tour in return.

In the beginning, Vivien felt more affection than real love for Jack. He was a balanced person who she could count on now that Olivier was out of her life. At the time Vivien had another admirer: John Harris, the son of the actress Ruth Gordon and Jed Harris. The young man showed his admiration for Vivien with expensive presents that were beyond Jack's means. But the courting suddenly stopped when Harris realized how close Vivien and Merivale had become.

Vivien was the one to take the initiative with Jack, asking him to kiss her and make love to her. In the beginning the relationship was hidden, but everyone who knew hoped that it would continue and become official because Jack seemed to have just the right character to match Vivien's strong personality.

On April 19, 1960, *Duel of Angels* opened at the Helen Hayes Theater in New York, winning unanimous consent from audiences and reviewers. *New York Times* critic Brooke Atkinson praised Vivien's performance: "Miss Leigh and Miss Ure give an amazing performance.... Their acting is a splendid demonstration of high style."[2]

What the audience and the reviewers did not know about that night was that shortly before the show had begun, Vivien had received a telegram from Olivier in which he asked her for a divorce. Peter Wyngarde, who was in the company, recalled how brave Vivien had to be to go on stage without showing any personal emotion even though she was devastated inside.

A few weeks before, Vivien had asked two of her dearest friends, Ruth

Gordon and her husband Garson Kanin, to make a last attempt on her behalf by writing a letter to Olivier to dissuade him from divorcing her. The result was catastrophic; Larry had written back to them stating clearly that they were not to interfere in his personal life. Therefore, for Vivien, receiving that telegram was definitive confirmation that Olivier wanted a divorce in order to marry Joan Plowright.

Merivale was a great comfort for Vivien, although he was warned by Peter Wyngarde and by Rex Harrison to pay careful attention to any strange behavior in her, to always try to calm her down when she looked nervous, and to help her refrain from drinking because she was mentally ill. Irene Selznick confirmed Vivien's mental disorders to Merivale a couple of days later because she was worried about her health. Selznick in fact, had received a phone call from Olivier, who had been shocked by a twenty-two page letter he had received from Vivien in which she begged him not to divorce from her and revealed Merivale's love for her. Olivier needed to make sure that someone made Jack aware of Vivien's disturbed mental state and wanted to make sure that he knew the absolute necessity that Vivien undergo electroshock treatment as soon as she became too agitated, which was usually the first symptom before an attack.

Selznick clearly explained the situation to Merivale, who later convinced Vivien to continue to be treated with that procedure, accompanying her personally to her medical sessions. During one of her previous attacks Vivien had given away a valuable diamond ring as a present to one of the nurses who assisted her. Merivale was always by her side, supporting her and praising her for her great courage.

At the end of the month of May, Vivien received a second letter from Olivier, in which he specifically insisted that she grant him the divorce, explaining clearly his reasons. His relationship with Joan Plowright was extremely serious, and he intended to marry her as soon as possible.

In a fit of madness Vivien, encouraged by Helpmann, who detested Olivier, made a unexpected public announcement on television: "Lady Olivier wishes to say that Sir Laurence has asked her for a divorce in order to marry Miss Joan Plowright. She will naturally do whatever he wishes."[3]

The reaction of the press from both sides of the world was immediate; reporters and photographers besieged Vivien's apartment in New York and Olivier's and Plowright's in London in order to get additional comments. It was exactly the type of situation that Olivier had hoped to avoid. Vivien's statement could, in fact, became an obstacle in obtaining the divorce. British law could see the situation as not consensual on both sides, and, therefore, the suit could last for years.

A couple of days later, Vivien told Merivale that she did not remember releasing such a statement. Jack realized that the situation was serious and took Vivien in for a second treatment of five sessions of electroshock therapy.

Then he decided to go with her to London, since the performances of *Duel of Angels* were temporarily suspended due to a dispute between New York theater managers and Actors' Equity. From Heathrow's airport to Eaton Square, Vivien was followed by a crowd of reporters who bombarded her with questions that she did not answer, because in her mind she was sure that she would be reconciled with Olivier. It was an impossible wish because Olivier had decided to marry Joan Plowright, and he had told a close friend that although he would never love anybody as much as he loved Vivien, it was not possible for him to live with her and do his work, because she was too exhausting.[4]

After an ineffective attempt at reconciliation, Vivien returned to New York and enjoyed a few days of vacation on Long Island with Merivale while the theater was still closed.

In July *Duel of Angels* toured to Los Angeles. During the long trip by train, Merivale wrote a letter to Olivier expressing all his feelings for Vivien and declaring his deep love for her. When he received it, Larry felt a sense of relief from his guilt and replied by communicating his eternal gratitude to Jack for taking care of Vivien.

One night in Los Angeles, Vivien went out with actor Tony Richardson and with writer Christopher Isherwood, who remembered in his diaries that after the theater he took Vivien with Merivale, Richardson and Helpmann to the Carousel, a gay bar on the beach in Santa Monica. Isherwood recalls in his entry that "Merivale, who is an almost unbelievable young-old British prude, who belongs in the last century, sat in the car after taking one horrified look.... Vivien loved the Carousel— where she was recognized.... Vivien didn't seem at all crazy; but neurotically self-obsessed and aggressive in her opinions of plays, etc. You feel her devotion to Larry, however. That's tragic. She talks of him constantly."[5]

Richardson remembered that evening in his memoir: "the arrival of Scarlett O'Hara ... passed unnoticed. Vivien wasn't going to be missed, so she climbed onto the bar and started pouring beer over the half-naked dancer. But that still didn't work—they only thought of her as some deranged drugster. And the evening had a sad consequence. Reports of Vivien's presence got into one of the gossip columns, and cops, saying the fire precautions were inadequate for the prominence of the persons now frequenting the beach, closed the bars and destroyed the buildings."[6]

After touring in Los Angeles, *Duel of Angels* went on to San Francisco, Denver, Chicago and Washington, DC. When the cast returned to New York, Vivien learned that Olivier was playing on Broadway in *Beckett* at the St. James Theatre, opposite Anthony Quinn, while Joan Plowright was starring in *A Taste of Honey* at the Lyceum next door.

Vivien surprised Olivier by visiting him back-stage unannounced after a performance, accompanied by Merivale, making both men uncomfortable. Nevertheless, the encounter was brief but pleasant.

The following day Vivien and Merivale boarded the Queen Elizabeth on their way to Europe, where Vivien was expected to make her next film, *The Roman Spring of Mrs. Stone*, which was to be shot in London and Rome two months later. It was based on a Tennessee Williams novel.

Once in Paris, Vivien went to Balmain to be fitted for the film's costumes. She chose sixteen outfits out of the thirty that were made exclusively for her.

Originally, Vivien had turned down *The Roman Spring of Mrs. Stone* after she had read the novel. She was alarmed by Williams' physical description of the character: an aged actress exploited by an Italian gigolo, which according to her, was "too cruel and too grotesque."[7] Then she read the script adapted by Gavin Lambert and changed her mind, accepting the offer from Warner Bros.

Before shooting, Vivien took a vacation with Merivale and other friends across France and later spent the Christmas holidays in Gstaad, Switzerland, at Noël Coward's. There she learned that *The Roman Spring of Mrs. Stone* was not to be shot on location in Italy anymore. The Italian censors, in fact, took one look at the screenplay and refused to issue permission for the company to shoot in Rome because they saw the plot as picturing Rome as a hole of prostitution and vice, which had already been presented in a different way that year by Federico Fellini in *La Dolce Vita*. Hence, the interiors were shot in a studio in Elstree in England. Later, the producer succeeded in persuading the Italian authorities to finally grant permission to shoot exteriors in Rome for two days without any actors present. Some of the filming was scheduled to be made in an apartment that overlooked the Spanish Steps in central Rome, but the owner saw the script and decided not to let the crew use his place, so it also had to be recreated in the studio.[8]

The Italian government was only one of the obstacles that producer Louis de Rochemont had to face in making the film. First, Vivien had to pass a medical examination in order to be approved by the insurance company for the production. Due to the precarious state of her health there was a fear she could not make it, however, miraculously she passed all the

tests. Second, there were some casting problems. The choice of the director Jose Quintero had been made by Tennessee Williams, but because
everybody knew that he had no previous experience with film and that
he had an exclusively theatrical background, most of the actors preferred
not to work with him.

In addition the starting date was approaching and no one had signed
to play Paolo, the Italian gigolo and male lead in the film. French heart-
throb Alain Delon was one of the many names proposed by the production, but Vivien refused to consider him because she felt he was "too
pretty." Warren Beatty, the star of Elia Kazan's *Splendor in the Grass*, was
also considered, but he was rejected because he did not look Italian
enough. But Beatty, who wanted the role at all cost, flew to Puerto Rico
to meet Tennessee Williams, who was on the island on vacation. "I was
in a gambling casino in Puerto Rico," said Williams, "when all of a sudden a waiter came up to me with a little glass of milk on a silver platter
and said 'A gentleman has sent this to you' [There had been stories in the
newspapers about Williams' ulcer caused by the bad reviews of his last
play *Sweet Bird of Youth*]. I said I did not appreciate that kind of sarcasm
and went on playing roulette. After I lost the amount of money I allowed
myself to lose, I started to leave. And there standing grinning at the door
was Warren Beatty. 'Tennessee, I've come to read for you,' he said. He
was very young then and a handsome boy. He wanted a part in *The Roman
Spring of Mrs. Stone* and somehow discovered where I was and had flown
to Puerto Rico. I didn't know Warren's work, and I thought that the role
should be play by a Latin type, since he's a Roman gigolo. I said, 'But
why, Warren? You're not the type to play a Roman gigolo.'

"He said, 'I'm going to read it with an accent, and without. I've come
all the way from Hollywood to read for you.'

"'Well, that's very lovely of you,' I said. And I went to his room, and
he read fabulously. With an accent and without. And I said, 'Warren, you
have the part.'"[9]

According to Williams' biographer Dotson Rader, there was a con-
tinuation to the story. He says that Williams told him that later that night,
Beatty came to his hotel room wearing only a bathrobe and the playwright
had sighed and said, "Go home to bed, Warren, I said you had the part."[10]

Beatty then had to win the favor of Vivien, who had casting approval,
but she was charmed by him, too.

The only objection Vivien had during the production period was her
demand to substitute a scene from Karen Stone playing Viola in *Twelfth
Night* for Williams' scene of her playing Juliet. "At forty-seven I would
be mad to play Juliet at all," was her explanation.[11]

Vivien hugging young Warren Beatty in *The Roman Spring of Mrs. Stone,* **1961.**

Two weeks before the film started, Vivien told the director and the screenwriter that she was not feeling well and that the following day she would go in for a shock treatment. The news was given with no more fuss than someone with a headache asking for an aspirin. Her lack of self-pity was touching and elegant, remembered Garson Kanin, adding that "The next afternoon at rehearsals Vivien appeared eager and energetic ... she'd go off for occasional treatments, but there was no crack in her composure, personal or professional."[12]

The first day on the set was the most terrifying for Quintero, since this was his first film experience. He humbly admitted his complete inexperience in front of the entire troupe and Vivien broke the ice by saying: "We are all with you, aren't we?"

During the six months needed to film *The Roman Spring of Mrs. Stone,* Vivien got along particularly well with Austrian actress Lotte Lenya, who was playing the part of the countess. Lenya had a lot of respect for Vivien, and they would often play cards together between takes.

Joan Collins was often visiting the set as she was Beatty's girlfriend and had been signed on as an extra. She described her great disappointment at her first meeting with Vivien: "I was thrilled finally to meet this icon, but when I did I was deeply disappointed. The powerful images of Scarlett O'Hara, Cleopatra, Lady Hamilton and Sabina were still etched in my mind, and I was unprepared for this thin, quirky, paper-skinned lady, who chain-smoked and had ugly hands."[13]

Vivien's opinion of Collins was not much better, and they often exchanged black looks. Tabloids wrote about a serious flirtation between Vivien and Beatty, and Collins herself was never sure if something really happened.[14]

Beatty was twenty-three years old. He had dyed his hair black and always wore dark, tan make-up and silk shirts for the part, trying to give off the image of a playboy or a sex-symbol like his character in the film, Paolo di Leo. Joan Collins remembers that she was once watching Warren play a scene in which he had to enter Mrs. Stone's drawing room, push her roughly aside and then admire himself in the mirror. Beatty was worried that this might make his character seem too unsympathetic, so he didn't shove Vivien roughly enough. After each take Quintero yelled, "Cut!" then insisted, "Do it again, Warren, but do it rougher this time." By the time Beatty had half-heartedly pushed her several times Vivien retired to her chair, lit another of her interminable cigarettes and remarked *sotto voce* to her hairdresser, "If that fool doesn't get it right the next fucking time, I'm getting the hell out of here." Then Quintero had a few words with Beatty who, gritting his teeth, finally pushed Vivien against the wall so hard that she almost went through it.[15]

There was some tension on the set when Vivien, according to assistant director Peter Yates (now a famous director), had an accident while she was riding a horse. The animal was startled by a sudden noise and started galloping under low-hanging branches. Vivien was quick enough to bend her head and avoid getting hurt, but she lost her blond wig and her hat. A doctor insisted that she rest for at least twenty-four hours, but Vivien refused and played the scene again right away.

Vivien shared the habit, along with Quintero and his driver Albert, of stopping on her way back home after shooting, at their favorite pub, The Purple Apple, where she would have a glass of her favorite drink, pink gin.

Two weeks before the film ended she nervously said to the director, "They are going to preview *Gone with the Wind* in Atlanta. They want to do it exactly like the same as they did it the first time. Gable is dead. Leslie Howard is dead. The only ones that are left are Olivia and myself. I would like to go again and they have invited me. I know it may delay you one or two days but maybe you can shoot some of the scenes with Warren or with Lotte. Oh Jose, I would like to go; please let me."[16]

The Panamanian director knew that Vivien wanted to go to Atlanta, but he also knew of her intention to stop in New York and meet Olivier, who was still playing *Beckett* on Broadway. Roger Furse and costume designer Bumble Dawson, two Vivien's close friends, begged Quintero not to give her permission to go because they were afraid of possible consequences to her mental health after a meeting with Olivier, who was now legally divorced from her. The director did not have the courage to say no to her, but told her, "Please don't harm yourself too much." Vivien thanked him, realizing exactly what he was referring to.

The following week Vivien left for New York, where she had dinner with Olivier at Sardi's. Larry had accepted the invitation to meet with her under the conditions that he was to be accompanied by Joan Plowright and that they would meet in a public place, such as a crowded restaurant. During the dinner, Olivier announced his imminent marriage to Joan and at the end he hugged Vivien, telling her that his affection and friendship for her would be always intact. The next day, Vivien, still devastated by the news she had to face, flew to Atlanta, where *Gone with the Wind* was presented on a big screen in the most spectacular way it had ever been shown.

Once back in London, Quintero went with other common friends to pick her up at home and take her to a party at the Embassy of Panama.

> As we approached her flat, we noticed that the sidewalk was crowded with reporters and cameramen. The press attacked the door and almost got into a car, and flashbulbs exploded everywhere.... I opened the door to help Vivien out.
>
> "Miss Leigh, what do you think about what happened today?" she was asked.
>
> "I think it was wonderful. We finished the picture," she answered.
>
> "That's not what I mean. Did you know about the marriage before?"
>
> "Are you and Sir Lawrence still friends?"
>
> "You know it happened this morning. Do you have anything to say?"
>
> "About what?" she said.
>
> "Don't you know that it was a quiet and a simple ceremony? They got married this morning in New York."
>
> "He bought a house for her in Brighton."
>
> I felt Vivien's body tighten. I thought for a moment she had stopped breathing, but then she smiled a Scarlett O'Hara smile, and we fought our way through into the building.
>
> "Of course I knew it, and when I went to New York I wished them all the happiness in the world."[17]

Olivier and Plowright had actually married in Wilton, Connecticut, a few days after Vivien had returned to London. Vivien reacted very bravely and slowly accepted the situation with the great support of Merivale, who was constantly by her side.

A party was organized to celebrate the end of the shooting of *The*

Roman Spring of Mrs. Stone and Vivien bought a gift for everyone who had worked with her. The party was held in the studios, where a Roman night-club had been reconstructed from one of the scenes. During that evening each actor gave a little thank you speech. When Beatty took the microphone, he said, "I want you all to know how much I've enjoyed being in England, even if the film turns out to be a bomb."[18] The statement created general embarrassment, and Vivien, who was sitting close to Merivale, suddenly stood up and invited him to dance, saving the situation.

When *The Roman Spring of Mrs. Stone* was over, Vivien proposed that she and Merivale take a holiday to Tobago in the Caribbean. Jack was worried about how much those few days of vacation would cost, but Vivien reassured him that she would use some money that she had saved in a Canadian account that Korda had given to her prior to filming *Lady Hamilton*.

The vacation in Tobago was perfect. Before the trip Vivien saw a doctor, who found her in good health, but in those three weeks she reached a perfect state of fitness.

Her manic-depressive crisis had caused an eating disorder and she had gained weight. Lying in the sun, playing cards or scuba diving helped her to lose the extra pounds, which worried her because she had planned to tour Australia by starring in three plays: *Twelfth Night*, *Duel of Angels* and *La Dame aux camelias*.

Vivien came up with the idea of an Australian tour while she was in the States playing *Duel of Angels*. She expressed her desire to go on with the successful show to Helpmann, and the director proposed the idea to Michael Benthall, director of the Old Vic. Benthall liked the plan and proposed that another two plays be added to the repertoire in order to diversify it and make the tour more complete. Thus Vivien chose Shakespeare's *Twelfth Night*, in which she had played in the past, and Alexander Dumas' *La Dame aux camélias*, which she had read in an English translation and found interesting.

Vivien's choice of Dumas' play was not based on the identification of herself with the character of Margherite Gauthier, who was also ill with tuberculosis, but on the possibility of playing one of the greatest female roles opposite Merivale, who was cast in the part of Armand, the lover.

Robert Helpmann, who planned to direct all three productions, just before leaving to Australia, suggested that the tour be extended to also include South Africa. The proposal generated many discussions; Jack did not think it was a good idea, especially for Vivien, who had always condemned the apartheid regime. If those opinions were to be publicly

Vivien as Margherite Gauthier in *La Dame aux Camélias*, 1962.

expressed there she could pay a high price. So instead of going to South Africa, they decided to tour the plays in Mexico and several South-American countries. This decision kept the company abroad for almost nine months.

On May 13, 1961, a few weeks before her departure to Australia, Vivien became a grandmother for the second time with the birth of Jonathan Farrington.

Following the advice of actor Dirk Bogarde, Vivien bought a new country house called Tickerage Mill in Blackboys, Sussex. The cottage was constructed in the Queen Anne style, had five bedrooms, 90 acres, woods and a barn. The fact that the house was very close to a beautiful lake was the main reason that Vivien bought the property. Later on, many friends expressed their opinion that the lake's dampness could have had a damaging effect on Vivien's tuberculosis.

Because she planned to be away touring for almost a year, Vivien left the renovation work and the job of furnishing the new house in her mother's hands. Gertrude was now seventy-two, and although she had suffered a heart attack she was completely recovered.

The three plays were rehearsed at the Finsbury Park Empire Theatre in London before the Australian tour. Vivien threw a party with all her friends at Tickerage, and during that evening she gave a Cartier lighter to Merivale as a present, engraved with the name *Angelica,* the nickname given to her by Jack.

The company flew to Australia via California and Hawaii, making a stop in the Fiji Islands. Vivien seemed very relaxed the entire trip. She brought her driver Bernard and her personal cook Trudi with her. The two had recently married and Vivien offered the trip to them as a wedding present. Her Rolls Royce was shipped two months before in order to have it in Australia when they arrived.

The debut of *Duel of Angels* in Melbourne was not a big success; Vivien found that the audience was not sophisticated enough for the play. The spectators would always arrive late, entering after the show had started or during the first intermission, and they did not welcome her warmly. She thought that the only good things in the city were its beautiful orchids, juicy oysters and bird watching.

Although all the shows quickly sold out, *La Dame aux camélias* was the one that both audiences and critics preferred.

After Melbourne, Vivien and Helpmann were interviewed in Burnie, Tasmania, on the Australian TV show *Advocate*, where they increased the visibility of their tour nationwide.[19]

Brisbane was the next tour stop. Vivien was welcomed with enthusiasm, and when the performances ended the company spent some days resting at a resort close to the Coral Reef.

In Sydney the plays had very good reviews, but the box-office did not reach the projected ticket sales. There she spent her forty-eighth birthday, as David Dodimead, an actor in the company, recalls:

> the plan was we crept out of the theater after the night of her birthday, and it was outrageous to run away from Vivien on her birthday .... She was furious. We rushed to this house and hid ourselves—put all the lights out—and Jack brought Vivien, who was furious—she was swearing like a trooper: 'Where in the hell do you think we're going? ...' All this was going on and we listened to it in the dark with great amusement. And suddenly we switched all the lights on .... I was there with her favorite drink in my hand, a large glass, gin— a lot of gin—a lot of water, a lot of ice and half lemon cut across.... She adored it. And of course forty years fell off her face the moment she realized.[20]

During the second week in Sydney, Vivien seemed less active than usual, and she started to refuse any public appearance she was invited to and tried to postpone those she had already accepted.

One night a couple of minutes before entering on stage, she started shaking, and once the show was over she ran into her dressing room sobbing uncontrollably.[21]

Merivale, who had brought all of Vivien's medical records with him, wanted her to be visited by a doctor before the depression transformed into a manic state, but Vivien refused and insisted that everything would be fine even without the electroshock treatments because she did not trust any doctor except her own.

The next day Vivien told Merivale that she intended to visit the Thompsons, a couple they had recently met who had invited them to their house that evening. John Thompson and his wife lived two hundred miles from Sydney and Jack discouraged her from taking such a long trip, especially when she was expected back the following night for a performance. She replied angrily that she would go with or without him and got into the car they had rented. She looked extremely upset and Jack did not feel right letting her go by herself, so he followed her into the car. The trip was a disaster. Vivien was silent for the entire drive; she mixed up the directions to the house and got a flat tire, which Merivale patiently changed in the midst of terrible heat and a swarm of mosquitoes.

They reached the destination completely exhausted from the stress and the heat. When they arrived they learned that the Thompsons had arranged a party in Vivien's honor. Vivien collapsed from exhaustion on the bed of her hotel room and wished not to be disturbed. Merivale apologized to their hosts. Just at that moment, news arrived that one of the guests of the party had committed suicide, shooting himself in the hotel where Vivien was resting. Fortunately, she had not noticed anything, although she was awakened suddenly by other people's screams and sobbing. If she was headed into a manic phase, as Jack feared, the shock of the suicide seemed to affect her like a session of electroshock, and she returned to her calm, sweet self.

After a while she confided to Jack: "I'm not afraid to die. But you won't let them put me away, will you?" "It would be over my dead body," Jack assured her.[22]

Everybody in the company was aware of Vivien's mental disorder, and they would support her by trying to cheer her up when she looked depressed. One of the first symptoms she showed when her mania was beginning was to start systematically taking off all the jewelry she was wearing and laying it down neatly on the table. Then she would begin compulsively cleaning everything in her path. When the actors realized that those were the first manifestations of an attack, they would start to do likewise, taking off their jewels and cleaning anything they could get their hands on so that she would not feel crazy or alone.[23] Often she would quickly assume another identity, like Dr. Jekyll and Mr. Hyde, and she was capable of stripping naked in public and screaming profanities.

After Sydney the tour stopped in Adelaide and Perth and then continued on to Wellington and Christchurch in New Zealand. Before leaving New Zealand, Vivien met Sir Ernest Davis, a great admirer and a very wealthy old New Zealander who owned considerable property in Auckland. He was obsessed with the idea of meeting Vivien and he did everything possible to get to know her when he heard that she was playing in his country. Vivien was flattered by the kindness of this bizarre old gentleman and gave a party on the occasion of his ninetieth birthday. Davis was very excited and officially proposed to her. Although Vivien did not accept, she kept receiving love letters and gifts from him for several months. When Davis died, he left her 17,000 pounds and a wad of shares in his will.[24]

In Wellington, Abel Farbman, a New York impresario, offered Vivien an audition for the lead in a musical version of the comedy *Tovarich*, the story of a noble Russian couple who worked as a butler and chambermaid in a bourgeois French household. Vivien was intrigued by the part because she would get to act, sing and dance for the first time on stage. The audition took place at the huge Wellington opera house. Vivien, accompanied by a piano, sang "I'll Be Loving You—Always." Her vocal qualities impressed Farbman, who promised to send her a record with the lyrics of all the songs before giving her a final answer.

The Old Vic tour traveled to Mexico and South America, making stops in Venezuela, Peru, Chile, Argentina, Uruguay and Brazil. The language difference did not appear to be an obstacle, as audiences were eager to see Vivien Leigh, the movie star, live and on stage. Vivien would often give little speeches in Spanish to welcome or thank the theatergoers.

In Buenos Aires, however, Vivien began misbehaving again. Once at a press conference she showed her temper when answering questions from journalists, and then during a fight with Merivale after a performance she tossed a heavy brass alarm clock out of their fourteenth-floor hotel window. The clock was a present from Merivale for their first anniversary together. Luckily the crazy act did not have any other consequences.

After taking an Easter break in Punta del Este they progressed to Rio de Janeiro, which Vivien called the most beautiful city in the world and where the tour concluded.

On May 25, 1962, the Old Vic Company flew back to England via New York. Vivien found Tickerage Mill in perfect condition; all the construction work was completed and Gertrude had furnished the house in great taste in her absence. She also found in her mail the record of *Tovarich* along with Farbman's offer, which she accepted.

While she was abroad, *The Roman Spring of Mrs. Stone* had opened in England with fair revenues at the box-office. The most interesting criticism came from Tennessee Williams, who wrote in his memoirs that the film was like a poem and was "the last important work of Ms. Leigh."[25] According to him *The Roman Spring of Mrs. Stone* was the only film of his body of work that remained completely faithful to the spirit of his original creation and avoided the accommodations to censorship to which the others works had been subjected.

Vivien still liked to entertain friends during weekends. Tarquin Olivier, who was always very fond of her, would often visit her, and Suzanne, who had by now had her third son, Rupert, would go to Tickerage with the children. In the beginning of September the French actor Jean Pierre Aumont, who had been cast as the male lead in *Tovarich*, started to spend a lot of time at Tickerage Mill, reading the script and listening to the songs he would have to perform with Vivien.

On November 2, Vivien, accompanied by her personal maid Trudy, left for New York, where she took singing, dancing and guitar lessons in preparation for the rehearsals of *Tovarich*. At the airport she was welcomed by the director Delbert Mann and by Farbman, who she had previously met in New Zealand, and they drove her to the Hotel Dorset, where they had reserved a suite for her.

Vivien would rehearse the songs with the piano accompaniment of maestro Lee Pockriss daily for at least three hours and then she would continue learning the choreography for the show from Norah Kaye. In *Tovarich* Vivien had to fake a Russian accent, and to be more precise in her pronunciation she consulted an old noble Russian émigré. Her strenuous work routine in preparing for the show and the absence of Merivale, who was in London shooting a film, led her to take pills to fight insomnia. Suddenly, her depression reappeared after *Tovarich*'s first general rehearsal.

Smoking like a chimney, Vivien announced her intention to leave the show, explaining that the part was not right for her and saying that she had found the daily changes made to the script unacceptable. Aumont recalls, "I thought that her behavior was a matter of caprice, but I was mistaken. Something profound and pathetic, which perhaps stemmed from faraway personal drama, was troubling her. I was wrong at the time not to attach any importance to these symptoms. Whenever the reason might have been, they were to prove tragic."[26]

Fortunately, Vivien changed her mind and went on with the show, which opened at the Erlanger Theater in Philadelphia with good reviews and grossed $72,000, an impressive amount of money at the time.

Noël Coward, who assisted with the premiere of *Tovarich*, saw Vivien backstage after the show and told her his opinion about the show. He felt that she had been crazy to accept that part since she was not a singer or a dancer, and in addition to the stupidity of the story he felt that the production was mediocre and the direction grotesque. He "forbade" her to appear on Broadway in it.[27] Vivien became so depressed that Merivale noticed it over the phone from London.

The show needed many changes, and the reviews had generally

Dancing and singing with Byron Mitchell in *Tovarich*, 1963.

praised the acting but considered the show to be out of style. So, the director Delbert Mann was replaced by Peter Glenville. But *Tovarich*'s greatest luck was that at the time of the Broadway debut, the newspapers went on strike for four days and the musical did not receive any reviews until many days later. The show had extraordinary success, especially at the box-office, and Vivien won a Tony Award as best actress of the year.

Vivien's health worsened because of her heavy drinking. She would often insult her colleagues and behave in a strange way. Once during a matinee, Aumont found her in tears in her dressing room with photographs of her grandsons in her hand while she was listening to the waltz from *Gone with the Wind*. Then when the performance began, Vivien was pale and trembling. She sang her first song three times quickly, while the musicians stood up, trying to understand what was happening on stage. Then, when the moment of her first duet with Aumont came, during which she was supposed to look at him in rapture, she turned her back to him, opened her pocketbook and began to read her personal mail.

In the second act, during a jealousy scene in which she was supposed to admit having been raped by her jailer, her repulsion for those lines made her claw, slap and kick poor Aumont. Since it was a quarrel scene, the audience did not notice anything strange, but Vivien suddenly stopped and wrapped herself in total silence, staring at her partner, who was trying to improvise to save the situation. Then Vivien moved to the edge of the stage, and looking at the audience said, carefully pronouncing each syllable: "An actress has to think before answering," before walking off.[28] The curtain dropped and the manager had to make some substitutions to the show. Vivien appeared at the end of the show, standing completely still in the middle of the stage while the rest of the company performed their last waltz.

That day director James Ivory and producer Ismail Merchant were in the audience. They went to the show with the idea of making a movie out of it with Vivien playing the lead, but after watching her strange performance they changed their minds.

Hours later when Aumont returned to his dressing room to prepare for the evening performance, he discovered that all the photographs of his family which had been attached to the wall had been torn off and ripped into pieces. There were two doctors in Vivien's dressing room trying to give her a shot of morphine. Although she was replaced by her understudy, the rest of the company could not concentrate that evening because of her screams. She was struggling like a wounded animal against those who were holding her to prevent her from making an entrance on stage, but the sedative did not affect her. Locked in her dressing room, Vivien wore her costumes and said every line, with her dresser and the two doctors as her only audience.

Finally, toward the end of April, Merivale arrived in New York, where he had a part in a production of Oscar Wilde's *The Importance of Being Earnest*. Gertrude soon joined him, but their presence did not help Vivien's situation.

One night during a formal dinner Vivien asked her mother in front of all the guests if she had ever had any homosexual experiences. Another time Noël Coward and his companion Graham Pym received a frantic phone call from Merivale in the middle of the night begging them to come over right away. When they arrived, they found Vivien completely naked, standing on the balcony over a flight of stairs, convinced that she could fly. Only the patience and the affection of her friends convinced her to return to her room.[29]

At one point Merivale thought that Vivien went completely crazy, and on October 6, 1962, after giving her a strong dose of sedatives, he put her on a stretcher and boarded a flight to London to leave her in Dr. Conachy's hands. For three months Vivien was hospitalized in a North

London clinic that specialized in mental disorders, and then she was transferred to Tickerage Mill under the twenty-four-hour supervision of an Australian nurse nicknamed "Adelaide" by Vivien. Her convalescence was very long and difficult because the electroshocks did not provide the results that they had hoped for, and Vivien had also started to neglect herself.

Dr. Conachy, who Vivien held in high esteem, died suddenly, but fortunately his successor, Dr. Linnett, was well acquainted with her pathologies and prescribed new drugs and also wrote a letter of advice to be given to any physician Vivien might need to call on in case of an emergency.

The visits that Vivien received during that period were very few and limited to her relatives and intimate friends. She was also having trouble sleeping and often would take long walks at night into the woods or near the lake in the company of Adelaide. Other times they would go into a close pub, where she would have a little glass of pink gin, disobeying her doctor's orders. Olivier would call her often and one day he showed up at Tickerage to surprise her. Vivien was as excited as a teenager and spent the entire afternoon with him, but after receiving a phone call from Plowright, Olivier had to go back to London.

Slowly her mental health seemed to recover, so she was able to go to a play with Gertrude and visit Suzanne and Leigh for Christmas in Zelas.

In January 1964, Jack and Vivien returned for a second vacation to Tobago in the Caribbean. Three months later, Vivien made her first public appearance, when she, Robert Helpmann and Michael Redgrave read some of Shakespeare's sonnets at the Yvonne Arnaud Theatre in Guildford to celebrate the author's 400th birthday.

Since her divorce from Olivier, Vivien had formed her own company called *Vivien Leigh Productions*, which financed the independent theatrical productions of new authors like Joe Orton and Leslie Storm. It was a profitable activity that helped her to partially pay her medical expenses.

Although she seemed to be completely recovered, Vivien was still reluctant to accept any of the offers of work she was receiving.

Producer and director Stanley Kramer was planning to film an adaptation of Katherine Porter's best-seller *Ship of Fools*. Kramer had beat Selznick in the battle to acquire the movie rights, and in collaboration with Porter had started to select the cast. For the role of the rich American divorcee on board the ship, Kramer had two actresses in mind: Katharine Hepburn and Vivien. Hepburn had been chosen over Vivien for the part of Mrs. Violet Venable in *Suddenly, Last Summer,* based on a Tennessee Williams play starring Elizabeth Taylor and Montgomery Clift, a role for which Vivien was actually considered uninsurable because of her health problems. But this time Kramer chose Vivien as Mary Tread-well and offered a salary of 50,000 pounds, an amount that she was unable not to accept. The French actress Simon Signoret and the actors Lee Marvin and George Segal completed the cast.

> "Vivien Leigh ... did an excellent job in a role with perhaps less depth than Signoret," Kramer later commented. "Leigh was a woman from whom happiness, or even contentment, always seemed to escape. We had her in mind when we created her role, and she had to have thought of herself when she was playing it. She is a drunk in the picture, filled with venom and dreaming about earlier days when she was beautiful, popular and happy. To punctuate the fact, I created a scene in which, alone and half looped, she breaks into a Charleston, a symbol of the carefree happiness she always wanted but never managed to achieve. I'm sure she realized that, in the picture, she was playing something like her own life, yet she never, by word or gesture, betrayed any such recognition. Nor did she ever complain about having to play a secondary role. She could no longer get starring roles because every producer in England and America knew how difficult it could be to get a performance out of her. I had an understanding with her in the beginning about what we wanted and what we had to have. I think she gave us everything we wanted, and her Charleston scene provides one of the most poignant moments in the picture."[30]

Vivien had to move to Los Angeles, where Katharine Hepburn and George Cukor had rented a magnificent villa in the hills of Hollywood. Since she was the bridesmaid at Vivien's wedding to Olivier, Hepburn had always been in touch with her, and she was aware of Vivien's mental illness. In fact, she would often accompany her to her periodic shock treatments that enabled her to show up on the set.[31]

Simon Signoret also knew of Vivien's troubles and she remembered in her autobiography: "From one moment to another she was scintillating or desperate."[32] Signoret was the real star of *Ship of Fools*, and she had written in her contract that her name had to be on the top of all the other actors in all the non-English speaking countries, while in the English speaking ones the honor was paid to Vivien.

Because Vivien's behavior had worsened again, Merivale tried to be by her side as much as possible with the help of Gertude, who arrived from London. Sometimes Vivien would hallucinate and insult the other actors in the cast for no reason, and some like Signoret understood and pretended that nothing had happened. Others, like a young actress,

Vivien and Lee Marvin in a "too real" scene from *Ship of Fools*, 1965.

protested during the production even though Merivale apologized to her profusely.

During the scene in which Lee Marvin is drunk and comes into her cabin by mistake and Vivien hits him in the face and on the head with the heel of her pump, she was so violent that Marvin had marks on his face for days.

She was always late on the set and one day, as Kramer recalls,

> She was making up for a scene when she fooled around at the makeup table for a long time and made life pretty miserable for all the makeup people for a period of about two and half hours.... Suddenly she looked up and must have looked at me for ten seconds, which is a long time when someone is piercing you, and said, "I ... Stanley, I can't do it today." And I knew that she was ill and she couldn't do it. I'll never forget that look. That was the look of one of the greatest actresses of our time. From that moment on I became, I think, probably the most on purpose, understanding and patient person that I could possibly be. She was ill and had the courage to go ahead—the courage to make the film was almost unbelievable.[33]

In one scene, Vivien hummed and sang pieces of a popular song from the 20s. If used in the film the song would have cost thousands of dollars in rights, so Kramer asked her to sing something else, but Vivien replied, "My husband was one of the greatest directors in the theater and film. He would permit me to do any song that I liked."[34] Kramer let her have it her way but the song was later dubbed by another actress singing a different tune.

Vivien was terribly embarrassed by the fact that everybody in Hollywood knew about her mental disorder. After at a party given by Rosalind Russell she stood up and sang a very filthy song in front of everybody.

"Everyone must know I'm as mad as a hatter," she told Merivale one day. Jack held her in his arms and said, "You're not! You are not mad. You have a mental condition and that's entirely different. That can be coped with."[35]

In May 1965, Kramer showed the final cut of *Ship of Fools* in London, and Vivien complained that one of her scenes, which she felt was very relevant for the plot of the film, had been cut.

At the New York premiere Noël Coward commented on how Vivien kept accepting the role of faded, beautiful women. The general reviews were negative, and critics spared only Vivien and Signoret. However, *Ship of Fools* won two Academy Awards, one for best photography and one for best set-design.

During her staying in Hollywood, Twentieth Century Fox offered Vivien a part in *Hush Hush ... Sweet Charlotte*. Bette Davis and Joan Crawford had been indicated as possible co-stars, after the recent success of *What Ever Happened to Baby Jane?* But Vivien told the press when she was asked if she would be interested in the role: "I could just look at Joan Crawford's face at seven o'clock in the morning, but I couldn't possibly look at Bette Davis's." Davis replied that she would never make a film

with Vivien because it would be more difficult than making a film with Joan Crawford because of her emotional problems and because of her "absurd" British accent. Davis seemed to have forgotten that Vivien won two Oscars playing two Southerners, Scarlett and Blanche, but she was still resentful over *Gone with the Wind*.[36]

Lee Marvin and Vivien as Mary Treadwell, another role of a faded beautiful woman, in *Ship of Fools*, 1965.

Chapter Seventeen

Breathless

*"I had shared a life that had resembled nothing so much
as an express lift skying me upwards and throwing me
downwards in insanely non-stop fashion."*
—Laurence Olivier talking about his life with Vivien Leigh

On August 25, 1964, Vivien returned to London with Jack. The following months were quiet and she spent her time at Tickerage trying to rest as much as possible by gardening, reading or inviting friends over for weekends. In October she threw an engagement party for Tarquin Olivier and his future bride Ridelle Gibson. She also received an unexpected visit from Princess Margaret and Lord Snowdon who were staying with mutual friends nearby.

Then she spent her fifty-first birthday with Leigh, while Merivale was in Hollywood working on a film. Taking advantage of Jack's long absence, Vivien decided to take a trip to India. She had not been back since 1920, when at the age of seven she had left for England.

The trip was organized by Henry Stebbins, the American ambassador to Nepal, who was a friend of their mutual friend, publisher Hamish Hamilton. The trip included a stop in Nepal and a stop on the Greek island of Corfu on the way back.

After having all the vaccinations required, she left with Lady Alexandra Metcalf, the daughter of Lord Curzon, the last viceroy of India. The flight was very long and stopped in Frankfurt, Vienna and Istanbul. After a day of rest in Delhi, Vivien proceeded to Katmandu on board a small aircraft that flew over the Himalayas and other places familiar to Vivien. In Nepal she was a guest of the British Embassy. She was very impressed with the mystical atmosphere of the places she visited, and by the kindness of the King of Nepal, who gave her his private airplane for her use.

Vivien was recognized everywhere she went as Scarlett O'Hara and she wrote all her emotions and impressions in long, daily letters addressed to Merivale. She wanted to go back to London in time to participate in Tarquin Olivier's wedding. The idea was not appreciated by Olivier, who was embarrassed at having all three wives reunited on that occasion.

Vivien also hosted Winston Churchill at Tickerage only a couple of months before his death, which saddened her profoundly.

Her next project was *La Contessa*, a play by Paul Osborn, based on a novel by Maurice Druon. The story was inspired by Marchesa Casati from Venice, who had lived in the 20s in a Palace overlooking the Canal Grande. She had become legendary for her numerous lovers and eccentricities, such as walking through the streets with a leopard on a chain.

The idea of having Vivien play in *La Contessa* had come from one of the most important Hollywood agents, Leland Hayward, who thought Vivien was right for the part. The production was very expensive because there were 14 different stage designs and many different costumes.

Vivien was playing a seventy-seven-year-old, the Countess Sanziani, and had to wear a bright orange wig and have her eyes rimmed with black tape. But despite the heavy make-up, Vivien still looked too beautiful and had a tone of voice that was too clear for a woman of that age. When a journalist asked her if she thought *La Contessa* was a good play, Vivien replied: "I think the idea of the play is very good. I think my part is a good one, but whether it was the right part for me to take I just don't know. If I knew that kind of things I would be a very rich woman."[1]

The play first opened in New Castle on April 6, 1965, and then toured in Liverpool and Manchester, but the reviews were dreadful, and the production decided not to risk losing even more money and closed before reaching London. In the '70s the film version of the play, *A Matter of Time*, directed by Vincent Minnelli, starring Ingrid Bergman and Liza Minnelli, would suffer the same destiny.

In 1966, Vivien and Jack went back to the United States to play together on Broadway in *Ivanov*, one of the last plays written by Chekhov. The play was directed by John Gielgud, who had personally staged the adaptation and was also playing the lead. Vivien was cast as Maria Petrovna, a secondary character who dies in the end of the third act. In the beginning she was undecided as to whether or not to accept a minor role, but the idea of working with Merivale convinced her to accept the part.

Vivien had organized her stay in New York by exchanging apartments with actress Joan Fontaine, Olivia de Havilland's sister. In her memoirs Fontaine stated that it had been a bad idea because Vivien did not tell her about the presence of her cat Poo Jones in the apartment, which "reeked of feline proximity." "Since I had left Vivien with my excellent Jamaican housekeeper in New York, had left out all my linens and silver for her use, I saw no reason why I should leave the Alfa Romeo on the street in Eaton Square when her garage was unoccupied. I rang the New York Apartment and explained my problem to Vivien, asking for housing of the convertible. 'You are not to use my gaz-zahge,' she regally commanded, and hung up the phone. My phone!"[2]

With John Gielgud in *Ivanov*, 1966.

The two actresses ended up hating each other after some valuable watches that Olivier had given Vivien disappeared from her apartment. Fontaine was suspected of theft and the news was printed by all the tabloids.

During the wide North American tour of *Ivanov*, the company was involved in a terrible fire that started in the hotel in which the actors were staying in Toronto. Fortunately nobody was injured, but the costumes smelled of smoke for a while.

Vivien suddenly started to cough again. Ironically, her character Anna dies of tuberculosis in the play. Although she was very annoyed because she was unable to cure the cold and the bad cough, nobody paid too much attention to the symptoms, thinking they were caused by the frigid winter weather.

Vivien was saddened by the scarce critical success of *Ivanov* and she told a reporter, "Let me assure you, that there is absolutely nothing romantic about being an actress. You slave over every role and are never satisfied. Of course, playing Chekhov was an irresistible challenge. I've longed to play Chekhov for thirty years. Finally, it came with *Ivanov*—and I was glad to have done it."[3]

The play was performed on Broadway for only two months and obtained modest results at the box-office. After *Ivanov* closed, Vivien and Merivale took a vacation in the Caribbean and then returned briefly to New York, where Vivien again showed serious symptoms of her mental illness.

One night at the Persian tea-room in the Plaza Hotel, where Jean Pierre Aumont and his wife Tina were acting in a cabaret show, Vivien, who was in the audience, suddenly stepped on stage and proposed that she and Aumont improvise a duet they had performed together in *Tovarich*. The French actor accepted with a hint of embarrassment, but as soon as the music began playing, Vivien forgot the lyrics of the song. She ended up dancing the Charleston while Aumont sang the entire piece. It was a total disaster, but the audience did not seem worried, just excited by this extra number being played by a famous movie star.

Once she returned to London Vivien resumed her electroshock sessions and started a new therapeutic treatment.

She was offered a part in a film on the life of Tchaikovsky, as Nadezhda von Meck, the mistress and producer of the great Russian composer. But producer Dimitri Tiomkin and Roy Moseley, Vivien's agent, did not reach an agreement, so the project remained unfeasible.

In 1967, Vivien's health deteriorated dramatically. She lost a lot of weight and often felt weak and unable to find a part she liked. She finally accepted a part in Edward Albee's *A Delicate Balance* opposite Michael Redgrave. They planned to open the show the following summer in London after a short provincial tour.

In preparing for the play, Vivien became confused about the text because of its complicated allegories and symbolism. For the first time in her career she tried to learn her lines before studying their meaning. Albee often visited her at Eaton Square in order to help her understand the part. In the past the playwright had wanted Vivien to star in another one of his plays, *Who's Afraid of Virginia Woolf?*, but she declined the offer due to previous engagements.

Vivien was invited to Oxford for a public reading of *Hazlitt in Florence* for a benefit event in support of the city of Florence, which had been hit by a flood. It was the last of Vivien's public appearances.

On a Sunday morning towards the end of May, while returning home from a weekend at Tickerage, Vivien suddenly fainted upon entering her apartment. She woke up with a strong cough and was spitting blood. Dr. Linnett took an X-ray in her bedroom, since she refused to go into a hospital, and he found a large black hole in her lung. Tuberculosis had returned in a very violent form.

Vivien had a very calm reaction, because she was confident that if she had already recovered once, she could do it again. The physician ordered absolute rest for her for at least three months and no drinking or smoking. Vivien reluctantly accepted the doctor's prescriptions without realizing the gravity of her illness.

As soon as the news of her tuberculosis spread to her friends, her apartment overflowed with flowers sent by friend and colleagues, who visited her or called her from all over the world, and she systematically replied to each gift or visit with thank-you notes.

Vivien seemed far more preoccupied by Olivier's health than her own. Larry had, in fact, been hospitalized in an emergency at the St. Thomas Hospital after being diagnosed with prostate cancer. Joan Plowright called her before the news of his health appeared in the media. Vivien would ask anyone who would visit her about Olivier's health.

During her period in bed she often chose not to follow Dr. Linnett's orders, smoking or walking around the apartment without taking her medications, especially when Merivale was not around to check on her. On the first day of July, Noël Coward and George Cukor visited her and they found her in better shape, even though she felt weaker and more tired in the middle of their visit.

Although she was in bed, Vivien continued to prepare for her role in *A Delicate Balance*. She received her hairdresser at home, who cut her hair according to the style of her character and showed her several wigs and hairstyles that she would have to wear in the show.

Although Merivale was busy playing in *The Last of Mrs. Cheyney* at the Guildford Theatre, he would spend all of his free time with her.

On the afternoon of July 7, 1967, Vivien watched the Wimbledon men's finals on television with Merivale, who then left to go to the theater for the evening performance. During the play's intermission Jack called her from his dressing room phone to see if she was all right. Vivien had a weak voice but told him not to worry.

Merivale arrived home around 11 P.M. and entered Vivien's bedroom, where he found her asleep with Poo Jones lying beside her on the bed. It seemed that everything was in order and he noticed that Vivien had already signed all the correspondence that had been typed by her secretary to be mailed the next day.

Merivale went into the kitchen to heat some soup, at 11.30 P.M., and he stepped into Vivien's bedroom again before going to bed. To his horror he found her lying on the floor unconscious. It looked like she had tried to go to the bathroom but had fallen. Her body was still warm but she had stopped breathing. He put her back in bed immediately and tried in vain to resuscitate her using cardiopulmonary resuscitation. He then called Dr. Linnett and his friends Bumble Dawson and Alan Webb, who lived nearby. Gertrude was on holiday in Scotland and Merivale was unable to reach her that evening.

Once he arrived, the doctor could only confirm Vivien's death.

The next morning at 8 A.M. Jack called Olivier at the hospital, where he was still recovering. Larry knew right away, before Merivale communicated the sad news to him, and left the hospital immediately even though he was still in pain. He had to take a secondary entrance into Vivien's building because the press was already there.

Merivale left Olivier alone in Vivien's bedroom, and as he recalled in his memoirs, "I stood and prayed for forgiveness for all the evils that had sprung up between us.... Looking for the last time at that beautiful dead face, I discerned a drawn look in her expression that I knew to be one of faint disgust."[4] Olivier also noticed a long stain of blood on the floor between the bed and the bathroom that, along with the expression on her face, confirmed the cause of her death to him.

The following day Gertrude arrived from Scotland and, along with Suzanne, they went to the morgue, where an autopsy was conducted. The medical report indicated that the cause of Vivien's death was chronic pulmonary tuberculosis. Both lungs were filled with fluid; she had suffocated.

"Scarlett O'Hara Is Dead" was the most popular headline among newspapers all over the world that covered the news of Vivien's death. Friends and fans of the actress were all astonished by her premature departure.

Merivale received sympathy cards and telegrams from all over the world, and at 10:00 that night, all of the theaters in London dimmed their lights as a tribute to Vivien.

On July 12, Gertrude organized a requiem mass for the funeral at St. Mary's in Cadogan Street, which was attended by relatives and close friends. Vivien's body was taken to Golders Green were it was then cremated. Cecil Tennant, one of Vivien's dearest friends and her former agent, who the Oliviers used to call "Uncle Cecil," died in a car accident on his way home after the funeral, hitting a tree with his Jaguar in Chertsey. For Olivier, the news of his death was almost as shocking as Vivien's.

In New York two requiem masses were celebrated in Vivien's honor; one in Manhattan, organized by Paula Lawrence, who had worked with her in *Duel of Angels*, and another in Staten Island, organized by her old friend, journalist Radie Harris.

Tennessee Williams sent a telegram to Jack with the message, "She was a definition of loveliness as a woman and artist."[5] Simone Signoret wrote, "I will miss her, her laughs and her screams, her humor and her toughness and her tenderness."[6]

On August 14, at St. Martin-in-the-Field's church in Trafalgar Square, a special service was held in Vivien's memory that was attended by many friends and colleagues. Gertrude, Leigh Holman, Suzanne and Robin Farrington, Jack Merivale, and Laurence Olivier sat in the front row, and behind them were many people who were paying their last tribute to Vivien. Among these were Richard Attenborough, Binkie Beaumont, Dirk Bogarde, Peter Brook, Jill Esmond and Alec Guinness. Noël Coward was unable to attend because he was too overcome by her death. During the ceremony Vivien's favorite poems by John Donne were read.

Later in October Vivien's ashes were scattered around the Lake in Tickerage in the presence of a few intimate people.

Vivien's estate was estimate at about 252,000 pounds, including her collection of paintings valued at 12,000 pounds, and in her will she left Merivale 6,000 pounds.

A few months after Vivien's death, Tickerage Mill was robbed, and Gertrude and Suzanne decided to sell the property for 40,000 pounds.

On March 17, 1968, at the University of Southern California in Los Angeles, movie stars and directors attended a special evening in Vivien's honor. Clips from her films were shown, along with Vivien's screen test for *Gone with the Wind*, and anecdotes were told by the celebrities who were present. It was a very moving occasion, in which Vivien was finally consecrated as a legendary movie star.

Among all the words said in Vivien's honor by the press from all over the world and out of the many tributes, the most significant and poignant were John Gielgud's:

> I'm very proud to have known Vivien as a close friend during the later years of her life–from the 1940's.... What can I write that will bring back the delight and sparkle that emanated from her? She hated getting old, but I thought her more beautiful than ever as the years went by, with her fine bone structure and delicate neck.
>
> She was an impeccable hostess and party-giver, thoughtful and generous to a fault, she had great ambition but was unceasingly self-critical of her acting talent, and working to perfect it with continual diligence.
>
> Away from the theater and film studio, she ran her household with infinite care, showed vigorous taste in choosing her clothes, tending and arranging her flowers, cherishing her animals, decorating her home and ordering meals for her guests.
>
> Working in plays and films she was loved by her colleagues and staff alike.

She was punctual, professional and a workaholic as well as being unfailingly interested in everyone and everything around her.

She was only too well aware of her darker side, and fought most gallantly to keep it under control, though in the end, she was fated to be overcome by its cruel demands upon her health.

How often I think of her calling me on the telephone with that imperious but affectionate "Johnnie?" and wish so much that I could hear that dear voice again.[7]

Film, Stage and Radio Appearances

FILM APPEARANCES

1935

Things Are Looking Up

Director: Albert de Courville; Producer: Michael Balcon; Screenplay: Stafford Dickens and Con West.

Cast: Vivien Leigh (Student), Cicely Courtneidge (Berta Fytte), Henrietta Watson (Miss MacTavish), Dick Henderson, Jr. (Money Junior), Max Miller (Joey).

The Village Squire

Director: Reginald Denham; Producer: Anthony Havelock Allen; Screenplay: Arthur Jarvis Black.

Cast: Vivien Leigh (Rose Venables), Leslie Perrins (Richard Venables), David Horne (Squire Hollis), Haddon Mason (Dr. Blake).

Gentleman's Agreement

Director: George Pearson; Producer: Anthony Havelock Allan; Screenplay: Basil Mason.

Cast: Vivien Leigh (Phil Stanley), Frederick Peisley (Guy Carfax), Anthony Hollens (Bill Bentley), David Horne (Sir Charles Lysle), Ronald Shiner (Jim Ferrin).

Look Up and Laugh

Director and Producer: Basil Dean; Screenplay: J.B. Priestley.

Cast: Vivien Leigh (Marjorie Belfer), Gracie Fields (Grace Pearson), Douglas Wakefield (Joe Chirk), Robb Wilton (Mayor), Helen Ferrers (Lady Buster).

1937

Fire Over England

Director: William K. Howard; Producer: Alexander Korda; Screenplay: Clemence Dane and Sergei K. Nolbandov, based on the novel by A.E.W. Mason.
Cast: Vivien Leigh (Cynthia Burleigh), Flora Robson (Queen Elizabeth), Laurence Olivier (Michael Ingolby), Lesile Banks (Count of Leicester), Raymond Massey (Philip II), Tamara Desny (Elena), James Mason (Hilary Vane).

Dark Journey AKA The Anxious Years

Director: Victor Saville; Producer: Alexander Korda; Screenplay: Arthur Wimperis. Based on a short story by Lajos Biro.
Cast: Vivien Leigh (Madeline Godard), Conrad Veidt (Baron Karl von Marwitz), Joan Gardner (Lupita), Anthony Bushell (Bob Carter), Austin Trevor (Dr. Muller).

Storm in a Teacup

Director and Producer: Victor Saville; Screenplay: Ian Dalrymple and Donald Bull. Based on the play Sturm in Wasserglas by Bruno Frank.
Cast: Vivien Leigh (Victoria Grow), Rex Harrison (Frank Burdon), Sara Algood (Mrs. Hegarty), Cecil Parker (Provost Gow), Robert Hale (Lord Skerryvore).

1938

A Yank at Oxford

Director: Jack Conway; Producer: Michael Balcon; Screenplay: Malcom Stuart Boylan, Walter Ferris and George Oppenheimer.
Cast: Vivien Leigh (Elsa Craddock), Robert Taylor (Lee Sheridan), Lionel Barrymore (Dan Sheridan), Maureen O'Sullivan (Molly Beaumont), Griffith Jones (Paul Beaumont), Edmund Gwenn (Dean of Cardinal).

St. Martin's Lane AKA Sidewalks of London

Director: Tim Whelan; Producer: Erich Pommer; Screenplay: Clemence Dane.
Cast: Vivien Leigh (Libby), Charles Laughton (Charles), Rex Harrison (Harley), Larry Adler (Costantine), Tyron Guthrie (Gentry), Maire O'Neill (Mr. Such).

Twenty-One Days AKA 21 Days Together

Director: Basil Dean; Producer: Alexander Korda; Screenplay: Basil Dean, Graham Green, based on the play The First and the Last by John Galsworthy.

Cast: Vivien Leigh (Wanda), Laurence Olivier (Larry Durrant), Lesile Banks (Keith Durrant), Robert Newton (Tolley), Francis L. Sullivan (Mander), Esme Percy (Henry Walenn).

1939

Gone with the Wind

Director: Victor Fleming (uncredited directors: George Cukor, Sam Wood, William Cameron Menzies and David O. Selznick), Producer: David O. Selznick, Screenplay: Sydney Howard and David O. Selznick, based on the novel by Margaret Mitchell.

Cast: Vivien Leigh (Scarlett O'Hara), Clark Gable (Rhett Butler), Lesile Howard (Ashley Wilkies), Olivia de Havilland (Melanie Hamilton), Hattie McDaniel (Mammy), Thomas Mitchell (Gerald O'Hara), Barbara O'Neil (Ellen O'Hara), Evelyn Keyes (Suellen O'Hara), Laura Hope Crews (Pittypat Hamilton), Harry Davenport (Dr. Mead), Rand Brooks (Charles Hamilton), Carrol Nye (Frank Kennedy), Ony Munson (Bella Watling), Alicia Rhett (India Wilkes), Butterfly McQueen (Prissy), Victor Jory (Jonas Wilkerson).

1940

Waterloo Bridge

Director: Mervyn LeRoy; Producer: Sydney Franklin; Screenplay: S.N. Behrman, Hans Rameau, George Froeschel, based on a play by Robert E. Sherwood.

Cast: Vivien Leigh (Myra), Robert Taylor (Roy Cronin), Lucile Watson (Lady Margaret Cronin), Virginia Field (Kitty), Maria Ouspenskaya (Madame Olga Kirowa), C. Aubrey Smith (Duke).

1941

Lady Hamilton AKA *That Hamilton Woman*

Director and Producer: Alexander Korda; Screenplay: W.C. Sherriff, Walter Reisch.

Cast: Vivien Leigh (Emma Hamilton), Laurence Olivier (Horatio Nelson), Alan Mowbray (Sir William Hamilton), Sarah Allgod (Mrs. Cadogan-Lyon), Gladys Cooper (Lady Nelson), Henry Wilcoxon (Capt. Hardy), Halliwell Hobbes (Reverend Nelson), Louis Alberni (King of Naples).

1946

Caesar and Cleopatra

Director and Producer: Gabriel Pascal; Screenplay: George Bernard Shaw, based on his play.

Cast: Vivien Leigh (Cleopatra), Claude Rains (Caesar), Flora Robson (Ftatateeta), Stewart Granger (Apollodorus), Francis L. Sullivan (Pothinus), Cecil Parker (Britannus), Basil Sydney (Rufio), Ernest Thesinger (Theodotus), Jean Simmons, Kay Kendall, Roger Moore (Extras)

1948

Anna Karenina

Director: Julien Duvivier; Producer: Alexander Korda; Screenplay: Julien Duvivier, Guy Moran, Jean Anouilh, based on the novel by Leo Tolstoy.

Cast: Vivien Leigh (Anna Karenina), Kieron Moore (Count Vronsky), Ralph Richardson (Alexei Karenin), Sally Ann Howes (Kitty Scherbatsky), Hugh Dempster (Stephan Oblonsky), Niall McGinnis (Levin), Martitia Hunt (Betty Tverskoy).

1950

A Streetcar Named Desire

Director: Elia Kazan; Producer: Karl Feldman; Screenplay: Elia Kazan, based on the play by Tennessee Williams.

Cast: Vivien Leigh (Blanche DuBois), Marlon Brando (Stanley Kowalski), Kim Hunter (Stella Kowalski), Karl Malden (Mitch), Rudy Bond (Steve), Peg Hillias (Eunice), Richard Garrick (Dottore), Nick Tennis (Pablo).

1954

The Deep Blue Sea

Director and Producer: Anatole Litvak; Screenplay: Terence Rattigan, based on the play by the same name by Terence Rattigan.

Cast: Vivien Leigh (Hester Collier), Kenneth More (Freddie Page), Emlyn Williams (Sir William Collyer), Moira Lister (Dawn Maxwell), Heather Thatcher (Lady Dawson), Dandy Nicholson (Mrs. Elton), Arthur Hill (Jackie Jackson).

1961

The Roman Spring of Mrs. Stone

Director: José Quintero; Producer: Louis de Rochemont; Screenplay: Gavin Lambert, based on the novel by Tennessee Williams.

Cast: Vivien Leigh (Karen Stone), Warren Beatty (Paolo Di Leo), Lotte Lenya (Countess Gonzales), Coral Brown (Meg), Jill St. John (Barbara Bingham), Carl Jaffe (Baron), Paul Stassino (Barber).

1964

Ship of Fools

Director and Producer: Stanley Kramer; Screenplay: Abby Mann, based on the novel by Katherine Anne Porter.

Cast: Vivien Leigh (Mary Treadwell), Simon Signoret (Contessa), Oskar Werner (Dr. Schumann), Michael Dunn (Glocken), Elizabeth Ashley (Jenny), José Ferrer (Rieber), Lee Marvin (Tenny), George Segal (David), José Greco (Pepe).

STAGE APPEARANCES

"The Green Sash"

Produced and Directed by Matthew Forsyth; Written by Debonnaire Sylvester and T.P. Wood.

Vivien Leigh (Giusta)

Q Theatre, London, February 25, 1935

"The Mask of Virtue"

Produced by Sydney Carroll; Directed by Maxwell Wray; Written by Carl Sternheim.

Vivien Leigh (Henriette Duquesnoy)

Ambassadors Theatre, London, May 15, 1935

St. James Theatre, London, May 29, 1935

"Richard II"

Directed by John Gielgud and Glen Byam Shaw; Written by William Shakespeare.

Vivien Leigh (Queen)

Oxford University, Dramatic Society, February 17, 1936

"The Happy Hypocrite"

Directed by Maurice Colbourne; Written by Clemence Byne; Based on a short story by Max Beerbohm.

Vivien Leigh (Jenny Mere)

His Majesty's Theatre, London, April 8, 1936

"Henry VIII"

Produced by Sydney Carroll; Directed by Robert Atkins; Written by William Shakespeare.

Vivien Leigh (Anne Bullen)

Open Air Theatre, London, June 22, 1936

"Because We Must"

Produced and Directed by Norman Marshall; Written by Ingaret Gifford.
Vivien Leigh (Pamela Golding-French)
Wyndham's Theatre, London, February 5, 1937

"Bats in the Belfry"

Produced by Sydney Carroll; Directed by A.R. Whatmore; Written by Diana
Morgan and Robert MacDermot.
Vivien Leigh (Jessica Morton)
Ambassadors Theatre, London, March 11, 1937

"Hamlet"

Produced by the Danish State Tourist Board and the Old Vic Theatre; Directed
by Tyron Guthrie; Written by William Shakespeare.
Vivien Leigh (Ophelia)
Kronborg Castle, Elsinore, Denmark (opening night performed at the Marienlist Hotel), June 3, 1937

"Midsummer Night's Dream"

Directed by Tyron Guthrie; Written by William Shakespeare.
Vivien Leigh (Titania)
Old Vic Theatre, London, December 27, 1937

"Serena Blandish"

Directed by Esme Percy; Written by S.N. Behrman; Based on the novel *A Lady
of Quality* by Enid Bagnold.
Vivien Leigh (Serena Blandish)
Gate Theatre, London, September 13, 1938

"Romeo and Juliet"

Produced and Directed by Laurence Olivier; Written by William Shakespeare.
Vivien Leigh (Juliet)
51st Street Theatre, New York, May 9, 1940

"Doctor's Dilemma"

Produced by H.M. Tennent; Directed by Irene Hentschel; Written by George
Bernard Shaw.
Vivien Leigh (Jennifer Dubedat)
Haymarket Theatre, London, March 4, 1942

"The School for Scandal" (two scenes)

Written by Richard Brinsley Sheridan.
Vivien Leigh (Lady Teazle)
Haymarket Theatre, London, April 24, 1942. Special performance on the occasion of Cyril Maude's eightieth birthday.

"Spring Party"

Revue produced by John Gielgud.
Tour in North Africa entertaining British troops, Spring 1943

"The Skin of Our Teeth"

Produced by H.M. Tennent; Directed by Laurence Olivier; Written by Thornton Wilder.
Vivien Leigh (Sabina)
Phoenix Theatre, London, May 16, 1945

"Richard III"

Written by William Shakespeare.
Vivien Leigh (Lady Anne)
Australian and New Zealand tour of the Old Vic Company, February 14–November 1, 1948

"The School for Scandal"

Written by Richard Brinsley Sheridan.
Vivien Leigh (Lady Teazle)
Australian and New Zealand tour of the Old Vic Company, February 14–November 1, 1948

"The Skin of Our Teeth"

Written by Thornton Wilder.
Vivien Leigh (Sabina)
Australian and New Zealand tour of the Old Vic Company, February 14–November 1, 1948

"The School for Scandal"

Produced by The Old Vic Company; Directed by Laurence Olivier; Written by Richard Brinsley Sheridan.
Vivien Leigh (Lady Teazle)
New Theatre, London, January 20, 1949

"Richard III"

Produced by the Old Vic Company; Directed by Laurence Olivier; Written by William Shakespeare.
    Vivien Leigh (Lady Anne)
    New Theatre, London, January 26, 1949

"Antigone"

Produced by the Old Vic Company; Directed Laurence Olivier; Written by Jean Anouilh; Translation by Lewis Galantiere.
    Vivien Leigh (Antigone)
    New Theatre, London, February 10, 1949

"A Streetcar Named Desire"

Produced and Directed by Laurence Olivier; Written by Tennessee Williams.
    Vivien Leigh (Blanche DuBois)
    Aldwych Theatre, London, October 11, 1949

"Caesar and Cleopatra"

Produced by Laurence Olivier; Directed by Michael Benthall; Written by George Bernard Shaw.
    Vivien Leigh (Cleopatra)
    St. James Theatre, London, May 10, 1951

"Antony and Cleopatra"

Produced by Laurence Olivier; Directed by Michael Benthall; Written by William Shakespeare.
    Vivien Leigh (Cleopatra)
    St. James Theatre, London, May 10, 1951

"Night of 100 Stars ('Terrible Triplets')"

Benefit organized by Charles Russell and Lance Hamilton.
    London, June 25, 1951

"Caesar and Cleopatra"

Produced by Gilbert Miller; Directed by Michael Benthall; Written by George Bernard Shaw.
    Vivien Leigh (Cleopatra)
    Ziegfeld Theatre, New York, December 19, 1951

"Antony and Cleopatra"

Produced by Gilbert Miller; Directed by Michael Benthall; Written by William Shakespeare.

Vivien Leigh (Cleopatra)
Ziegfeld Theatre, New York, December 20, 1951

"The Sleeping Prince"

Produced by H.M. Tennent and Laurence Olivier; Directed by Laurence Olivier; Written by Terence Rattigan.
Vivien Leigh (Mary Morgan)
Phoenix Theatre, London, November 5, 1953

"Night of 100 Stars"

Benefit organized by Charles Russell and Lance Hamilton.
London Palladium, London, February 1954

"The School for Scandal" (one scene)

Written by Richard Brinsley Sheridan.
Vivien Leigh (Lady Teazle)
One performance to honor Dame Sybil Thorndike.
Royal Academy of Dramatic Art, London, May 31, 1954

"Twelfth Night"

Directed by John Gielgud; Written by William Shakespeare.
Vivien Leigh (Viola)
Shakespeare Memorial Theatre, Stratford-upon-Avon, April 12, 1955

"Macbeth"

Directed by Glen Byam Shaw; Written by William Shakespeare.
Vivien Leigh (Lady Macbeth)
Shakespeare Memorial Theatre, Stratford-upon-Avon, June 7, 1955

"Titus Andronicus"

Directed by Peter Brook; Written by William Shakespeare.
Vivien Leigh (Lavinia)
Shakespeare Memorial Theatre, Stratford-upon-Avon, August 16, 1955

"South Sea Bubble"

Directed by William Chappell; Written by Noël Coward.
Vivien Leigh (Alexandra Shotter)
Lyric Theatre, London, April 25, 1956

"Titus Andronicus"

Directed by Peter Brook; Written by William Shakespeare.

Vivien Leigh (Lavinia)
Paris, Venice, Belgrade, Zagreb, Vienna, Warsaw, May 6–June 22, 1957
Stoll Theatre, London, July 1, 1957

"Duel of Angels"

Produced by Laurence Olivier; Directed Jean-Louis Barrault; Translation of the play *Pour Lucrèce* by Jean Girardoux; Translated by Christopher Fry.
Vivien Leigh (Paola)
Apollo Theatre, London, April 24, 1958

"Look After Lulu"

Produced by H.M. Tennent and Laurence Olivier; Directed by Tony Richardson; Written by Noël Coward, based on the play *Occupe-toi d'Amelie* by Georges Feydeau.
Vivien Leigh (Lulu d'Arville)
Royal Court Theatre, London, July 29, 1959
New Theatre, London, September 8, 1959

"Duel of Angels"

Produced by Roger L. Stevens and Sol Hurok; Directed by Robert Helpmann; Translation of the play *Pour Lucrèce* by Jean Girardoux; Translated by Christopher Fry.
Vivien Leigh (Paola)
Helen Hayes Theatre, New York, April 19, 1960, followed by a tour of Los Angeles, San Francisco, Denver and Washington.

"Twelfth Night"

Directed by Robert Helpmann; Written by William Shakespeare.
Vivien Leigh (Viola)
Australian and South American Tour of the Old Vic Company, June 26, 1961–May 25, 1962

"Duel of Angels"

Directed by Robert Helpmann; Translation of the play *Pour Lucrèce* by Jean Girardoux; Translated by Christopher Fry.
Vivien Leigh (Paola)
Australian and South American Tour of the Old Vic Company, June 26, 1961–May 25, 1962

"La Dame aux Camélias"

Directed by Robert Helpmann; Written by Alexandre Dumas fils.
Vivien Leigh (Marguerite Gauthier)

Australian and South American Tour of the Old Vic Company, June 26, 1961–May 25, 1962

"Tovarich"

Musical produced by Abel Farbman and Sylvia Harris; Directed by Peter Glenville, based on the play by Jacques Deval and Robert E. Sherwood.
Vivien Leigh (Tatiana)
Broadway Theatre, New York, March 18, 1963

"La Contessa"

Produced by H.M. Tennent and Leland Hayward; Directed by Robert Helpmann; Written by Paul Osborn.
Vivien Leigh (Contessa Sanziani)
Newcastle, April 6, 1965, Liverpool, April 19, 1965, Manchester, May 4, 1965

"Ivanov"

Produced by Alexander H. Cohen; Directed by John Gielgud; Written by Anton Chekhov.
Vivien Leigh (Anna Petrova)
Shubert Theatre, New York, May 3, 1966

"Hazlitt in Florence"

Reading of poems by William Hazlitt, Oxford, May 1967

RADIO APPEARANCES

A British Tribute to King George and Queen Mary (February 1939), NBC Radio USA
A Broadcast Tribute to the British Stage and Screen Royalty (December 1940), NBC Radio USA
For Us the Living (April 8, 1941), BBC UK
My Life in the Theatre (May 11, 1941), BBC UK
The School for Scandal (May 8, 1942), BBC UK
Sunday Night Poetry Reading (February 10, 1944), BBC UK
Lux Radio Theatre Presents Rebecca (1950), USA
Look Awards (February 26, 1952), NBC Radio
Desert Island Discs (September 2, 1952), BBC UK
Theatre (Italian exchange program) (May 5, 1956), BBC UK
A Message to India (August 8, 1956), BBC UK
Intervista (April 28, 1957), BBC UK
Intervista (July 31, 1957), BBC UK
Antony and Cleopatra (August 20, 1957), BBC UK
Woman's Hour: Conversation in Ebony Street (September 24, 1957), BBC UK
Toast of the Town (May 8, 1958), BBC UK
What Makes an Actor? (June 6, 1966), BBC UK

DOCUMENTARIES

Guide Dogs for the Blind (September 1935)
The Valiant Years (June 1961)—a documentary on Winston Churchill's life

TELEVISION APPEARANCES

The Skin of Our Teeth (March 17, 1959), Granada Television, UK

Notes

Chapter One: Scent of India

1. Gwen Robyns, *Light of a Star* (New Jersey: A.S. Barnes and Co., 1970), p. 245.
2. Hugo Vickers, *Vivien Leigh* (Boston: Little, Brown & Co., 1988), p. 7.
3. *Ibid.*

Chapter Two: Inside a Convent

1. Alexander Walker, *Vivien: The Life of Vivien Leigh* (New York: Weidenfeld & Nicolson, 1987), p. 30.
2. Alan Dent, *Vivien Leigh: A Bouquet* (London: Hamish Hamilton, 1969) p. 44.
3. *Ibid.*, 47.
4. Anne Edwards, *Vivien Leigh: A Biography* (New York: Simon & Schuster, 1977), p. 28.
5. Thomas Kiernan, *Sir Larry: The Life of Laurence Olivier* (New York: Times Books, 1981), p. 119.
6. Hugo Vickers, *op. cit.*, p. 24.
7. David Lewin, "Vivien Tells," *Daily Express*, August 15, 1960, p. 4.
8. Hugo Vickers, *op. cit.*, p. 25.

Chapter Three: Wedding Interlude

1. David Lewin, *op. cit.*, p. 4.
2. Alexander Walker, *op. cit.*, pp. 38–39.
3. Hugo Vickers, *op. cit.*, p.33.
4. Alexander Walker, *op. cit.*, p.41.
5. Angus McBean, *Vivien: A Love Affair in Camera* (Oxford: Phaidon, 1989), p. 15.
6. Hugo Vickers, *op. cit.*, p. 38.
7. Hugo Vickers, *op. cit.*, p. 40.

Chapter Four: A Star Is Born

1. Hugo Vickers, *op. cit.*, p. 43.
2. *The Times*, February 26, 1935.
3. Basil Dean, *Mind's Eye* (London: Hutchinson, 1973), p. 207.
4. Cynthia Marylee Molt, *Vivien Leigh: A Bio-Bibliography* (Westport, CT: Greenwood Press, 1992), p. 14.
5. Anne Edwards, *op. cit.*, p. 50.
6. *Ibid.*
7. Alexander Walker, *op. cit.*, p. 54.
8. Peter Cotes, *Thinking Aloud. Fragments of Autobiography* (London: Owen, 1993), p. 173.
9. Paul Tabori, *Alexander Korda* (London: Oldbourne, 1959), pp. 187–188.
10. Anne Edwards, *op. cit.*, p. 52.
11. Hugo Vickers, *op. cit.*, p. 55.
12. James Agate, *Sunday Times*, May 19, 1958.
13. Hugo Vickers, *op. cit.*, p. 55.
14. Thomas Kiernan, *op. cit.* p. 128.
15. Laurence Olivier, *Confessions of an Actor* (New York: Simon & Schuster, 1982), p. 100.
16. Anne Edwards, *op. cit.*, p. 55.
17. Laurence Olivier, *op. cit.*, p. 100.
18. John Cottrell, *Laurence Olivier* (Englewood Cliffs, N.J.: Prentice Hall, 1975), p. 109.
19. Alexander Walker, *op. cit.*, p. 74.
20. McBean, *op. cit.*, p. 11.
21. *Ibid.*, p. 13.
22. Lewis Funke and John E. Booth, *Actors Talk About Acting* (New York: Random House, 1961), p. 239.

Chapter Five: Larry, Larry, Larry

1. Laurence Olivier, *op. cit.*, p. 18.
2. *Ibid.*, pp. 85–86.
3. Gwen Robyns, *op. cit.*, p. 54.
4. Hugo Vickers, *op. cit.*, p. 69.
5. Paul Tabori, *op. cit.*, p. 188.
6. Hugo Vickers, *op. cit.*, pp. 68–69.
7. Oswald Frewen Diary, 29 October 1936.
8. Tarquin Olivier, *My Father Laurence Olivier* (London: Headline, 1992), p. 67.
9. *Ibid.*
10. Cynthia Marylee Molt, *op. cit.*, p. 23.
11. Rex Harrison, *Rex: An Autobiography* (New York: Morrow, 1975), p. 51.
12. Laurence Olivier, *op. cit.*, p. 101.
13. Anthony Holden, *Laurence Olivier: A Biography* (New York: Collier, 1988), p. 127.
14. Hugo Vickers, *op. cit.*, cit., p. 81.
15. Cynthia Marylee Molt, *op. cit.*, p. 27.

16. Oswald Frewen Diary, 28 June 1937.
17. Tarquin Olivier, *op. cit.*, pp. 70–71.
18. *Ibid.*, p. 75.
19. Alexander Walker, *op. cit.*, p. 93.
20. *Ibid.*, p. 94
21. *Ibid.*, p. 95.
22. *Ibid.*, p. 96.
23. *Daily Mail*, February 26, 1938.
24. Laurence Olivier, *op. cit.*, p. 105.
25. Hugo Vickers, *op. cit.*, p. 90.
26. Anne Edwards, *op. cit.*, p. 78.
27. Rex Harrison, *A Damned Serious Business* (New York: Bantam, 1991), p. 65.
28. Alexander Walker, *op. cit.*, p. 104.
29. Axel Madsen, *William Wyler* (London: W.H. Allen, 1974) p. 185.

Chapter Six: Gone with the Wind

1. Stewart Granger, *Sparks Fly Upward* (New York: Putnam, 1981), pp. 43–44.
2. Holden, *op. cit.*, p. 139.
3. Hugo Vickers, *op. cit.*, p. 97.
4. Paul Boller, *Hollywood Anecdotes* (New York: Morrow, 1987), p. 274
5. Bette Davis, *The Lonely Life: An Autobiography* (New York: MacDonald, 1962), p. 84.
6. David O. Selznick, *Memo from David O. Selznick*, ed. Rudy Behlmer (New York: Modern Library, 2000), p. 187.
7. Alexander Walker, *op. cit.*, p. 113.
8. Bob Thomas, *Selznick* Doubleday, New York 1970, p. 152.
9. David Thomson, *Showman: The Life of David O. Selznick* (New York: Knopf, 1992), p. 281.
10. David O. Selznick, *op. cit.* p. 187.
11. Hugo Vickers, *op. cit.*, p. 104.
12. Bob Thomas, *op. cit.*, pp. 154–155.
13. Anne Edwards, *op. cit.*, p. 94.
14. Laurence Olivier, *op. cit.*, p. 108.
15. David Thomson, *op. cit.*, p. 284.
16. Margaret Mitchell, *Margaret Mitchell's Gone with the Wind: Letters 1936–1949* (New York: Macmillan, 1976), p. 245.
17. David Thomson, *op. cit.*, p. 285.
18. George Eels, *Hedda and Luella* (New York: Putnam, 1972), p. 173.
19. Thomson, *op. cit.*, p. 285.
20. Peter Hay, *Movie Anecdotes* (New York: Oxford University Press, 1990), p. 233.
21. Gavin Lambert, *On Cukor* (New York: Putnam, 1972), p. 149.
22. Sheila Graham, *Hollywood Revisited* (New York: St. Martin Press, 1985), p. 54.
23. Emanuel Levy. *George Cukor: Master of Elegance* (New York: Morrow, 1994), pp. 119.

24. Sheila Graham, *op. cit.*, p. 54.

25. Emanuel Levy, *op. cit.*, pp. 117–118.

26. William Harris, *Gable and Lombard* (New York: Simon & Schuster, 1974), p. 112.

27. Roland Flamini, *Scarlett, Rhett and a Cast of Thousands* (New York: Collier, 1975), p. 256.

28. Alan Dent, *op. cit.*, p. 65.

29. Carlton Jackson, *Hattie: The Life of Hattie McDaniel* (New York: Madison Books, 1990), p. 43.

30. Hugo Vickers, *op. cit.*, p. 113.

31. Alexander Walker, *op. cit.*, p. 122.

32. *Ibid.*

33. Gary Carey, *Cukor & Co.* (New York: Museum of Modern Art, 1971), pp. 48–49.

34. Alexander Walker, *op. cit.*, p. 129.

35. Gary O'Connor, "Damn Larry! Who Is He Sleeping with Now," *The Mail on Sunday*, July 9, 2000, p. 50.

36. Alexander Walker, *op. cit.*, p. 130.

37. Tad Mosel, *Leading Lady: The World and the Theatre of Katherine Cornell* (Boston: Little Brown, 1978), p. 430.

38. Joan Fontaine, *No Bed of Roses* (New York: Morrow, 1978), p. 116.

39. William Harris, *op. cit.*, pp. 116–117.

40. Frank Nugent, *New York Times*, 20 December 1939, sec. 31, p. 2.

Charter Seven: Romeo and Juliet

1. Mervyn LeRoy, *Mervyn LeRoy: Take One* (New York: Hawthorn Books, 1974), pp. 146–147.

2. Gwen Robyns, *op. cit.*, p. 83.

3. Whitney Stine, *I'd Love to Kiss you: A Conversation with Bette Davis* (New York: Pocket Books, 1990), p. 64.

4. Hugo Vickers, *Op. cit.*, p. 122.

5. *Ibid.*

6. Bosley Crowther, *New York Times* 11 May 1940, sec. 2, p. 23.

7. Alexander Walker, *op. cit.*, p. 142.

8. Anthony Holden, *op. cit.*, p. 156.

9. *Ibid.*, p. 156.

10. Jared Brown, *The Fabulous Lunts* (New York: Atheneum, 1986), p. 300.

11. David Lewin, "Vivien Tells," *Daily Express*, 18 August 1960, p. 9.

12. Douglas Fairbanks, *The Salad Days* (New York: Doubleday, 1988), p. 344.

13. Alexander Walker, *op. cit.*, pp. 148.

14. *Ibid.* p. 149.

15. *Ibid.*

Chapter Eight: Times of War, Times of Love

1. Hugo Vickers, *op. cit.*, p. 1.

2. David Lewin, "Vivien Tells," *Daily Express*, 18 August 1960, p. 9.

3. Michael Korda, *Charmed Lives: A Family Romance* (New York: Random House, 1979) pp. 151–152.

4. Paul Tabori, *op. cit.*, p. 225.

5. Alexander Walker, *op. cit.*, p. 153.

6. Henry Wilcoxon, *Lionheart: The Autobiography of Henry Wilcoxon* (Metuchen, NJ: Scarecrow, 1991), pp. 132–133.

7. Gwen Robyns, *op. cit.*, p. 91.

8. *Vancouver Herald News*, 28 November 1940.

9. Richard Huggett, *Binkie Beaumont* (London: Hodder & Stoughton, 1989), p. 272.

10. *Ibid.*, p. 273.

Chapter Nine: Cleopatra

1. Cecil Beaton, Unpublished Diary, 24 November 1941, Cecil Beaton Papers.

2. John Gielgud, *Backward Glances* (London: Hodder & Stoughton, 1989), p. 24.

3. Richard Huggett, *op. cit.*, p. 281.

4. *Ibid.* p. 284.

5. *Ibid.*

6. *Ibid.* p. 285

7. Alexander Walker, *op. cit.*, p. 167.

8. Dan H. Lawrence, *Bernard Shaw: Collected Letters 1926–1950* (New York: Viking, 1988), p. 713.

9. Anne Edwards, *op. cit.*, pp. 137–138.

10. *Ibid.* p. 139.

11. Stewart Granger, *op. cit.*, p. 80.

12. Alexander Walker, *op. cit.*, p. 155.

13. Gary O'Connor, *op. cit.*

14. Stewart Granger, *op. cit.*, pp. 83–84.

15. Anne Edwards, *op. cit.*, p. 140.

Chapter Ten: Lady Olivier

1. Cynthia Marylee Molt, *op. cit.*, p. 56.

2. Alan Dent, *op. cit.*, p. 19.

3. Laurence Olivier, *op. cit.*, p. 139.

4. Alexander Walker, *op. cit.*, p. 175.

5. *Ibid.*

6. Hugo Vickers, *op. cit.*, pp. 166–167.

7. *Ibid.*, p. 169.

8. Gary O'Connor, *op. cit.*

9. Cecil Beaton Diary, 11 May 1954, Papers.

10. Anne Edwards, *op. cit.*, p. 160.

11. Michael Korda, *op. cit.*, p. 150.

12. Hugo Vickers, *op. cit.*, p. 176.

13. Gwen Robyns, *op. cit.*, pp. 118–119.

14. Gary O'Connor, *Darlings of the Gods: One Year in the Lives of Laurence Olivier and Vivien Leigh* (London: Hodder and Stoughton, 1984), p. 74.

15. Laurence Olivier, *op. cit.*, p. 158.

16. Gwen Robyns, *op. cit.*, p.119.

17. Yolande Finch, *Finchy* (New York: Wyndham Books, 1981), p. 28.

18. Gina Guandalini, *Non solo Via col vento* (Roma: Edizioni Logos, 1990), p. 140.

19. Hugo Vickers, *op. cit.*, p. 192.

20. Laurence Olivier, *op. cit.*, pp. 161–162.

21. Donald Spoto, *Laurence Olivier: A Biography* (New York: HarperCollins, 1992), p. 222.

Chapter Eleven: Blanche DuBois

1. Richard Huggett, *op. cit.*, p. 414.

2. Donald Windham, *Tennessee Williams: Letters to Donald Windham 1940–1965* (Athens, GA: University of Georgia Press, 1996), p. 241.

3. Richard Huggett, *op. cit.*, pp. 413–417.

4. *Ibid.*

5. David Lewin, "Vivien Tells," *Daily Express*, 14 August 1960.

6. *Daily Express*, 28 September 1949.

7. Alexander Walker, *op. cit.*, pp. 192–193.

8. *Ibid.* pp. 197–198.

9. Anne Edwards, *op. cit.*, p. 177.

10. *Ibid.*, p. 178.

11. David Lewin, "Vivien Tells," *Daily Express*, 16 August 1960.

12. Alexander Walker, *op. cit.*, p. 202.

13. David Lewin, *op. cit.*

14. Marlon Brando, *Songs That My Mother Never Taught Me* (New York: Random House, 1994), p. 152.

15. Peter Manso, *Brando* (New York: Hyperion, 1994), p. 298.

16. Elia Kazan, *A Life* (New York: Knopf, 1988), p. 386.

17. *Ibid.* p. 387.

18. Jeff Young, *Kazan: The Master Discusses His Films* (New York: Newmarket Press, 1999), p. 81.

19. Karl Malden, *When Do I Start: A Memoir* (New York: Simon & Schuster, 1997), pp. 192–193.

20. Donald Spoto, *op. cit.*, pp. 228–229.

21. Martin Gottfried, *Nobody's Fool: The Lives of Danny Kaye* (New York: Simon & Schuster, 1994) pp. 167–168.

22. David Lewin, *op. cit.*.

23. *Ibid.*

24. Phillip Gene, *The Films of Tennessee Williams* (Philadelphia: Art Alliance Press, 1980), p. 78.

25. Elia Kazan, *op. cit.*, p. 384.

Chapter Twelve: Fire and Air

1. Jill Bennet, *Godfrey: A Special Time Remembered* (London: Hodder & Stougton, London 1983), p. 137.

2. Kathleen Tynan, *The Life of Kenneth Tynan* (New York: Morrow, 1987), p. 134.

3. John Gielgud, *op. cit.,* p. 24.

4. Anne Edwards, *op. cit.*, p. 185.

5. Jill Bennet, *op. cit.*, pp. 139–140.

6. *The Valiant Years—Goodbye Mr. Churchill,* 11 January 1961, New York Museum of Radio and Television.

7. Laurence Olivier, *op. cit.*, p.172.

8. Brooks Aktinson, *New York Times*, 21 December 1951, sec 2, p. 22.

9. Lewis Funke and John Booth, *op. cit.*, p. 256.

Chapter Thirteen: Peter Finch

1. Hugo Vickers, *op. cit.*, p. 208.

2. Anne Edwards, *op. cit.*, p. 192.

3. Elaine Dundy, *Finch: Bloody Finch* (New York: Holt Rinehart and Winston, 1980), p. 179.

4. *Ibid.*, pp. 179–180.

5. *Ibid.*

6. *Ibid.*, p. 181.

7. *Ibid.*, p.186.

8. Sheridan Morley, *The Other Side of the Moon* (New York: Harper & Row, 1985), pp. 180–181.

9. Laurence Olivier, *op. cit.*, pp. 189–190.

10. Donald Spoto, *A Passion For Life: The Biography of Elizabeth Taylor* (NewYork: HarperCollins, 1995), p. 94.

11. Laurence Olivier, *op. cit.*, p. 191.

12. Gary O'Connor, *op. cit.*, p. 50.

13. Graham Payn and Sheridan Morley, *The Noël Coward Diaries* (Boston: Little Brown, 1982), p. 211.

Chapter Fourteen: Stage Door

1. Michael Darlow and Gillian Hodson, *Terence Rattingan: The Man and His Work* (London: Quartet Books, 1979), p. 218.

2. Elaine Dundy, *op. cit.*, p.198.

3. Rachel Kempson, *Life Among the Redgraves* (New York: Dutton, 1988), p. 165.

4. Elaine Dundy, *op. cit.*, p. 199.

5. Kirk Douglas, *The Ragman's Son: An Autobiography* (New York: Simon & Schuster, 1988), pp. 289–290.

6. Hugo Vickers, *op. cit.*, p. 219.

7. *Ibid.*, p. 220.

8. Ronald Hayman, *John Gielgud* (London: Heinemann, 1971), p. 192.

9. Ivor Brown, *Theatre 1954–55* (London: Max Reinhardt, 1955).

10. Kenneth Tynan, *Curtains* (New York: Atheneum, 1961), p. 99.

11. Laurence Olivier, *op. cit.*, p. 200.

12. John Russell Taylor, *Vivien Leigh* (London: Elm Tree Books, 1984), p. 99.

13. Alexander Walker, *op. cit.,* p. 222.

14. Hugo Vickers, *op. cit.,* p. 229.

15. Elaine Dundy, *op. cit.,* pp. 206–207.

Chapter Fifteen: Madness, Madness, Madness

1. Alexander Walker, *op. cit.,* p. 224.

2. Anne Edwards, *op. cit.,* p. 212.

3. Barbara Leaming, *Marilyn Monroe* (New York: Crown Publishers, 1998), p. 252.

4. Oswald Frewen Diary, 11 June 1956.

5. Alexander Walker, *op. cit.,* pp. 224–225.

6. Anthony Holden, *op. cit.,* p. 308.

7. Gina Guandalini, *op. cit.,* p .201.

8. Alexander Walker, *op. cit.,* p. 234.

9. *Play and Players*, August 1957, no.11 vol.4 p. 3.

10. Hugo Vickers, *op. cit.,* p. 255.

11. Claire Bloom, *Leaving a Doll's House: A Memoir* (Boston: Little Brown, 1996), p. 103.

12. Angus McBean, *op. cit.,* p. 38.

13. Claire Bloom, *op. cit.,* p. 104.

14. Lauren Bacall, *By Myself* (New York: Knopf, 1978), pp. 321–322.

15. Alexander Walker, *op. cit.,* p. 237.

16. Anne Edwards, *op. cit.,* p. 224.

17. *Country Life*, 13 August 1959.

18. Cynthia Marylee Molt, *op. cit.,* p. 89.

Chapter Sixteen: Jack Merivale

1. Alexander Walker, *op. cit.,* p. 245.

2. Brooks Aktinson, *New York Times*, 20 April 1960, sec. 2, p. 22.

3. Alexander Walker, *op. cit.,* p. 250.

4. *Ibid.,* p. 252.

5. Christopher Isherwood, *Diaries 1939–1960* (New York: HarperCollins, 1997), pp. 882–883.

6. Tony Richardson, *The Long Distance Runner: An Autobiography* (New York: Morrow, 1993) p. 148.

7. Danny Peary, *Close-ups: Intimate Profiles of Movie Stars* (New York: Workman Publishing, 1978), p. 314.

8. Gene Philips, *op. cit.,* p. 260.

9. John Parker, *Warren Beatty: The Last Great Lover of Hollywood* (New York: Carroll & Graf, 1994), pp. 63–64.

10. David Thomson, *Warren Beatty and Desert Eyes: A Life and a Story* (New York: Doubleday, 1987), p. 219.

11. Gene Philips, *op. cit,* p. 265.

12. Danny Peary, *op. cit.* p. 314.

13. Joan Collins, *Second Act* (New York: St. Martin Press, 1997), p. 125.

14. Joan Collins, *Past Imperfect: An Autobiography by Joan Collins* (New York: Simon & Schuster, 1984), p. 181.

15. Joan Collins, *Second Act*, p. 126.

16. José Quintero, *If You Don't Dance They Beat You* (New York: St. Martin's Press, 1988), p. 275.

17. *Ibid.*, p. 277.

18. Alexander Walker, *op. cit.*, p. 266.

19. *Advocate TV,* Tasmania, Australia, 24 July 1961.

20. Hugo Vickers, *op. cit.*, p. 295.

21. Anne Edwards, *op cit.*, p. 250.

22. *Ibid.*, p. 251.

23. John Russell Taylor, *op. cit.*, p. 116.

24. John McCallum, *Life with Googie* (London: Heinemann, 1979), p. 138.

25. Tennessee Williams, *Memoirs* (New York: Doubleday, 1972), p. 138.

26. Jean-Pierre Aumont, *Sun and Shadow* (New York: Morrow, 1977), p. 218.

27. Alexander Walker, *op. cit.*, p. 277.

28. Jean Pierre Aumont, *op. cit.*, pp. 233–234.

29. Graham Payn, *My Life with Noël Coward* (New York: Applause, 1994), p. 235.

30. Stanley Kramer, *A Mad, Mad, Mad, Mad World: A Life in Hollywood* (New York: Harcourt, Brace & Co., 1997), pp. 208–209.

31. Christopher Andersen, *An Affair to Remember* (New York: Morrow, 1997), p. 290.

32. Simon Signoret, *Nostalgia Isn't What It Used to Be* (New York: Harper & Row, 1978), p. 308.

33. Peter Hay, *op. cit.*, p. 274.

34. Anne Edwards, *op. cit.*, p. 268.

35. Alexander Walker, *op. cit.*, p. 284.

36. James Spada, *More Than a Woman: An Intimate Biography of Bette Davis* (New York: Bantam, 1993), p. 383.

Chapter Seventeen: Breathless

1. "Vivien Leigh's Comeback Play Hits Trouble," *London Daily Mail,* 24 April 1965, p. 1.

2. Joan Fontaine, *op. cit.*, pp. 281–282.

3. John Guren, "Vivien Leigh and Simon Signoret," *Close Up Magazine,* pp. 23–24.

4. Laurence Olivier, *op. cit.*, p. 274.

5. Hugo Vickers, *op. cit.* p. 327.

6. *Ibid.*, p. 328.

7. Roddy McDowall, *Double Exposure: Take Two* (New York: Morrow, 1989), p. 70.

Bibliography

Andersen, Christopher. *An Affair to Remember*. New York: Norton, 1997.

Aumont, Jean Pierre. *Sun and Shadow*. New York: Norton & Company 1977.

_____. *Dis-moi d'abord que tu m'aimes*. Paris: Editiones Jade, 1986.

Bacall, Lauren. *By Myself*. New York: Knopf, 1978.

Barrow, Andrew. *Gossip*. New York: Coward McCann Geoghegan, 1979.

Base, Ron. *Starring Roles*. London: Little, Brown, 1994.

Bennet, Gill, and Suzanne Goodwin. *Godfrey. A Special Time Remembered*. London: Hodder & Stoughton, 1983.

Bikel, Theodore. *Theo: The Autobiography of Theodore Bikel*. New York: HarperCollins, 1994.

Billips, Connie: *Maureen O'Sullivan: A Bio-Bibliography*. Westport, CT: Greenwood Press, 1990.

Black, Kitty. *Upper Circle: A Theatrical Chronicle*. London: Methuen, 1984.

Bloom, Claire. *Leaving a Doll's House: A Memoir*. Boston: Little, Brown, 1996.

Bogarde, Dirk. *A Particular Friendship*. London: Viking, 1989.

Bogdanovich, Peter. *Who the Devil Made It*. New York: Knopf, 1997.

Boller, Paul, and Ronal Davis. *Hollywood Anecdotes*. New York: Morrow, 1987.

Brando, Marlon. *Brando: Songs My Mother Taught Me*. New York: Random House, 1994.

Braun, Eric. *Deborah Kerr*. New York: St. Martin's Press, 1977.

Brook, Peter. *Threads of Time: Recollections*. Washington D.C.: Counterpoint, 1998.

Brown, Ivor. *Theatre 1954–55*. London: Heinemann, 1971.

Brown, Jared. *The Fabulous Lunts*. New York: Atheneum, 1986.

Buckle, Richard. *Self Portrait with Friends: The Select Diaries of Cecil Beaton*. New York: Times Books, 1979.

Callow, Simon. *Charles Laughton: A Difficult Actor*. London: Methuen, 1987.

Carey, Garey. *Cukor & Co*. New York: Museum of Modern Art, 1971.

Clark, Colin. *The Prince, The Showgirl and Me*. New York: St. Martin's Press, 1996.

Clark, Kenneth. *Another Part of the Wood*. New York: Harper & Row, 1974.

_____. *The Other Half*. New York: Harper & Row, 1977.

Collins, Joan. *Past Imperfect: An Autobiography by Joan Collins.* New York: Simon & Schuster, 1984.

_____. *Second Act.* New York: St. Martin's Press, 1997.

Considine, Shaun. *Bette & Joan: The Divine Feud,* New York: Dutton, 1989.

Cotes, Peter. *Thinking Aloud: Fragments of an Autobiography.* London: Peter Owen, 1993.

Cottrell, John. *Laurence Olivier.* Englewood Cliffs, NJ: Prentice-Hall, 1995.

Cowles, Fleur. *She Made Friends and Kept Them: An Anecdotal Memoir.* New York: HarperCollins, 1996.

D'Amico, Silvio. *Enciclopedia dello Spettacolo.* Rome: Le Maschere, 1959.

Darlow, Michael, and Hodson Gillian. *Terence Rattigan: The Man and His Work,* London: Quartet Books, 1979.

Davis, Bette. *The Lonely Life: An Autobiography.* New York: MacDonald, New York 1981.

Dean, Basil. *Mind's Eye.* London: Hutchinson, 1973.

Dent, Alan. *Vivien Leigh: A Bouquet.* London: Hamish Hamilton, 1969.

Dexter, John. *The Honorable Beast.* New York: Theatre Arts Books, 1993.

Douglas, Kirk. *The Ragman's Son: An Autobiography,* New York: Simon and Schuster, 1988.

Dundy, Elaine. *Finch, Bloody Finch.* New York: Holt, Rinehart and Winston, 1980.

Edwards, Anne. *Vivien Leigh.* New York: Simon & Schuster, 1977.

Eels, George. *Hedda and Louella.* New York: Putnam, 1972.

Epstein, Edward. *Portrait of Jennifer: A Biography of Jennifer Jones.* New York: Simon & Schuster, 1995.

Fairbanks, Douglas, Jr. *The Salad Days,* New York: Doubleday, 1988.

_____. *A Hell of a War.* New York: St. Martin's Press, 1993.

Fairweather, Virginia. *Olivier. An Informal Portrait.* New York: Coward-McCann Inc., 1969.

Finch, Yolande. *Finchy,* New York: Wyndham Books, 1981.

Flamini, Roland. *Scarlett, Rhett, and a Cast of Thousands,* New York: Collier, 1978.

Fontaine, Joan. *No Bed of Roses.* New York: William Morrow, 1978.

Forbes, Bryan. *Ned's Girl: The Life of Edith Evans,* London: Elm Tree Books, 1977.

Forsyth, James. *Tyron Guthrie: A Biography.* London: Hamish Hamilton, 1976.

Funke, Lewis. *Actors Talk about Acting.* New York: Random House, 1961.

Gielgud, John. *Distinguished Company.* New York: Doubleday, 1973.

_____. *Backward Glances.* London: Hodder & Stoughton, 1989.

Givner, Joan. *Katherine Anne Porter: A Life.* London: University of Georgia Press, 1982.

Gordon, Ruth. *Myself Among Others.* New York: Atheneum, 1971.

_____. *Ruth Gordon: An Open Book.* New York: Doubleday, 1980.

Gottfried, Martin. *Nobody's Fool: The Lives of Danny Kaye.* New York: Simon & Schuster, 1994.

Graham, Sheila. *Hollywood Revisited.* New York: St. Martin's Press, 1985.

Granger, Stewart. *Sparks Fly Upward.* New York: Putnam, 1981.

Guandalini, Gina. *Vivien Leigh: Non solo Via col vento.* Roma: Edizioni Logos, 1990.

Guinness, Alec. *Blessing in Disguise.* New York: Knopf, 1986.

Guthrie, Tyrone. *A Life in the Theatre.* New York: McGraw Hill, 1959.

Harris, William. *Gable and Lombard.* New York: Simon & Schuster, 1974.

Harrison, Rex. *Rex: The Autobiography of Rex Harrison.* New York: Morrow & Co., 1975.

_____. *A Damned Serious Business.* New York: Bantam Books, 1991.

Hay, Peter. *Hollywood Anecdotes.* New York: Oxford University Press, 1989.

_____. *Movie Anecdotes.* New York: Oxford University Press, 1990.

Hayman, Ronald. *John Gielgud.* London: Heinemann, 1971.

_____. *Tennessee Williams: Everyone Is an Audience.* New Haven: Yale University Press, 1993.

Higham, Charles. *Charles Laughton: An Intimate Biography.* Garden City: Doubleday, 1976.

Hoare, Philip. *Noël Coward: A Biography.* New York: Simon & Schuster, 1995.

Holden, Anthony. *Laurence Olivier: A Biography.* New York: Collier, 1988.

Houghton, Norris. *Entrances & Exits.* New York: Limelight Editions, 1991.

Howard, Leslie Ruth. *A Quite Remarkable Father.* New York: Harcourt Brace & Company, 1959.

Howard, Ronald. *In Search of My Father: A Portrait of Leslie Howard.* New York: St. Martin's Press, 1981.

Huggett, Richard. *Binkie Beaumont.* London: Hodder & Stoughton, 1989.

Isherwood, Christopher. *Diaries: Volume I: 1939–1960.* New York: HarperCollins, 1997.

Jackson, Carlton: *Hattie: The Life of Hattie McDaniel.* New York: Madison Books, 1990.

Kanin, Garson. *Tracy and Hepburn: An Intimate Memoir.* New York: Viking, 1971.

_____. *Hollywood.* New York: Viking, 1974.

Kashfi, Anna. *Brando for Breakfast.* New York: Crown Publishers, 1979.

Kaufmann, Beatrice. *The Letters of Alexander Woollcott.* London: Cassell, 1946.

Kazan, Elia. *A Life.* New York: Knopf, 1988.

Kempson, Rachel. *Life Among the Redgraves.* New York: Dutton, 1988.

Kiernan, Thomas. *Olivier: The Life of Laurence Olivier.* New York: Times Books, 1981.

Kobal, John. *People Will Talk.* New York: Knopf, 1985.

Korda, Michael. *Charmed Lives: A Family Romance.* New York: Random House, 1979.

Kramer, Stanley. *A Mad, Mad, Mad, Mad World: A Life in Hollywood.* New York: Harcourt Brace & Company, 1997.

Kulik, Carol. *Alexander Korda.* London: W.H. Allen, 1975.

Lahr, John. *Prick-Up Your Ears.* New York: Knopf, 1978.

_____. *The Orton Diary.* New York: Harper & Row, 1986.

Lambert, Gavin. *On Cukor.* New York: Putnam, 1972.

_____. *Norma Shearer: A Life.* New York: Knopf, 1990.

Lasky, Jessie, and Pat Siver. *Love Scene: The Story of Laurence Olivier and Vivien Leigh.* London: Angus & Robertson, 1978.

Lawrence, Dan H. *Bernard Shaw: Collected Letters 1926–1950*. New York: Viking, 1988.

Leaming, Barbara. *Marilyn Monroe*. New York: Crown Publishers, 1998.

Leonard, Jeff, and Jerold Simmons. *The Dame in the Kimono*. New York: Grove Weidenfeld, 1990.

Leonard, Maurice. *Montgomery Clift*. London: Hodder & Stoughton, 1997.

LeRoy, Mervyn. *Mervyn LeRoy: Take One*. New York: Hawthorn Books, 1974.

Lesley, Cole. *Remembered Laughter: The Life of Noël Coward*. New York: Knopf, 1976.

Levy, Emmanuel. *George Cukor: A Master of Elegance*. New York: William Morrow, 1994.

Lewis, Roger. *The Real Life of Laurence Olivier*. New York: Applause, 1997.

Linet, Beverly. *Ladd: The Life, the Legend, the Legacy of Alan Ladd*. New York: Arbor House, 1979.

Logan, Joshua. *Movie Stars, Real People and Me*. New York: Delacorte Press, 1978.

Macnee, Patrick, and Marie Cameron. *Blind in One Ear*. San Francisco: Mercury House, 1989.

Madsen, Axel. *William Wyler*. London: W.H. Allen, 1974.

Mafioly, Serge. *Vivien Leigh: D'Air et de Feu*. Paris: Henry Veyrier, 1990.

Malden, Karl. *When Do I Start? A Memoir*. New York: Simon & Schuster, 1997.

Manso, Peter. *Brando: The Biography*. New York: Hyperion, 1994.

Manvell, Roger. *Theater and Film*. London: Fairleigh Dickinson, 1979.

Marvin, Pamela. *Lee: A Memoir*. London: Faber & Faber, 1997.

McBean, Angus. *Vivien Leigh: A Love Affair with the Camera*. Oxford: Phaidon, 1989.

McCallum, John. *Life with Googie*. London: Heinemann, 1979.

McClintic, Gunthrie. *Me and Kit*. Boston: Little, Brown, 1955.

McDowall, Roddy, *Double Exposure. Take Two*. New York: Morrow, 1989.

McGilliagan, Patrick. *George Cukor: A Double Life*. New York: St. Martin's Press, 1997.

Meyer, Michael. *Words Through a Windowpane*. New York: Grove Weidenfeld, 1989.

Miller, John. *Ralph Richardson: The Authorized Biography*. London: Pan Books, 1995.

Mitchell, Margaret. *Margaret Mitchell's Gone with the Wind Letters 1936–1949*. New York: Macmillan, 1976.

Molt, Cynthia Marylee. *Vivien Leigh: A Bio-Bibliography*. Westport, CT: Greenwood Press, 1992.

Morley, Margaret. *The Films of Laurence Olivier*. New Jersey: Citadel Press, 1978.

Morley, Sheridan. *Tales from the Hollywood Raj*. New York: Viking, 1983.

_____. *The Other Side of the Moon: The Life of David Niven*. New York: Harper & Row, 1985.

Mosel, Tad. *Leading Lady: The World of Katherine Cornell*. Boston: Little, Brown, 1978.

Moseley, Roy. *Rex Harrison: A Biography*. New York: St. Martin's Press, 1987.

_____. *Bette Davis: An Intimate Memoir*. New York: Donald I. Fine, 1990.

Niven, David. *The Moon's Balloon.* New York: Putnam, 1972.

O'Connor, Gary. *Ralph Richardson: An Actor's Life.* London: Hodder & Stoughton, 1982.

_____. *Darlings of the Gods: One Year in the Lives of Laurence Olivier and Vivien Leigh.* London: Hodder & Stoughton, 1984.

_____. *Alec Guinness: Master of Disguise.* London: Hodder & Stoughton, 1994.

_____. *The Secret Woman: A Life of Peggy Ashcroft.* London: Weidenfeld & Nicolson, 1997.

Offen, Ron. *Brando.* Chicago: Henry Regnery Company, 1973.

Olivier, Laurence. *On Acting.* New York: Simon & Schuster, 1982.

_____. *Confessions of an Actor.* New York: Simon & Schuster, 1982.

Olivier, Tarquin. *My Father Laurence Olivier.* London: Headline, 1992.

Paris, Barry. *Garbo: A Biography.* New York: Knopf, 1995.

Parker, John. *Five for Hollywood.* New York: Carol Publishing Group, 1991.

Parker, Josh. *Warren Beatty: The Last Great Lover of Hollywood.* New York: Carroll & Graf Publishers, 1994.

Payn, Graham,. *My Life with Noël Coward.* New York: Applause 1994.

Payn, Graham and Morley Sheridan. *The Noël Coward Diaries.* Boston: Little, Brown, 1982.

Peary, Danny. *Close-ups. Intimate Profiles of Movie Stars.* New York: Workman Publishing, 1978.

Philips, Gene. *The Films of Tennessee Williams.* Philadaelphia: Art Alliance Press, 1980.

_____. *George Cukor.* Boston: Twayne Publishers, 1982.

Powell, Michael. *Million-Dollar Movie.* London: Heinemann, 1992.

Quintero, José. *If You Don't Dance They Beat You.* New York: St. Martin's Press, 1988.

Quirk, Lawrence. *The Great Romantic Films.* New Jersey: Citadel Press, 1974.

_____. *The Films of Warren Beatty.* New Jersey: Citadel Press, 1990.

Richardson, Tony. *The Long-Distance Runner: An Autobiography.* New York: William Morrow, 1993.

Riese, Randall. *All About Bette: Her Life from A to Z.* Chicago: Contemporary Books, 1993.

Robyns, Gwen. *Light of a Star.* London: Leslie Frewin, 1968.

Rossi, Alfred. *Astonish Us in the Morning: Tyrone Guthrie Remembered.* London: Hutchinson of London, 1977.

Salter, Elizabeth. *Helpmann.* New York: Universe, 1978.

Selznick, David O. *Memo from David O. Selznick.* New York: Modern Library, 2000.

Selznick, Mayer. *Irene: A Private View.* New York: Knopf, 1983.

Shaw, Bernard. *Collected Letters 1926–1950.* New York: Viking, 1988.

_____. *The Lure of Fantasy: Volume III 1918–1950.* New York: Random House, 1991.

Sheridan, Morley. *The Great Stage Stars.* New York: Facts on File Publications, 1986.

Signoret, Simone. *Nostalgia Isn't What It Used to Be.* New York: Harper & Row, 1978.

Sinclair, Andrew. *Spiegel. The Man Behind the Pictures.* Boston: Little, Brown, 1987.

Spada, James. *More Than a Woman: An Intimate Biography of Bette Davis.* New York: Bantam Books, 1993.

Spoto, Donald. *Lenya: A Life.* Boston: Little, Brown, 1989.

_____. *Laurence Olivier.* New York: HarperCollins, 1992.

_____. *A Passion for Life: The Biography of Elizabeth Taylor.* New York: Harper-Collins, 1995.

Stine, Whitney. *I'd Love to Kiss You: A Conversation with Bette Davis.* New York: Pocket Books, 1990.

Stockman, Martin. *The Korda Collection: Alexander Korda's Film Classics.* London: Boxtree Limited, 1992.

Tabori, Paul. *Alexander Korda.* London: Oldbourne, 1959.

Taylor, Elizabeth. *Elizabeth Taylor: An Informal Memoir.* New York: Harper & Row, 1964.

Taylor, Helen. *Scarlett's Women: Gone with the Wind and Its Female Fans.* New Brunswick, NJ: Rutgers University Press, 1989.

Taylor, John Russell. *Vivien Leigh.* London: Elm Tree Books, 1984.

Thomas, Bob. *Selznick.* New York: Doubleday, 1970.

Thomas, Tony. *Films of the Forties.* New Jersey: Citadel Press, 1975.

Thomson, David. *Showman: The Life of David Selznick.* New York: Knopf, 1992.

_____. *Warren Beatty and Desert Eyes: A Life and a Story.* Garden City: Knopf, 1992.

Tims, Hilton. *Once a Wicked Lady: A Biography of Margaret Lockwood.* London: Virgin, 1989.

Tornabene, Lyn. *Long Live the King: A Biography of Clark Gable.* New York: Putnam, New York, 1996.

Troyan, Michael. *A Rose for Mrs. Miniver: The Life of Greer Garson.* Lexington, Kentucky: University Press of Kentucky, 1999.

Tunney, Kiernan. *Interrupted Biography & Aurora.* London: Quartet Books, 1989.

Tynan, Kathleen. *The Life of Kenneth Tynan.* New York: Morrow, 1987.

Tynan, Kenneth. *Curtains.* New York: Atheneum, 1961.

_____. *Profiles.* New York: Random House, 1998.

Utilov, Vladimir. *Vivien Li.* Moscow: Iskustvo, 1980.

Vermilye, Jerry. *The Great British Films.* New Jersey: Citadel Press, 1978.

Vertrees, Alan David. *Selznick's Vision.* Austin, Texas: University of Texas Press, 1997.

Vickers, Hugo. *Cecil Beaton: A Biography.* Boston: Little, Brown, 1985.

_____. *Vivien Leigh.* Boston: Little, Brown, 1988.

Vinemberg, Steve. *Method Actors.* New York: Schirmer Books, 1991.

Walker, Alexander. *Vivien Leigh: The Life of Vivien Leigh.* New York: Weidenfeld & Nicolson, 1987.

_____. *Fatal Charm: The Life of Rex Harrison.* New York: St. Martin's Press, 1994.

Wapshott, Nicholas. *Carol Reed: A Biography.* New York: Knopf, 1989.

Wayne, Jane Ellen. *Robert Taylor*. New York: St. Martin's Press, 1992.

Welles, Orson, and Peter Bogdanovich. *This Is Orson Welles*. New York: Harper-Collins, 1992.

Wilcoxon, Henry. *Lionheart in Hollywood: The Autobiography of Henry Wilcoxon*. Metuchen, NJ: Scarecrow Press, 1991.

Williams, Tennessee. *Memoirs*. New York: Doubleday, 1972.

_____. *Five O'Clock Angel: Letters of Tennessee Williams to Marie St. Just 1948–1982*. New York: Knopf, 1990.

Windham, Donald. *Tennessee Williams' Letters to Donald Windham 1940–1965*. Athens, GA: University of Georgia Press, 1996.

Winn, Godfrey. *The Positive Hour*. London: Michael Joseph, 1970.

Winters, Shelley. *Shelley Also Known as Shirley*. New York: William Morrow, 1980.

Young, B.A. *The Rattigan Version*. New York: Atheneum, 1988.

Young, Jeff. *Kazan: The Master Director Discusses His Films*. New York: Newmarket Press, 1999.

Zierold, Norman. *The Moguls*. New York: Coward-McCann, 1969.

Zolow, Maurice. *Stagestruck: The Romance of Alfred Lunt and Lynn Fontanne*. New York: Harcourt, Brace & World, 1964.

Index

211